T0077889

THE BALOCH NATIONAL STRUGGLE IN PAKISTAN: EMERGENCE AND DIMENSIONS

JAN MUHAMMAD DASHTI

Order this book online at www.trafford.com
or email orders@trafford.com

Most Trafford titles are also available at major online book retailers.

Print information available on the last page.

ISBN: 978-1-6987-0395-4 (sc)
ISBN: 978-1-6987-0397-8 (hc)
ISBN: 978-1-6987-0396-1 (e)

Library of Congress Control Number: 2020921093

Trafford rev. 11/12/2020

 www.trafford.com

North America & international
toll-free: 844-688-6899 (USA & Canada)
fax: 812 355 4082

CONTENTS

ABBREVIATIONS

BELF   Balochistan Exile Liberation Front
BLF   Balochistan Liberation Front
BLO   Balochistan Liberation Organization
BPDO   Balochistan Peoples Democratic Organization
BPLF   Balochistan Peoples Liberation Front
BMDTH   Baloch Musala Defais Theanzen
BRZ   Baloch Raaj e Zrombesh
BRP   Baloch Republican Party
BLA   Balochistan Liberation Army
BNA   Balochistan National Party
BNDP   Balochistan National Democratic Party
BNYM   Balochsitan National Youth Movement
BNM   Baloch National Movement
BPLF   Balochistan Peoples Liberation Front
BUF   Balochistan United Front
BSU   Balochistan States Union

HF   Hizbul- Fuqan
ISI   Inter-Services Intelligence agency

JUI   Jamiat-e-Ulema-e-Islam
JWP   Janmhoori Wathan Party

LJ   Lashkar e Janghwi
LK   Lashkar e Khurasan

MRD	Movement for the Restoration of Democracy
NAP	National Awami Party
NDP	National Democratic Party
NP	National Party
NWFP	Northwest Frontier Province
PONM	Paksitan Oppressed Nations Movement
PYM	Progressive Youth Movement
PEAR	Popular Front for Armed Resistance
PNA	Pakistan National Alliance
PNP	Pakistan National Party
PPP	Pakistan Peoples Party
RCD	Regional Cooperation for Development
SBPF	Sindhi BalochPakhtun Front
SSB	Sepha Shuhda e Balochistan
WBO	World Baloch Organization

PROLOGUE

Countless racial or linguistic groups overwhelmed other peoples and civilizations in ancient times. But the conditions have undergone a tremendous change in modern times. Territories and peoples can no longer be conquered in what was practiced during earlier ages. I feel that if Islam had been introduced to twentieth-century Arabia, it could hardly have achieved a breakthrough in other parts of the world. There would have been no Muhammad Bin Qasim to subjugate the Great Sindhi nation or a Khalid Bin Waleed to lay waste Syria and Iraq; nor could the great Persians or the Romans have been defeated by Arabs much inferior in arms and civilization. The main obstacle, apart from many other relevant factors, is the new spirit of nationalism- an inspiring force and certainly the strongest deterrent to all invaders of the modern ages.

In the written history, the earliest manifestation of nationalism can be traced among the Israelites during their bondage in Egypt or in the Roman conflict with Carthage. In the modern era, we have witnessed this in many regions of the world. Algeria and Vietnam defeated great imperial powers. Many Asian and African nations forced mighty colonial powers to withdraw from their countries. In the sub-continent, imbued with a sense of patriotism, the Bengalis fought a successful war of independence in 1971. A small people organized under ethnoreligious nationalism; the Israelites are visibly withstanding an onslaught from the same Arabs who had overrun the entire Middle East within a few decades in the early stages of Islam. Conversely, the modern Persians under Ayatollah Khomeini, inspired by the same religious zeal, cannot defeat an Iraq much smaller in size and population, because it is fighting its battle in the name of Arab nationalism, which is proving much stronger than the fanaticism of Shia Islam.

Baloch nationalism has its genesis in a culture which has never been analyzed in its true historical perspective, or in the context of present-day socio-political conditions. It is sometimes argued that the "Baloch issue" no longer exists. The state-hired analysts in Pakistan believe that the allocation of funds for the development of the region coupled with reforms of the socio-cultural structure will render dormant the Baloch aspirations to national self-determination for many years to come. The more optimistic among the ruling circles in Pakistan think that, without intervention by an external power, directly or by proxy, the Baloch will progressively be assimilated into Pakistani 'nation and culture'. However, they are forgetting that patriotism pervades the entire Baloch socio-cultural approach from the very beginning of their historical journey as a nation. In the contemporary Balochistan, a deep national consciousness is beginning to emerge among the Baloch masses led by their first generation of intellectuals. This volume is a modest contribution to this emergence, analyzing the geopolitical imperatives, seeking to ask many questions and supplying many answers which are animating the minds of the Baloch youth and of those interested in comprehending the new trends in Baloch politics.

In the following pages, the philosophical and historical rationale of the Pakistani state and the justification of its continued existence in the context of the principle of the right of national self-determination will be discussed and its applicability to the Baloch and other ethnic groups in Pakistan. It will also be discussed that how long the Panjab will be able to unite the country through coercion and whether its western allies have the will and strategic compulsion to perpetuate the present socio-ideological and political shape of the country in the face of strong resentment from the ethnic minorities. I have also considered in a hypothetical way the physical and political shape "greater Balochistan" may assume should Pakistan disintegrate either through internal subversion or external attack.

Balochistan is divided into three parts: Western Balochistan is under Iranian rule; a considerable portion of the territory is in Afghanistan and the major part lies in Pakistan. I have taken the entire Baloch land as an indivisible Unit, as considered by the Baloch people. However, given my limitations and the non- availability of any reliable data on the western and the Afghan parts of the country, this study is mainly confined to Pakistani Balochistan. None the less, since all the Baloch are living almost under the same strained circumstances, with a historic sense of national destiny, I have assumed that this work applies to a large extent to all the Baloch throughout their country.

I would also like to mention that it has been difficult to obtain bibliographical notes or document the huge stock of material consulted. Frequent citations have been avoided because such references would not have been beneficial to the readers other than providing an impressive maze of unnecessary numbers strewn throughout the text. Therefore, many authors may not have been credited who must have contributed to my understanding of the Baloch history, their cultural personality and their quest for a separate national identity.

Jan Muhammad Dashti
Kohlu, Balochistan
7th September 1985

CHAPTER I

BALOCHISTAN – THE COUNTRY AND ITS PEOPLE: AN INTRODUCTION

1- The Political History from Ancient o Medieval Times

The evidence of human settlement in Balochistan is not much older than 5000 BC. The archaeologists believe that by about the fourth millennium BC, Balochistan was inhabited and the population growth and expansion were fairly rapid. Analyses of the remains of Neolithic settlement give results typical of the late Stone Age. The recent finds in Mehrgad discovered by a French Archaeological Team, from the Scientific Research Institute, Paris, show that the population of the area had become familiar with agriculture and the use of wild animals. The people lived in clay-brick houses. Stone-made ornaments and Jewelry or precious stones and seashells were also found.

It appears that important cultural changes occurred in north-central Balochistan as the result of a settled lifestyle and material development in the area coinciding with extensive settlements in the Indus Valley. There is a marked cultural similarity between settlements in Balochistan and those of the Indus civilization. The material remains found in Nal, Quetta, and Mehrgad support this assertion. Another significant fact is that settlements have also been found in mountainous regions and in some cases in the isolated valleys located at considerable heights.

Balochistan undoubtedly served as an intermediary link between the cultures of South Asia, Central Asia, and the Middle East. The finds in Jahlaawan bear a striking resemblance to the pottery of the eighth century BC discovered in Cyprus and Phoenicia [1]. Antiques including pottery so far found in Makkuraan and along the Persian coast appear to be of Arabian and Egyptian origin, probably brought to the coast in Arab ships [2].

A proper religious-cultural evaluation of an ancient people depends largely upon the intelligibility of the archaeological finds. It is difficult to establish a proper relationship of the primitive unrecorded ages to subsequent cultures of the same place or region. In fact, the evidence we have of cultural development reflects no more than the ancient peoples' progress in their struggle against the forces of nature, and the archaeological remains give us no more than a glimpse of the socio-economic conditions or some clue regarding religious beliefs of the people. Thus, we have no conclusive evidence from the first settlements in Balochistan to whether terracotta figurines, both human and animal, were really cult objects. However, in the pre-Harrapan period, the heavily ornamented female figures with exaggerated features can generally be interpreted as mother goddesses. Similarly, painted figures of bull certainly signify some religious beliefs. In Jahlawaan, many places of the fire-worshippers have been spotted. Tombs have been located, indicating a system of subterranean burial, and vaulted burial chambers cut in the slopes have been discovered in the hills near Pandaran. In graveyards in Mehrgad pieces of clay utensils and other ornaments have been found alongside the human remains, which indicate a belief in a life after death.

Significantly, relics of Greco-Bactrian rule and Buddhist settlements have been identified in major parts of Afghanistan and central and northern Balochistan. The Sindhi ruler of Lasbela was a Buddhist priest as late as the seventh century AD. Indo-Scythian coins have also been discovered in Afghanistan and the Panjab [3]. Traces of considerable Buddhist influence are found in folk stories still told in Balochistan [4].

Balochistan is not an isolated landmass of high mountains and inhospitable regions. It has been the meeting ground of ancient civilizations and empires: those of Persia, Bactria, and the Indus

2

Valley. Moreover, the region has been visited by many people during the last 4000 years. The first-ever recorded intrusion of a tribal people is that of the Aryans which began after the disintegration of Sumer and Akkad. The empire of Sumer and Akkad was founded by the Sumerian Ur-Engur of Ur and lasted until the reign of the Amorite Hammurabi (e.1792-1750 BC), after whose death the empire rapidly collapsed. There is no direct evidence that the Sumerian empire was ever extended to India, but the possibility may not be ruled out in the face of archaeological discoveries of civilization in the Indus valley apparently related to that of the Sumerians of Mesopotamia [5].

The Aryans are generally believed to have begun settling in India around 1500 BC [6]. They came from the north-west along what is now known as the traditional routes. They probably belonged to the Indo-Iranic group of tribes, as is apparent from the close kinship between Sanskrit and the earliest surviving Iranian languages. Furthermore, the Rig-Vedic religion contains elements from three evolutionary strata: an early element common to most of the Indo-European tribes, a later element held in common with early Iranian and an element acquired in the Indian sub-continent itself after the Aryan settlement [7].

The Aryan influx into India brought with it great cultural and religious changes as the ancient Dravidian civilization gave way to the Aryan. The "Aryanization" of most of the population was achieved by the first millennium BC, the diverse ethnic groups amalgamating to produce Indo-Aryan tribal unions. This is supported by the extension of the important geo-ethnic notion, Aryavarota (Aryana), the country of the Aryans. The researchers are not in agreement with the exact location of the Aryana but many believed that Aryavarota originally stood only for the central part of northern India [8].

We find mention of the area by ancient writers and chroniclers, especially the Greeks. Ptolemy's seven provinces of Ariana include Gedrosia, which is regarded as comprising most parts of the present Balochistan. It was also known as Karmania Altera, which lives on in the name of present Kirmaan in Iran. After the voyage of the Greek Admiral Nearchus and Alexander's march through Makkuraan and Las, there is a considerable record of Maka or Gedrosia in Greek writings, but no conclusion can be deduced from such sketchy narratives regarding the people, their culture and society or their possible affinity with the present inhabitants of Balochistan. Some account of the people is, however, mentioned by Arian of Las and

Maka. He mentions Ichthyophagai and Oreitai as two distinct people. Ichthyophagaiis said to live on fish, a possible reference to the people of the coastal belt, while the Oreitai are believed to be Huth.

Balochistan has occupied an important strategic position since the dawn of history. The difficult wasteland of Greek description changed hands not infrequently between the great empires of ancient epochs. It also provided routes both for trade and for invaders of the Indian sub-continent. The Behistun inscriptions of Darius (522-468 BC) mention Arachosia, Sattagydia, Maka and Gandhara as part of the Darian Empire. After the Greek conquest of Persia and some parts of India, Balochistan came under Greek domination and subsequently that of the Mouryan Empire. The Greek sources maintain that in 305 BC Emperor Mouriya engaged in a conflict with Seleucus I Nicator in the trans-Indus region. The hostilities terminated in a treaty by which Seleucus abandoned the frontier provinces to Mauriya, including all of Balochistan and most part of Afghanistan. The Asokan edicts discovered at Kandahar and Pol-e-Daruntah confirm Indian rule in these areas.

It is not established whether the Huna invasion during the reign of Chandra Gupta Mouriya had any political impact on Balochistan. The Huna was a branch of the Ehthalite or white Huns, one section of which migrated to the Volga valley and another to the Oxus, invading Persia and Afghanistan. Yet another group separated and swept into northern India to form the Huna Kingdom in the early 6th century. The most significant result of the Huns invasion of India was that northern India once again came into social and cultural contact with Central Asia by the periodic migration of many tribes to the sub-continent.

Another important event was the invasion by the Saka, who advanced south from Central Asia to the borders of Parthia and the Graeco- Bactrian states. A section of the Saka swept through eastern Iran and occupied Drangiana and southwestern part of present-day Afghanistan. The territories were then called Sakastan, the country of the Saka, a name that has survived to the present day in the historical province of Seistan [(9)]. At the beginning of the first century BC the Saka moved through southern Afghanistan and northern Balochistan up to the Indus, and later on made their way to India, where they ruled for nearly four hundred years [(10)].

From 227 AD to 590 AD, Balochistan came under the Sassanian rule with Ephatalite Turks controlling the central and northern regions from 470 to 520 AD, leaving only the southern coastal region. Subsequently, the weakened Sassanians were replaced by the rulers of Sindh, who extended their rule to western Balochistan as far as Kirmaan until the advent of the Arabs [11].

The Arabs attempted to conquer Makkuraan during the reign of Caliph Omar. Initially, the incursions were for booty collection (Ghazwa) and there was no permanent presence of Arabs in the region. However, after some years, they tried to occupy the region and made it part of the Arab Empire. The Arab invasion under the command of Budail, who was killed in the battle, proved disastrous. Another expedition, sent under the command of Kakam Ibn al Taghlabi, defeated the forces of the ruler of Makkuraan who was joined by an expeditionary force sent by the king of Sindh in late October 644 A.D. However, it appears that the Arab suzerainty over Balochistan was limited and their rule never went far beyond the walls of the fortified cities in which the garrisons were lodged [12]. There are nevertheless indications in some accounts about broader Arab control of the region. For example, Ibn Haukal, who visited India around 976 A.D maintains that an Arab Governor was ruling Jahlawaan.

The Arabs rule collapsed after 150 years and major parts of Balochistan came under the suzerainty of Ghaznavi, and Ghori rulers till the end of the twelfth century when Balochistan fell under the Seljuks who held sway till the end of 13th century AD. The Baloch tribes who had migrated into Sistaan and Kirmaan carried out occasional forays into the Ghaznavid domains, resulting in bloody battles. After a few indecisive skirmishes, the Ghaznavid troops were mobilized to a large extent and sent to Kirmaan, who defeated the Baloch around Khabis. The entire area of Sistaan then came under Ghaznavid rule, and most Baloch tribes migrated further east as far as Panjgur, reinforcing the earlier Baloch settlements. The Ghaznavid ruler Masood pursued his conquests to Makkuraan and defeated the Baloch at Bampur. The Seljuk rule gave way to the Mongol hegemony. During the fifteenth century, the country fell into the hands of the Arguns and subsequently the Mughal.

Balochistan often changed hands between Persia and Mughal India. Safavid rule was replaced by that of the Mughal in 1596 AD. In 1638 the country again came under Persia. However, Sivi, part of the Multan province had effectively remained under the Mughal since the reign of Akbar. The present Pakhtun-speaking districts of Balochistan were governed by the rulers of Kandahar and Hirat and were also under Sadozai and Barakzai chieftains for a considerable time up to the mid-nineteenth century.

Balochistan appears to have served as one of the major trade routes between Persia, Central Asia, and India in ancient times. Trade was carried on from various points in Balochistan to Kandahar, Ghazni, and Kabul via Kasarkand and Chahbaar in the coastal belt. Although we do not have any sound evidence for seaborne trade on any scale between India and the Middle East, especially Assyria and Mesopotamia, however, some of the historical accounts suggest that maritime trade appears to have flourished in that period. Such trade might have existed during the reign of the Assyrian King, Tiglat Pileser III (745-727). From Greek accounts and archaeological references, there is evidence of coastal trade between India and the Persian Gulf during the reign of Hiram, King of Tyre. It might be that the Syrians and Phoenicians operated trade activities along the coast of Makkuraan and western India for the purpose of acquiring spices and gold. Relics found in Makkuraan are yet to be decoded, preventing firm conclusion regarding trade and commerce, art and architecture, language and literature and above all the races who occupied the southern belt of Makkuraan [13]. There is archaeological evidence of considerable trade between the Indus valley and Mesopotamia: the Harrapan seals on Bundles of goods to be sent to Ur and other Mesopotamian centers signify commercial activities. Although it is difficult to imagine the volume or the nature of trade, the discovery at Lothal of a type of seal characteristic of the Persian Gulf suggests flourishing maritime trade.

It appears that the Tehran-Mashad route served as the trade highway which linked Mesopotamia with Bactria. Another route ran through Yezd and Kirmaan via Makkuraan to Sindh. The Major commercial centers mentioned by Ibn Haukalare Dizzek, Geh, and Kasarkand: other flourishing centers of trade were Bampur, Kech, and Panjgur. Marco Polo noted growing agriculture, commerce, and trade in the area. The fertile region of Kach-Gandhawa also formed a major economic nucleus in the northeast [14].

The overland track to India through Makkuraan, linking with the Middle East, was probably one of the best trade routes in ancient times. Another route linked the Oxus region with Kabul and central reaches of the Indus.

2- The Original Roots of the People

There are numerous theories regarding the inhabitants of present-day Balochistan. A lot of confusion has been created by the hired writers who tried to present an account of the people of this region which could serve the interests of colonial or dominant powers controlling Balochistan. A brief discussion on the ethnic composition of the region is imperative in order to give a relatively factual account.

A. The Brahui

There is a lot of confusion regarding the racial origin of the Brahui faction of the Baloch. They have been classed as Dravidians because of their language, and Arabs, Turco-Iranians or Semites in view of some common cultural traits. The word Biroea, the Greek name for Aleppo, has conveniently been connected with Brahui to assert their Syrian origin.

By some authors, the racial cognation of the Brahui with various peoples has been sought on the basis of faint archaeological evidence. ; It is not uncommon in their theories to refer to a supposed similarity in place-names or identical sounds in certain words in proposing a racial kinship [15]. An etymological connection with Brahui-speaking Mengal has been traced in Min, a Scythian tribe. The Scythian tribes of Sagatae and Saka have been claimed as progenitors of the Brahui tribe Sajedi; and similarly, the Sarparra is said to be the descendants of the Thracian tribe Sarapaarae [16].

Brahui has also been identified as antonym of Narohi, the inhabitants of the plains of Alborz Mountain; or since the Brahui came from Burzkoh, (Alborz mountain in Kirmaan), under Brahim, it is suggested they were at first called Brahimi after their leader, Brahim or Braho, which ultimately changed to Brahui [17].

However, the common fallacy is the unsubstantiated assertion that the Brahui are the remnants of the Dravidians [18] inhabiting this part of Balochistan. This claim is made on the basis that their language, also classed as Dravidian is connected with the languages spoken in southern India.

We have little evidence regarding the racial origin of the Brahui apart from the general belief that they are Baloch and must belong to the same racial group as the Baloch. They might have lost some ingredients of Balochi, their original language, through political domination or intermarriage, intermingling with the indigenous Turks or Dravidian population of Central Balochistan over a long period. We have at least trace of such a Dravidian language in central Balochistan before the arrival of the Baloch tribes, which might have given Brahui speech its present structural form.

There is historical evidence that the Brahui were living in Fars in the 10th century AD. Ibn Haukal mentions Brahui tribes along with the Baloch. It can safely be presumed that the Brahui was the first to move from eastern Iran to Thuran. This migration might have occurred during the last century of Sassanid rule, with the bulk of the Baloch tribes following a few hundred years later. Many centuries later, the Brahui tribes established themselves in Naal and Khuzdar after securing political authority by defeating the Sindhi ruler of Kalat during the last decades of the sixteenth century [19].

The argument that the Brahuis are the remnants of Dravidian people, driven out by invading Aryan hordes, is thus baseless; nor we have any proof what so ever that the Brahuis are a people inhabiting their present abode since the ancient past. Therefore, it is generally believed that the Brahuis are not the Dravidians of Indian civilization but are part of migrating Baloch tribes from Iran, escaping economic and political pressure.

The Brahui language has generally been classed as belonging to the Dravidian family of languages [20], in spite of the fact that except a few, nearly all of the nouns used by Brahui speakers are Balochi. However, this fact can not be denied that there are traces of Turkish and Dravidian languages in Brahui's speech. The fact is that if the foreign overgrowth which has twined itself so luxuriantly around the Brahui stem is chopped off, we would lay bare the trunk of a language whose structure is still an unscathed Balochi speech [21].

B. The Kurd

The Kurds are of Aryan origin and believed to have come to Bohtan [22] from the region of Lake Urmia, in the seventh century B.C. Many etymologists believe that the Kurds belong to the Median branch of the Aryan tribes, who intermixed with many peoples of indigenous origin and later invaders including Semites, Armenians, and Turkomans [23]. The Kurdish mountainous region [24] was inhabited from time immemorial by a people who fought and sometimes defeated the forces of Babylonia and Assyria. The region of modern Kurdistan was settled by the seventh century BC, either through assimilation or displacement of the indigenous people, by Iranized progenitors of the modern Kurds [25]. Nevertheless, Kurdish settlements have been traced from 2400 BC. Some researchers asserted that the Gutie or Kurtie people are believed to be the ancestors of the Kurds: these people mixed with the surrounding stock, both Semites and Aryans.

Clay tablets found in ancient Babylon confirm the geographical location, as well as the name, that was given to the ancient Kurdish country. They indicate a Kingdom of Gutium (2211-2120 B.C) in that country, with twenty-one Kings according to Sumerian King-list. A king of this dynasty proclaimed himself the king of the four corners of the world. In a Sumerian inscription dated 2000 BC a country known as Kardala is mentioned and afterward the Assyrian king Tiglath-pileser II (C.745-727 B.C) appears to have fought a tribe referred to as Kur-ti-e. Xenophon (c.434-355 B.C) also speaks of Kardukai a mountain folk who harassed his march towards the sea [26].

Another thesis asserts the indigenous character of the Kurd, who are related to the Semites, especially the Chaldaeans, Georgians, and Armenians. Their original language is supposed to have been replaced by a later Iranized one [27]. The Kurds have been living in the Kurdish region and the Zagros area since the Semitic conquest of Assyria. They are said to have constituted a permanent nuisance for the weak rulers of Assyria by organizing raids on the Tigris mainland [28]. They were well organized and always resisted any penetration into their country by powerful neighbors. There are considerable pieces of evidence that the Guitie tribes used to raid the Mesopotamian outposts of the Semitic empire [29]. Herodotus maintains that they organized raids on Greek troops and settlements. The Greeks were restricted and did not dare to penetrate the Kurdish hills. He also talks of Kurdish movements at that time further east where there are some Kurdish tribes living alongside the Baloch tribes. The Kurds were also a threat to the Iranian Monarchs. The founder of the Sassanian dynasty, Ardashir 1 (226-241 A.D) mentions among his opponents, the Shah-e-Kurdan [30].

Linguistically, Kurdish belongs to the family of northwestern Iranian languages. It is strikingly closer to Balochi than any other tongue. Kurdish is generally grouped into three main divisions:

northern, central and southern. Akre, Amadiyah, Dahuk, Shaythun, and Zakhu are grouped as southern; Irbil, Bingird, Pizhdar, Sulemaniya, and warmawah as central. The Mukri dialect is spoken to the south of Lake Urmia, west of Iran. Another grouping of Kurdish dialects has been made, giving Kirmaanji and Kurdish prominence in the northern and southern regions, while a third dialect is Macho-Macho, which is called Zaza in Turkish and Gorani in Persian. Many linguists, however, doubt the Kurdish affinity or origin of the dialect [31]. Kurdish has undergone considerable phonetic changes, yet it is distinct in grammar, syntax, and vocabulary from any other neighboring speech.

C. The Indigenous Tribes

It is difficult to identify the tribes who may be of purely Baloch or non- Baloch origin [32]. Since their migration from north-west Caspian region and their movement eastward, most probably in waves which started at the end of the second millennium BC and continued to the 16th century of the Christian era, when they reached Multan in the east and as far as Gujrat in India, the Baloch must have absorbed many indigenous tribes along the way [33], some of them losing their identity, some blending with others and quite a few maintaining their distinctive character against tremendous pressure. A wide variety of invaders came to Balochistan and greatly influenced the racial and cultural environment of the region. After a long journey from their abode in the northwestern Caspian region, it took the Baloch two and half millennia to reach the Indus valley; it is inevitable that there must have been a considerable admixture of peoples during their constant movement.

As regards, the non-Baloch tribes of the region, there are sketchy accounts in the Greek, Persian and Arab chronicles. There are references to the existence of Cushites among the possible Kiprat-arbat of Mesopotamia. The Biblical discourses and the Greek authors mention of Kuch, Kach or Kaj, interpreted as the names of certain tribes probably Cushitic. Kach Candhawa or Kech Makkuraan are presumed to have been named after the chief of these tribes, called Gandara and after whom the country was called Gedrosia [34]. In a similar vein the Gadurs of Las, who are certainly of Rajput origin, have been said to belong to Gedrosia [35] in the ancient past. The Meds, who possess many attributes of Arrian's Ichthyophagoi, are also said to be of indigenous stock, while the Sajidi in Mushkey is guessed to be the remnants of the Sacae or Scythians [36]. The Greeks also mention Oreitai, Oxoi, and Parikanoi, the latter meaning mountaineers, does not connote any tribal appellation. The former two words are attributed largely to Houth faction [37] of the Baloch. The Arab chronicles mention Korak or Med: both are found in the coastal belt of Balochistan.

The Jath or Jadgaal are considered to be Dravidian and their Language is of Sindhi origin. The early Arab Historians describe them as holding the country between Kirmaan and Mansura in Sindh. They are believed to have migrated from east to west and must have a racial affinity with the Jamotes and Sungurs [38].

The Lasi claim descent from Summas and Sumras of Sindh. The Lasis and their subsection can clearly be identified with the Jaths. The Dehwaars of Kalat and Mastung are mostly Tajiks with elements of Chamakzai who have migrated from Bactria. Their language is a corrupt form of Persian. The Noushervanis of Kolwah has an unsubstantiated claim of a Perian connection through Kiani Maliks.

D. The Afghan

The north-east of Balochistan is populated by Pakhtuns/ Afghan tribes. The word Afghan is believed to have been derived from the Sanskrit Avagen which goes back to the Sumerian word for a mountainous region, Ab-bar-gan "the high country" [39]. A 6th century AD Indian astronomer, Varahamihira, was the first to use the name Afghan in his writings. Historically, the area, Afghanistan, has been mentioned since the 6th century B.C. Although we cannot derive any firm conclusions from the sketchy accounts of the Greeks or the inscriptions found in the area, which date back the Achaemenian era, the main regions mentioned, Bactria, Arachosia, and Aria, have generally been interpreted as the region up to the Indus including the Afghan plains around the Amu River, Kandahar, and Herat. The Greek's Drangiana must have been a region in the southeast of Afghanistan, including probably some parts of Sistaan.

Some of the Afghans consider themselves descendants of Afghan, the grandson of the Biblical King Saul. They claim that Saul was forty-fifth in descent from Abraham, while Kais, Kish or Kesh was the thirty-seventh from Saul. In some Afghan traditions, Kais has been regarded as contemporary of the Prophet Muhammad. They maintain that seventy-six tribesmen, representing the principal Afghan tribes under their leader Kais, visited Hijaz and embraced Islam. Prophet Muhammad renamed Kais Abdur Rashid and bestowed on him the title of Pihtan, which means the "rudder" of a ship in the Syriac language. However, the claim of their migration from the Middle East to present Afghanistan and later to the northeast of Balochistan and their relationship with the Israelites cannot be substantiated by any sound historical evidence.

Their language, Pashthu, an Aryan tongue, is most probably the Pactypae mentioned by the Greeks. It is said that the Afghan may have adopted the language after their settlement among Pashthu-speaking people. Linguistically, the Afghans who do not claim Perso-Turkish origin, are Pathan, but ethnologically all Pathans are not Afghans [40]. The Afghans, unlike their Baloch neighbors, are deeply religious to the extent of bigotry.

The political organization of the Pakhtun is essentially tribal and constituted from a number of kindred groups through common ancestry. Many tribes or sections are normally affiliated with others who may be alien but such kinship endures not through common blood but through mutual benefits. The office of the tribal chief, the Khan, is elective and depends on the goodwill of the people. However, the leadership of the entire tribe is generally hereditary, the dynasty running in some particular family.

Although the Pathan chief has tremendous power and can exercise those without consulting the clan elders, the individual Pakhtun is democratic in his approach and can be persuaded only by the Jirga or through common consent. Individuality has a greater scope for expression among the Afghans. Every Pakhtun thinks it his inalienable right to do himself justice. The right to private revenge is not only lawful but considered honorable. A self- respecting Afghan will not kill a woman, a minor or a racial inferior. Generally, Afghan has cultural characteristics common to most people of Central Asia in a tribal set-up.

E. The Baloch

There are differences among scholars regarding the racial origins of the Baloch. Some believe that they belong to the Chaldean branch of the Semitic people, owing to their name to the Babylonian King Belus, which was also the name of their God. An Assyrian, Turco-Iranian and Aryan origin has also been mentioned by many writers.

The origin and etymology of the name Baloch are still obscure; E Herzfeld believes that it is derived from a Median term which he reconstructs as brza-vaciya from brza-vak, loud cry, in contrast to namravak, quite polite way of talking [41]. Alternatively, it is maintained that Baloch is made of two Sanskrit words, *Bal* and *Och*. Bal means strength or power and Och high or magnificent [42]. Another line of etymology is suggested by East India Company spy and writer Longworth Dames, who says the word is a nickname meaning a "cock's comb" [43]. A seventeenth-century Persian dictionary, Burhan-e-Kathih, mentions the Baloch as a cock's comb crest or the name of a barbarian people who inhabit the mountains on the border of Kirmaan [44].

The Baloch are generally referred by Arab and Persian writers as Koch o Baloch. Both are considered to be one people, with two names being synonymous except for the difference of language. A tenth-century geographical treatise, Hudud al Alam, localizes the Kufij or Koch in the south-eastern mountainous region of Iran [45]. Nizamul Mulk in Sistaan Nama refers to the Kufij and maintains that they lived in the neighborhood of Kirmaan [46]. The Arab writer Al Istakhri says the Kufij lived on the eastern fringe of the Kirmaan Mountains, which he terms *Jabal al kufs* [47]. The Moroccan Abu Abdullah Muhammad, known as Al Idrisi, writing at the end of the eleventh century A.D, also mentions Kufs and Belus living in the west and south as far as the sea. He gives the impression that the Belus apparently lived separately from the Kufs. Another Arab writer, Yakut, also mentioned Koch and Belus living in the Kirmaan Mountains: and Masudi and ibn Haukal likewise refer to Koch and Belus inhabiting the mountainous fringe of Kirmaan. The kufs are said to have divided into seven tribes with a different language from the Baloch. Some of the Baloch writers believed that it is possible that the contemporary Brahui tribes might have been regarded as Koch [48].

Beginning from ancient history, the Baloch appear to have been in constant conflict with their neighbors. The first organized attack on them on a large scale came from the Persian monarch Khusraw I, the Anushervan (531-578 A.D), around 531 A.D. After the collapse of Sassanids, various regional rulers of Iranian peninsula also fought occasional battles with the Baloch to keep the trade routes open through Baloch territories and also keep Baloch in their areas to a minimum. The Baloch in Kirmaan and Sistaan continued to be a formidable threat and came into a bloody conflict with the Buwaihi rulers. They defeated the forces of the dynasty under the command of Abul Hasan Ahmad bin Buwaihi. However, another expedition under Abidbin Ali defeated the Baloch and occupied areas up to Makkuraan. Most of the Baloch leaders were killed in the battle, the invading forces capturing the southern limits of the Baloch region as far as the sea [49].

It seems that the first Baloch migration from Kirmaan [50] and Sistaan toward the east started generally in the early sixth century A.D after the Iranian thrust into their region during the reign of the Anushervan. The Ephthalite inroads into northern Iran must be another factor. Up to the late 10th century A.D, the Baloch or Koch o Baloch inhabited the western and northern areas of Kirmaan, Sistaan, and Makkuraan. Their migration eastward may have been the result of pressure, first from Persian rulers, then from the Turkish Seljuk tribes. Mongol hordes of Genghis Khan also forced many Baloch tribes to move eastward towards present-day Balochistan. By the 14th century, some of the Baloch tribes moved into central Balochistan up to the Jahlawaan hills, where they came into conflict with a group of the Baloch tribes-Brahuis who were already settled there. Further eastward migration of these tribes to the Indus valley or Punjab took place at a much later date. The movements of the Baloch tribes were also witnessed from Seistan to the Helmand valley as far as Farah and southward to Shorawak [51].

From linguistic evidence, it appears that the Baloch migrated eastward from the region of the Caspian Sea-a theory borne out by the clear relationship obtaining between Balochi and Kurdish [52]. Balochi language is one of the descendants of ancient Iranian dialects dominant in the territory of Media and Parthia. It is this consideration that furnishes one of the major arguments in support of the proposition that areas adjacent to the southern coasts of the Caspian were the original Baloch homeland [53]. These ancient dialects, while disclosing some features common to Parthian, have a number of peculiarities that distinguish them from other languages. Of the movement of the Baloch south-eastwards from northwestern areas of Iran we possibly find evidence in the parallel between the Baloch and Iranian dialects Farsi and Khuri to the south of the Dasht-e-Kavir, a parallel which stems from the prolonged existence of Baloch tribes in the area [54].

The Baloch kinship with the Chaldean branch of Semitic people is still asserted. The suggestion that they may be original inhabitants of the Sistaan, Kirmaan or present-day Balochistan has also been propounded. The hypothesis of an Arab origin and migration from Aleppo or Hijaz is based simply on one so-called "genealogical poem" of doubtful attribution.

The Semitic connection of the Baloch was first suggested by George Rawlinson in 1862 in his three-volume book, the five Great Monarchies of the Ancient Eastern World. He maintains that the word Baloch might have been derived from Belus, the Babylonian king, identified as Nimrod. According to usual theory and mostly supported by Scriptures, the Babylonian or Chaldean empire extended from the mouth of the Euphrates-Tigris to Euxine, the river Halys and Palestine, parts of eastern Iran and the southern shores of the Persian Gulf. The empire comprised of many people- including Hamites, Semites, Ethiopians, and Aramaeans. These peoples spoke various Semitic languages, prominent among them Chaldean, Aramaean, Hebrew, and the Syriac and Turanian dialects with Ethiopian or Cushite vocabulary [55] or more precisely the kiprat-arbat, interpreted as the four nations, or the four tongues; that is Cushite, Turanian, Semitic and Aryan. The early inscriptions contain considerable Cushite, Semitic and a small Aryan element. These languages were presumed to be not merely local dialects but distinct tongues representing four great families of human speech [56].

The Baloch connection with Chaldea comes with reference to Asiatic Ethiopians, of whom physical comparison has been made to some people in ancient Balochistan well before the arrival of the Baloch. Two possible theories have been put forward. Firstly, the Chaldean Cushite or Asian Ethiopians might have spread east and west, on the one hand to Susiana, Persia proper, Karmania (Carmania), Gedrosia and India; and on the other hand, to Arabia and the east coast of Africa. The second proposition is that the Cushites might have colonized the coastal region of Arabia and from there spread to Makkuraan, Kirmaan, and areas bordering India [57].

The very existence of a Chaldean people supposed to be a race entirely distinct from the early Babylonians, Armenians, Arabs, Kurds, or Sclaves, who came from the north long after the historical period and settled as the dominant people in the lower Mesopotamian valley– is based mostly on conjecture and very much disputed by scholars [58]. Moreover, the Asiatic Ethiopians who constituted one of the major races of Chaldea obviously are not the Baloch of today. They may have a certain relationship with the people inhabiting ancient Balochistan, but the Baloch settlements in Gedrosia by all accounts date from centuries later than the referred Asiatic Cush. However, the physical description of the Asiatic Cush fits many people in the sub-continent and Balochistan. As regards their affinity with the Baloch, the description could apply to a great extent to the Darzadag factions among the Baloch in southern Balochistan. A critical study of Baloch hereditary characteristics, physical features, socio-cultural and religious traditions amply demonstrates the Baloch racial kinship with Aryan people and reveals the Caspian Sea region as their original homeland.

3- Balochi

The ancient vocabulary, the breakdown of sounds, grammatical structure, forms of inflection and pattern of reconstruction of such form are the factors usually analyzed to establish any relationship among various languages. Mere loan-word which has crept into a language as a result of contacts with the speakers of other tongues cannot be the proper criterion for determining language kinship. Normally, there are three main sources of word entering Balochi: foreign words such as English or Arabic, the latter through religious influence; words derived from neighboring languages such as Persian, Pashthu, or indigenous languages such as Jadgaali, Saraiki or quite recently Urdu; and words coined from original Balochi sources to meet modern scientific and technological requirements. Another interchange of words occurred in Balochi due to frequent change of speech among the many linguistically separated Baloch and Brahui clans. Many Baloch tribes speak Brahui, while Brahui tribes speak Balochi. Moreover, almost all the Brahui tribes in Iranian Balochistan now speak Balochi. Sometimes it becomes difficult to assert with certainty whether there is a Brahui substratum in Balochi or whether it is Brahui that has been influenced by Balochi. It is, however, probable that Balochi had some influence and that the original Dravidian phonetical system of Brahui has been adapted to that of its Balochi neighbor.

Linguists are generally in agreement that Balochi belongs to the Persian branch of the Aryan sub-family of the Indo-European languages. Balochi bears striking resemblance to Kurdish and Persian. There is also an overlay of Indo–Aryan loan words or an underlay from some older indigenous non-Indo-European tongue [59]. What was the ancient source of present-day Balochi, is difficult to claim with confidence. It is maintained that Balochi derives neither from Parthian nor from Middle Persian. The original source is sometimes held to be a lost language that must, however, have a certain affinity with Parthian or Middle Persian. Balochi has a pronounced individuality which is greatly influenced by Median speech and the Kurdish dialects [60]. It occupies a distinct position among all the Iranian languages, resembling most other Iranian tongues in showing a nearer relationship to ancient Avesta than to Old Persian [61] -the court language of the Achaemenians from which modern Persian is descended. The affinity of Balochi with any language of the Semitic family [62] is absolutely untenable. All linguists are unanimous in the belief that Balochi is an Indo-Aryan language of the Iranian family [63].

Balochi is not homogeneous. The people of various regions speak their own variety of dialects with an overriding influence from neighboring tongues. Balochi dialects can be classified into two main groups, northern and southern. Dialects spoken in Kach-Gandhawa, the Suleiman Mountains, parts of Dera Ghazi Khan and Jacobabad can be categorized among the north while southern dialects said to be spoken in Makkuraan and Persian Balochistan, excluding the dialects of Kharan and Sistaan [64]. Linguist, Dr. J.H Elfenbein, establishes six major dialects. The eastern hill dialects; Rakhashani, subdivided into Kalati, Chagai, Kharani, Afghani, and Panjguri; Sarhaddi, which includes dialects of the Marv region; Sarawaani; Kechi and Lotuni; and the Coastal. He further groups these dialects into three categories on a philological basis as 'oldest', 'transitional' and 'youngest'. He places the eastern hills and coastal dialects as the oldest with the centrally located dialects, Rakhshani, as the youngest and Sarawaani, Kechi and Lotuni as the transitional. His criteria for such an arbitrary grouping are those dialects that have preserved more archaic features versus those which display greater tendencies towards innovation and change [65].

Balochi is spoken by the majority of people in the Pakistani, Irani and Afghani parts of Balochistan. Other languages spoken in Balochistan are mainly Pashthu, Persian, Brahui, Saraiki, and Jadgaali. In central Balochistan, the region occupied by the Brahui tribes, the people are mostly bi-lingual; speaking Brahui along with Balochi.

Balochi has been influenced by the Indo-Aryan languages such as Sindhi, Panjabi and a variety of other tongues such as Saraiki on the east and Pashthu on the north, with Persian influence on the west easily observed. But it has remarkably resisted phonetic change. Many ancient words have been retained in Balochi in their original form and meaning. However, many words have entered the language from neighboring languages that diluted its Iranian heritage to some extent [66].

Balochi literature is available today mostly in the form of folk tales, primitive in any sense but extending over many thousand years. The poetic literature is available in a very advanced and developed form from the fifteenth century AD.

Poetry is still one of the main sources of Baloch history and culture. Being unwritten, however, its authenticity with regard to many events sometimes becomes doubtful. Most of the poems must invariably have been edited throughout history and many of them have been lost. The Poetry which has come to us takes the form of epics, lyrics, lullabies, fables, and riddles, knitting together a great mass of ancient traditions, customs, legends, proverbs, religious-mythological beliefs and cultural traits of the people. The epics can be compared in forcefulness and lucidity and for their content of prudential sayings with Greek and Hindu epics. They depict a pastoral and nomadic culture of a proud and warrior people. Balochi poetry is not merely an arrangement of words and phrases devoured of any purposefulness or indifferent to geo-social and political happenings. It undoubtedly shows a certain amount of poetic imagination and artistry and there is only the slightest degree of exaggeration. It depicts the culture and tradition of the people in a vigorous, simple and very appropriate manner. These poems appear to have been constructed either by the individuals involved in a war or romance or the court poets of various tribes, called Zangi Shahi [67].

4- Socio-cultural Behavior

Baloch society places immense importance on the individual and accords him an honorable status. Consequently, he is highly egoistic and deeply proud. *Kay mani gahgeerien sara guddieth?* —who can cut off my majestic head" is a true manifestation of the Baloch attitude. He disdains intermarriages with social inferiors [68]. However, there is no caste system among the Baloch the one that is being practiced in Indian society [69]. All people were noble, enjoying equal social status. The inferiority and superiority come with the deeds, not by descent.

It is an open society where men and women work in unison. The Baloch give women privileges which to a great extent are identical to the equal social rights advocated in the ancient Iranian religious work Din Kard. The society is organized on patriarchal lines with the formal authority vested in the males, who are primarily the holders and inheritors of property; though the woman does inherit and manage the property and also play an important role in managing family affairs. Polygamy is practiced but divorce is rare.

The Baloch tribal society is based on the concept of mutual benefit and loss. The political, economic and social nucleus is the tribe, whose structure is firm and permanent for the good of every member. It is constituted from a number of kindred groups but forms a closely-knit unit of fighting men, ready to defend individual and tribal interests.

Every individual had equal access to natural resources and a vested right to exploit them, in a system based on common economic responsibility. The land was jointly cultivated by groups of tribesmen or clans. Private possession of lands is clearly a later phenomenon.

The tribal organization and its external structure have been witnessing transformation mainly through external socio-economic and political influences but without any mark or drastic effect on the existing social conditions. The tribe organized mainly on the pattern of ancient Aryan tribes [70] was, therefore, a self-sufficient political, social, economic and cultural unit, headed by the tribal chief, who enjoyed considerable authority. The post of the chief was not hereditary: before the occupation of Balochistan by the British, the tribal chiefs were appointed through election by headmen [71].

The Baloch cultural traditions are based on moral principles of good conduct beneficial to the entire people. Such traditions are acquired by the individual through a constant process. He is brought up in a specific social environment where he is taught to respect the rules sanctified by society. He is never insulting. Even punishments meted out to criminals were never degrading. There was never hanging or maiming or blinding, which were prevalent among many ancient people. The honorable way of the beheading was always used to kill a criminal or an enemy.

A respected Baloch is truthful and honest. Telling lies is considered an insult. He will keep his word at any cost: once he vows to do something, he will do it by whatever means in total disregard of the consequences. The woman's dishonor is washed off only by blood. Prostitution, abhorred as a vitiating act of perversion and highly intolerable, is punished with death.

The Baloch has a penetrating sense of individual and collective justice. He considers it his duty and inalienable right to take revenge. The right to do himself justice is never delegated to others. Once a wrong is committed the wrongdoer will be paid in the same coin. Sometimes the revenge is taken even after generations. He who does wrong is symbolized as evil while those taking revenge are thought noble and virtuous. The fight should not be equal: virtue must overwhelm the evil. The Baloch always sides with the oppressed because he has a just cause. The tradition of *Baahot* in all its theoretical aspects is to help the weak and withstand hardship in defense of the oppressed who have sought help. Defending a person or his interests when he seeks help is by no means helping the wrong side. Basically, it is weak who request help and such help is always forthcoming.

The Baloch respects the brave while despising the coward. He has great regard for the fallen hero, even belonging to the enemy, whom he buries with full honors. Enemy leaders are neither ridiculed nor belittled, even if defeated. In the Baloch epics, heroes from both sides are equally praised for their bravery and courage. This attitude is evident during the Rind Lashaarconflict and tribal wars and before and after this period. The principles are upheld even in individual conflicts. Baalach, a folk hero who avenges his brother's death by fighting an entire tribe single-handedly, respects Beebagr, who killed his brother. Conceptually, he considers him evil incarnate and vows to fight to the last, but he praises him for his skilled use of the sword. In another folk story, a mother, while mourning the death of her fallen son in the hands of a young foe who also dies, profusely praises the enemy for his courage and bravery, boasting that her son is killed not by a scoundrel but by a brave and honorable youth [72].

The Baloch is frank and deeply affectionate. Once obliged he remembers it for life. *'Thaase aap ware sad saala wapa bedaar'*-you should have affection for the person for a century who once offered you a glass of water, - so goes the saying.

5- Mythological beliefs

Religion has always been a part of human intellectual behavior [73]. But the Baloch can truly be called to have been secular if the term is appropriate to denote a people who have not allowed religion to overwhelm their traditions and socio-economic beliefs. We cannot trace Baloch religious thinking in ancient epochs, apart from the fact that their religious view was very much closer to the beliefs of migrating Aryan tribes [74] and they generally belonged to the religious fraternity of the Central Asian peoples, especially the Iranians. We can deduce certain viewpoints on the basis of Baloch religious behavior during the last two thousand years. It appears that there are elements in their social life which have a bearing on religion while beliefs, social or cultural, firmly held by the Baloch undoubtedly have elements of religious ecstasy.

After the fall of the Sassanid empire, like the other nations in the Iranian plateau, the Baloch, by and large, adopted the Arabian religion of Islam. However, from the very beginning, the Baloch were not considered perfect Muslims by the orthodox section of the Muslim community. The earliest reference regarding the Baloch secular approach is found in the account of the Arab historian, Al Muqaddasi, in the 10th century A.D. He observed that Baloch was Muslims only by name and that they never observed the tenets of the new faith in letter and spirit. It appears that even after 300 hundred years, Islam, which, in spite of the political force behind it, could not diffuse throughout the Baloch society [75]. Pre-Islamic thinking was still prominent among the bulk of the people [76]. In many ways, the Baloch's religious outlook is still not shaped entirely by his acceptance of Islam more than fourteen hundred years ago. It achieved no breakthrough to the point of fanaticism among the Baloch which it easily inculcated among many other people. Instead, ancient Baloch religious thoughts perfected throughout entries and which must be a fine amalgam of Iranian and Indian religious views held full sway and proved much stronger than the tenets of Islam. All the writers of the nineteenth and twentieth centuries are unanimous in their observation that the Baloch are not religious fanatics. Compared to other neighboring people, they have no high regard for clergy, who wear no particular dress and are not encouraged to be distinguished. Although *Mullah* or *Peer* has a role in countering the evil of *jinn,* sorcerers or monsters, there was no established clergy or priesthood, nor did Peer or Buzurg or the so-called religious celebrities exist among the Baloch.

The Baloch are still inexact in their duties, considering the religion as purely a personal affair. Their attitude towards religious matters is one of the philosophical calm. Any attempt on the part of the *Mullah* to transgress reasonable limits is strictly resisted and his influence other than religion is also curiously limited. He is neither Sunni nor Shia, he is simply a Baloch first and a Muslim next. To a Baloch Sunni or Shia makes no difference. The Zikris among the Baloch, who are the followers of one of the numerous Muslim sects (Seventy-two factions of Islamic faith are officially identified), are never discriminated against; although, to an outside observer, the Zikris may be violating some Orthodox Islamic views.

The ignoble attempts by certain Mullahs enjoying the active support and connivance of the ruling faction in Pakistan to create bitterness among the Baloch by importing sectarian feeling from other parts of the country or elsewhere, where the clergy not infrequently exploit the common people on Shia-Sunni divide or other frivolous issues, miserably failed to attract the people who generally regarded the entire game as an attempt by the state to divide the Baloch masses.

The Baloch is superstitious. He draws auguries from almost everything or happening which may be slightly unusual. The cry of the wild beast, sight of a serpent, a bird on the wing in the early morning or at night, a black cat or a hare crossing his path when he starts on a journey; and a host of other happenings are sufficient for him to perceive things auspicious or inauspicious for him or for the entire tribe. He has certain days considered unpromising for a journey or for ceremonies such as marriage. Sorcery also plays an important role. The sorcerer or Jathu is the most feared person and his evil influence can be lessened by a *Shey* or *Mullah*. The Baloch believe in Jinii or fairies or monsters in an overwhelming way.

References

1. Imperial Gazetteer of India, provincial series, Balochistan: Calcutta, 1908, reprinted: Orient Publishers, Lahore, 1976, pp 21-22

2. Thomas Holdich: The Gates of India-being a Historical Narrative. London,1877 reprinted: Goshae- Adab, Quetta, 1977, p 30.

3. Charles Masson: Narrative of A Journey to Kalat, London, 1843, reprinted: Indus Publications, Karachi,1976, p 8

4. Gul Khan Naseer: Balochi RazmiaShairi, Balochi Academy, Quetta,1979, p 14

5. Arnold J. Toynbee: A Study of History (in two volumes), Vol 1 Oxford, London 1978, pp 45-46

6. The Aryan migration has been steady and taken place in successive waves. The first to arrive on the Iranian Plateau, around the middle of the second millennium B.C, from the region of the Oxus and Laxartes rivers.

7. Encyclopedia Britannica: Vol 8, p 908

8. Yu.V. Gankovsky: The Peoples of Pakistan, Nauka, Moscow, 1971 p 146

9. Ibid. pp 80-81

10. The Sakas, whom Herodotus calls Scythians, were a semi-nomadic people from the Eurasian steppe. It appears that their settlement in Iran was of historic significance when the Medes were defeated at Nineveh by the Assyrians and Scythians. Later, the Scythians dominated the Medes and also devastated most of Asia Minor, including Palestine. The Cynthiana interregnum in the Median dynasty falls between the reign of Khashathrita Prorates (675-653 B.C) and Cyaxares (653-585 B.C).

11. The first mention of the Name "Arab" is found in the inscriptions of Shalmaneser III (858-824 B.C) of Assyria who in 853 B.C defeated Ahab, the King of Israel, supported by many Princes including "Jundibu, the Arab". The Arab kings and Queens are also referred to in later Assyrian cuneiform tablets and in an inscription in the Nabataean script.

12. Ibid. p 145

13. Thomas, Holdich" Op cit., pp 55-57

14. Yu.V. Gankovsky: Op Cit., p 149

15. Muhammad Sardar Khan Baloch (History of the Balochi Race and Balochistan. Process Pakistan, 1958; The Great Baloch, Balochi Academy, Quetta,1965: and A literary History of Baloch, Vol 1 Balochi Academy, Quetta, 1977) give etymological clues to establish supposed kinship among people or entire races. He refers to the names of places or tribes in ancient Mesopotamia, linking them ingeniously with the Baloch regardless of the fact that the scientific evidence on race or the hereditary characteristics of a people can be deduced on the basis of the comparative anatomy of skeletal and external features such as hair texture, skin color, and nasal breadth; anatomy of brain and central nervous system and of internal organs such as the heart, lungs and glands; and study of physical and intellectual growth and mental pathology. Studies are also carried out to determine the degree

of inventiveness or potential creativeness in diverse races and the nature and impact of socio-cultural and geographical factors.

16. Denys Bray: The Brahui language Vol, II London, 1931, reprinted Brihui Academy, Quetta,1978, pp35-36

17. Ahmad Yar Khan; Mukhtaser Tharikh-e-Baloch aurKhawanine-e- Baloch, Aiwan Kalat, Quetta, 1972, pp 7-8.

18. The Vedic hymns describe the native Dravidians as Dasyus, a term which has been interpreted as a "foe". The ancient writers have narrated strange tales about them. They were mentioned as "five or even three spans in height" some "noseless" they are hairy "with dog-shaped heads armed with claws".

19. Noor Ahmad Khan Fareedi: Baloch Qoumaur us ki Tharikh. Qasr-e-Adab Multan,1968, p 14.

20. Some writers have connected Brahui Language with the Aryan group while others with Kol language of Central India. Dr. Caldwell, an oriental linguist deleted Brahui in his list of Dravidian tongues though he believed that it contained a strong Dravidian element.

21. Denys Bray: Op Cit.Vol l, pp.7-8

22. Basile Nikitine: Les Kurds. Quoted in DerkKinnane: The Kurds and Kurdistan. Oxford, London,1970, p.21

23. Hasan Arfa: The Kurds-A Historical and Political Study. Oxford London,1968 P 1

24. The name Kurdistan, the country of the Kurds, was first used by the Seljuk Sultan Sanjar in the 12th century when he created a province of that name. By the 15th century, the province was reduced in size, but in both the Ottoman and Turkish empires the area was called Kurdistan.

25. DerkKinnane: Op Cit. p 21.

26. Hasan Arfa: Op Cit. P 21.

27. DerkKinnane: Op Cit. P 21

28. J.L Myres: The Dawn of History. Williams and Norgate, London,1918 p 128.

29. Sheikh A. Waheed: The Kurds and their country. Publishers united Lahore,1955, pp 46-47.

30. Kurdistan is divided among Syria. Iraq, Turkey, and Iran, the first division came after the Battle of Chaldiran in 1541 A.D when the area was practically partitioned between the Turks and Iranians. The Kurds have never accepted the partition of their homeland. Their struggle against alien rule has continued since 1832, but achieving a sovereign independent Kurdistan has been an elusive dream.

31. DerkKinnane: Op Cit. 3.

32. Race and nation are two mutually exclusive terms. A race will have certain genetically inborn physical features in common, while a nation has common socio-cultural attributes and a strong desire to achieve given political objectives. Race can not be determined by speech classification. Speakers of various languages may form one racial grope while people belonging

to one race may speak different languages. The case of the Baloch, the Kurds, and the Brahuis is similar. They belong to the same racial stock but speak three different languages. Our Afghan neighbors speak Pashthu as well as Persian. The Ugandan tribe Amba speaks two different languages but they are considered as one people. The term Aryan and Semite denote groups of people speaking closely interrelated languages but the speakers of these languages may not racially be as close as the languages they spoke. Therefore, the division of people by race does not correspond to their division in terms of speech.

33. The race has been in a continuous state of transformation. They have drifted frenetically: new genes have been introduced by explorers, conquerors and a variety of others. Thus, the notion of purity of race or blood appears to be untenable in view of the vast intermingling of peoples throughout history. Movement of the population in prehistoric as well as historic epochs with apparent free interbreeding have resulted in admixtures of various peoples.

34. Thomas Holdich Op Cit. pp 34-36.

35. A difference of opinion persists regarding the etymology of the word Mekran, Makkuraan or Maka. It has been presumed to have derived from Mah (Town) situated on the shores of the sea, Keran. Some Arab writers believe the word has been derived from Mokran, grandson of Noah. It is also considered to be a corruption of the Persian Mahi Khoran, Fisheaters-the Ichthyophagoi of the Greeks; or Maka meaning deceit. The word is also thought to be derived from the Dravidian word Mokara which occurs in Brihat Samhita in the 6th century A.D. Yet another interpretation is that the world Makraan is the Sanskrit Aryana or Irinya which signifies waste or swamp.

36. Charles Masson: Op Cit. pp 340- 344.

37. A few clans of Huth migrated about 1459 A.D from Makkuraan to Multan under the leadership of Mir Suhraab, who became a confidant of the Multan ruler Husain Langah, a Rajput by descent. Mir Suhraab's two sons, Ismail and Fateh, later ruled two separate districts of Multan called after them Dera Ismail and Fateh.

38. Balochistan-Through the Ages- A selection from the Government Record. Op Cit. Vol 11. p 549.

39. John C. Griffiths: Afghanistan- Key to a continent. Andre Deutch, London,1981, p. 13.

40. Mountstaurt Elephantston: Op. Cit, pp 290-293.

41. E. Herzfeld: Zoroaster and His word Vol II quoted in Yu V. Gankovsky. Op.Cit. p144

42. Husain Bakhsh Kousar: Quoted in Dost Muhammad Dost: The languages and Race of Afghanistan. Pashthu Academy, Kabul, 1975, p 362.

43. In 1010 A.D, Abdul QasimFirdousi (935-1020 AD) completed the Shahnama, which deals with nearly four thousand years of Persian history. He mentions that the Baloch sided with the Persian army under Cambyses (530-522 B.C) who fought the Median monarch Astagos. "After

Gustasham, came Ashkash. His army has formed the wanderers of the Koch and Baloch, intent on war with exalted 'cock-cob' and 'crest', whose back none in the world ever saw, nor was one of their figures bare of armor."

44. Mir Khuda Bakhsh Mari: Searchlights on the Baloch and Balochistan. Op Cit. P 15.

45. Hudad al Alam: quoted in yu v Gankovsky, Op Cit. P 34.

46. Nizamul Mulk: Siasat Nama, quoted in yu. V. Gankocsky, Ibid.

47. Ibid.

48. Henry George Raverty: notes on Afghanistan and Balochistan. London 1878, reprinted, GoshaeAdab, Quetta, 1976, p 1.

49. Mir Khuda Baksh Mari, The Baloches through the Centuries – History Vs Legend. Islamic press. Quetta, 1964 pp 17-18.

50. A Persian Chronicler has narrated that the Baloch chief of Kirmaan picked a quarrel with the ruler, who had demanded a girl for his harem from each of the forty Baloch clans. The Baloch dressed up and sent boys in girls disguise, and then fearing his wrath migrated from Kirmaan. (quoted by Edward. E Oliver Op. Cit.p 30.

51. Muhammad Sardar Khan Baloch: The Great Baloch, Op.Cit, pp 40-42.

52. Muhammad Abdur Rahman Barker and Aqil Khan Mengal: A course in Balochi. Vol, 1. Institute of Islamic Studies, Mcgill University Montreal,1969, P xiii.

53. Yu.V. Ganovsky: Op Cit. 144

54. Ibid.

55. Rawlinson: The five Great Monarchies of the Ancient Eastern World Vol I. John Murray, London, 1862, p 65.

56. Ibid. pp 69-70.

57. Ibid. p 67

58. Ibid. p 70-71

59. Muhammad Abdur Rahman Barker and Aqil Khan Mengal: Op Cit, Pxiii.

60. Mir Khuda Bakhsh Mari: Searchlights on the Baloches and Balochistan. Op. Cit. p 31.

61. George Abraham Grierson: A linguistic Survey of India-Specimens of Language of the Iranian Family. Calcutta. 1921, p 33.

62. Semitic, like Aryan, is exclusively a linguistic term coined in 1781 by a German anthropologist, Schlosser, qualifying a family of language which subsequently applied to those who speak or spoke any of the Semitic tongues. They are Akkadian (Assyro-Babylonian), Canaanite (Amorite and Phoenician) Aramaic (Syriac) Hebrew, Arabic and Ethiopic. The cuniform sources reveal a striking similarity among the various dialects spoken by these peoples. The pronouns and the nouns denoting blood relationships, numbers and the main organs of the body are identical in many Semitic tongues. The speakers of these languages are traditionally presumed to have descended from Sem, the eldest son of the Biblical Noah. They include the Babylonians', the Abyssinians, the Sabaeans, the Arabs, the Amorites, and the Chaldeans.

63. Muhammad Sardar Khan Baloch maintains that Balochi, its origin, its basic vocabulary, and sound, come close to the ancient Semitic family. (A Literary History of the Baloches, Op Cit. pp 9-17). He further asserts that if all the loan words of neighboring languages are discarded from Balochi, there remains a trunk of a language which is a profound relic of the ancient Semitic family both in roots and sound (History of Baloch Race and Balochistan, pp 3-4). In his enthusiasm to find a Semitic connection for the Baloch and their language, the author forgets that there may not necessarily be any relation between language and race. People who may speak mutually unintelligible tongues may belong to one racial stock. Furthermore, there are numerous languages categorized as spoken by certain groups of people known after these languages as Semites. From which branch of the Semitic speech Balochi may have descended has never been explained. Even the original founder of the idea, George Rawlinson, who tried to find some connection between Asian Ethiopians and those of Mesopotamia, did not suggest language affinity between Balochi and any of the ancient Semitic tongues. Muhammad Sardar Khan Baloch's supposition has found no favor with any linguist. His assertion can be classed with the 'Theories' on Baloch and Balochi by late Muhammad Husain Unqa, in his book Baloch QoumkeDoureQadeem Ki Tharikh (Pakistan Pres, Quetta, 1974).

64. M. Longworth Dames: Quoted in AbdurRehaman Barker and Aqil Khan Mengal, Op, Cit. pxxiv.

65. J.H. Elfenbein: "The Balochi Language- A Dialectology with the text" Royal Asiatic Society Monographs, Vol, xxvii, London,1966, p10

66. A.J. Arberry(ed): The legacy of Persia, Oxford, London, 1953 pp 194-195.

67. Gul Khan Naseer: Op. Cit. p 20.

68. The classification and comparison of races based on physical observation and measurement or upon differences in genetic makeup or both have largely been misinterpreted, often giving rise to false notions of the superiority or inferiority of various races and peoples. Discrimination against dark-skinned people appears to be very old. The Greek philosopher, Aristotle, has been dubbed the first racist in recorded history, but his theory appears to be based not on biological but on cultural premises. The ancient Hebrews attributed to themselves the idea of a "chosen people". Later, one can find a similar religious notion with the Muslims. Such conceptions, religious or social are not new. The ancient Chinese, Egyptian, Greeks, Romans, and Indians made a distinction between human groups, mostly on cultural accounts. When the Aryans invaded the sub-continent, they called the original inhabitants 'dark-skinned barbarian', and themselves as dvija. The Chines distinguish themselves from a people described as resembling donkeys, from whom they descended. The social differences among the Egyptians themselves were painted in wall paintings. Even as late as 7th century A.D when the Arabs, after accepting Islam set out to conquer civilized people like the Romans and the Persians, both distinguished themselves from Arabs calling them 'lizard eating beasts'. In Pakistan the

Baloch identify immigrants from India, as 'Kallu' and Panjabis as 'Tundo' (a person with an egg-shaped head), denoting an inferior position to them.

69. The distinctive feature of Hindu socio-religious behavior was the caste system, which is considered to be the off-shoot of the doctrine of reincarnation and varna, which divides men into four major castes: the Brahmans, the priest; the Kshatriya, the fighters; the Vaisyas, the workers; and the Sudras, the dependent, who were from the indigenous non-Aryan section of the people. The incarnation theory gave religious justification to the caste institution, which was seen as ordained by the Divinity, who made it hereditary, from father to son. Rebirth to a higher social grade, however, depended upon the goodness and honesty of the individual in his former life. Salvation could be attained on the basis of the observation of the doctrine of dharma, variously interpreted as virtues, order, law, and ideals.

70. The Aryan tribal union or Kingdom, Rashtra, comprised the tribes and their section down to their family, kula. The head of the tribal kingdom, gifted with divine authority, was assisted in political and legal administration by a council of advisors comprising almost all tribal chiefs and probably the priest. The Aryans were divided into three main classes: the aristocracy, the priesthood, and the common man. There was absolutely no caste consciousness at the beginning. However, the Aryans, who were the victors, kept themselves aloof from the indigenous colored masses which ultimately strengthened the caste system, which either already existed or was perfected as a social institution later, well after the Aryan interregnum.

71. Muhammad Sardar Khan Baloch: History of the Baloch Race and Balochistan, Op Cit,85.

72. Qazi, Abdur Rahim Saabir: Balochistan ke Janbaaz. Balochi Adabi Board, Karachi, 1979, pp 82-83

73. Religion is man's intellectual commitment to the recognition of a supernatural source who is supposedly responsible for human comforts as well as miseries both during his life and afterward, depending upon the honest or dishonest behavior of the individual. Religions that differ in practice have an identical approach to the fundamentals. They are neither good for social discipline or control even today, but certain religious attributes that were appropriate for the primitive mind may have lost their utility and have little relevance in today's socio-cultural environment. Religions appear to be in conflict with human intelligence and socio-economic progress. As a historical phenomenon, however, it provided comfort and patience to the ancient man in his helpless struggle against the forces of nature.

74. The religious ideas of the Aryans are those of primitive animism. The forces of nature were personified as male or female deities. Their pantheon of Divas, the shining ones, were Indira, the god of strength; Agni the god of fire; Surya, the sun god; Soma, the god of intoxicating juice soma: Vanuma, the spirit of Order; Yama, the god of death. Other Gods were Savitri, Gandharvas, Apsaras, Maruts, and Vishedevas. The Cardinal point in

religious belief was the sacrifice, both individual and communal. The belief in life after death, which appears rudimentary, was in terms of punishment for sin and reward for holiness.

75. Al Muqasi: AhsanulThaqasim, quoted in Dost Muhammad Dost, Op Cit, p363.
76. Yu.V. Gankovsky: Op Cit. p 145.

CHAPTER II
NATION, NATIONALISM, AND THE NATION-STATE

1- Nation

The word nation in its present sense can be traced in early writings in Europe especially in Latin and French literature. However, the nation as a doctrinal notion goes back to the German philosophers of the Romantic era. Johann Gottlieb Herder gave an imaginative interpretation of the nation, opposing the 19th-century theory of mankind as a single uniform group of animals. Although he never espoused racist notions, he differentiated between separate natural groupings on the basis of geography, which he believed would cause internal unification of each group as a result of specific heredity.

Renan, in the 19th century, provided an inspiring definition of a nation. 'A nation is a soul... great solidarity created by the sentiments of sacrifices. It presupposes a past. It resumes itself in the present by a tangible fact: the consent, the clearly expressed desire to continue living in common' [1]. Herder believed that perpetual self-perfection is not attainable by the individual in isolation but only through corporate activity in groups, each of which becomes a composite unity and develops a "soul" or spirit of its own. This spirit of the group or nation is distinctive for each nationality. Each nation thus forms a separate, independent entity, expressing itself in its language and culture, setting its own standards of values and conduct, and is thus entirely self-determining [2]. Barker asserted that the nation must be an idea as well as a fact before it can become a dynamic force [3]. The nation is invariably a collective personality: the racial element in nationalism is one of the strongest factors.

A feeling of solidarity and love for a homeland and a desire to live under the government of one's choice can be cited as a significant criterion of nationhood necessary for arousing the national sentiments in a community or group. Common traditions and a shared historical past knit people together to a single nation. Smith observed that people who grasp its sense of nationality with pleasure and love can always celebrate its rebirth [4].

The nation came to be regarded as the ultimate summit of human loyalty directed to achieve prosperity and a high level of morality and justice. The nation thus becomes the highest source of allegiance and the greatest images of man's social identification and loyalty. In the meantime, nationalism gave impetus to aggressive instincts aimed against foreigners, or to be more precise against the stronger people dominating the weaker. It urged unity and vigilance against the enemy in a deep sense of national self-interest. From a wider perspective, people who have a common historical background, ethnic affinity, linguistic kinship or group consciousness can be classed as a nation. The attributes of nationhood are numerous and varied: such as possession of a compact territory, common racial origin with a single language, a distinct culture, and common religious traditions and above all a desire to live under some political authority as a free people. However, all the national groups do not conform to this interpretation. Take the example of the Jewish people. They have been scattered all over the world with no compact territory common tongue or a common culture. But they still regard themselves as Jews and have strong impulses of national solidarity. The case of the Baloch and other nationalities can be seen in the same light. Baloch live in three different countries. They do not speak the same language, although the majority of them speak Balochi or its various dialects. A considerable number of them live in areas other than Balochistan proper. They have their linguistic differences, with Brahui faction. Moreover, linguistic and geographical isolation have had some bearing on their culture, which sometimes appears very dissimilar, as in the Pakistani provinces of Punjab and Sindh, while it has developed distinct traits in the Irani and Afghani part of Balochistan.

Nevertheless, the Baloch are imbued with an intense sense of a national identity or nationhood.

2- Nationalism

Nationalism can be regarded as the most essential characteristic which provides the state or a nation with its true identity and an inspiring will. It is an emotional outlook and has its sway in the inalienable right of self-determination and the principle of national sovereignty. In a broader sense, nationalism is a progressive step towards equality, at least among a people speaking one language and with a common historical background. It removes the distinction, at least theoretically, between the ordinary man and the nobility, and harks back to primitive tribalism, where all members of the tribe had equal rights and privileges. Inseparably linked with the nation and nationalism is the fatherland or the national state, to which the people give unreserved loyalty. In a national state, obedience and subjugation to the rulers are transferred to the state, where the people find historical solidarity.

The national instinct or consciousness, without which nationalism could not be conceived, would have an easy path if identified with a nation-state or the sovereign independence of a people. The people cannot easily forget the pride of national belonging and there are many examples in the history where people kept their national ambitions even being subjugated for hundreds of years. The Ethiopian Jews waited thousands of years to be reunited with their fellow Jews of Israel in 1985. An occupied Poland had kept the national awareness alive throughout the period of foreign rule. Hungarians, Czechs, and Bulgarians remained under foreign hegemony for many centuries, as did many other people of diverse ethnic and cultural origin, but remarkably, they preserved their national identity and culture. The Baloch and the Kurds retained their identity despite tremendous odds.

Nationalism is regarded as a state of collective mentality which represents the peoples' political will aimed at achieving a national state where it can live for the good of all its members. It became a force among those who had developed a perception of nationhood. But such nationalism can be destructive if directed against other people. Ziring pointed out this aspect of nationalism by remarking that in its positive form nationalism is a demand for individual freedom and self- expression, while in its negative form it threatens a tenuous equilibrium [5].

The growth of nationalism had a different origin in various countries under varying circumstances but historically, it would be invidious to give a firm date to the rise of nationalism. Man, however, has always made a distinction between different peoples and has always been loyal to his own linguistic or religious-cultural group. Early tribalism or the Greek city-states are examples of primitive nationalism. Modern nationalism is the magnified and most sophisticated form of promotive group loyalties and sentiments. Historical development and past adventures against a common enemy arouse national sentiments that bind the group together with a deep sense of national pride. The same feelings ultimately merge with a desire to attain national and political independence.

The greatest feat of national consciousness and pride was displayed by the Greeks of Xanthe. Such acts could not be motivated by the mere threat of subjugation but only by deeply resented provocation and a burning hatred of the alien rule. According to Herodotus, the Persians who had overrun the neighboring country were approaching Xanthe. Seeing no way out to resist the invaders, the men of Xanthe collected together their goods as well as the women, children and elderly people, set fire to them and vowed not to give up to the Persians and die rather than surrender. In later years, the Greeks held in high esteem those who laid down their lives in defense of their country. Similar examples are witnessed in Baloch history when they vowed to fight to the last. In the Panjab, the Baloch performed courageous acts against the expected attack by the Mughal army out of intuitive national feeling. In the more recent past, the Baloch elders bound themselves together to die during the battle of Hadab against the British forces. These are acts by people with a high spirit of national sentiment and deep hatred for foreign rule.

The genesis of contemporary nationalism can be traced to ideas linked with human dignity and equality, freedom and solidarity. The French revolution not only signified patriotism and national pride; it also legitimized governments identified with the peoples' interests as against monarchic rule. It also provided a base for intellectual discussions regarding the nation and the general concept of nationalism, which resulted in the argument that human beings are divided into nations and that the government can claim validity only if it is backed by the free will of the people. It thus gave legitimacy only to national self-government. The French Revolution negated many primitive ideas regarding the nature and style of government and emphasized the indivisible personality of the nation. The concept of loyalty to the nation emerged as a progressive theory in subsequent decades.

Giuseppe Mazzini (1805-1872) gave a further boost to the liberal theory of nationalism by presenting national self-determination as a universal principle for the solution of all political issues. Mazzini was a staunch supporter of national self-rule and any form of individual self-seeking was considered a betrayal of the national cause. Giuseppe Garibaldi and Thaddeus Kosciuszko exemplified the doctrine of nationalism and the national state, The French count de Lafayette and America's Kazimierz Pulaski expounded the same cause by observing that nationalism and a free democratic society to be very much compatible. Lenin considered nationalist movements as a progressive approach to peoples' freedom. He supported the minorities against the imperial West, but he made a clear distinction between progressive and reactionary nationalism. The former is tolerable because it emerges from modern feudal conditions, while the latter is the tool of imperialist power and an ignoble means to exploit the smaller peoples.

Nationalism, in all its historical instances, has been seen initially as a movement for liberation embracing all good things, including the freedom to the individual to pursue his own destiny in the democratic company of common people of the same nationality. It had a conspicuous beginning but through the passage of time, it has absorbed ideas and notions which ultimately not only retarded its progress to a considerable extent but also falsified most of its ideals. Since the present territorial states cannot accommodate the national sentiments of many of the nationalities, only militancy is considered useful to achieve the goal of national independence. Present-day political upheavals and radical dissent which often take the form of communal riots in many developing countries are the results of suppressing the national aspirations of the smaller ethnic groups who are living quite unwillingly within the state which they hardly consider their own. The subjugated nations consider the present political boundaries unsatisfactory and beyond their national requirements. It is certainly not ideological motivations, which are being expressed largely in the form of militancy. Even groups that claim loyalty to socialism, communism or capitalism cannot detach themselves from these nationalistic ideals.

It is generally argued that in the age of scientific and cultural closeness the communality or categorical ethnic distinction may give way to an affinity of socio-cultural traits, which will ultimately prove to be a check on extreme national urges among the nations within a territorial state. But national appeal or ethnicity never depends on such affinity. Cultural and national differences will persist in spite of inter-ethnic contacts and dependence. In India, although linguistic and cultural differences of the Sikh religious minority with the other Indian people are insignificant, many of them are still expressing emotive solidarity with their own group. Similarly, the Kurds in Iran are not altogether a community segregated from other Iranians, but this has never proved strong enough for them to renounce their claim for separate nationhood. The majority of the Baloch have been part of Pakistan for many decades. Its youth are being educated in its schools and universities and for the most part, is being influenced by the official national culture of Pakistan: but the sense of nationalism and the demand for separate nationhood is stronger among the educated youth than in any other section of the population. Quebecois, Basques, Irish and Tamils are not isolated entities, nor do they reject cultural influences from other groups but their demand for national self-rule is overwhelming.

Nationalism is undoubtedly a remarkable force. It can withstand the severity of alien rule, invigorate the masses in a spirit of national pride and honor and give energy to the people to fight for national freedom, usually at enormous cost. It is a spirit that resists divisive forces within an ethnic, linguistic or geographical community and motivates a desire to stick together for the common good of the entire people. Nationalism distrusts foreigners, not without justification. The stronger groups have always oppressed the weaker within the conceptual framework of aggressive nationalism, which ultimately borders on the imperialism of ancient and modern times. Therefore, nationalism suspects others and in this, it has become a force to be skeptical about. Nationalism mobilizes and activates a group's energies towards certain definite or illusory objectives of a political nature. It may bank on a separate religious background or cultural distinction and aims at mobilizing a people demanding the right of self-rule or cultural, religious and economic autonomy for the people of the group.

The spirit of nationalism has been the guiding spirit throughout history. The forces of nationalism were undoubtedly at work during the Arab conquest of most of the Middle East and Asia in the early days of Islam, and later when the Arabs rose to defend their faith against Byzantium. During the heyday of the Arab empire at Damascus and Baghdad, in spite of the professed universality of Islam, the Arabs developed sentiments of nationalism on the basis of race and culture. There was yet another aspect of the issue. The Arabs felt that their religion was in danger due to the influence of alien practices entering their land through new settlers, including scholars, artists, and merchants. More recently the war between Iraq and Iran has its roots more in history than in the conflict on *Shat al Arab*. Jordan's King Hussein's threat of organizing an *al Qadisia* volunteer force reminds the Arabs of defeating the Iranians at Qadisia in 635 AD, during the time of Caliph Umer. The Iraqis are laying emphasis on Arab nationalism and clearly giving the impression that they are fighting an Arab war against an aggressive non – Arab nation. The Iran-Iraq conflict also can be traced from the days of the Persian Monarch Cyrus, who in 529 BC laid waste a major portion of ancient Mesopotamia (now modern Iraq) or more precisely from the early days of Islam when Arab troops marched victoriously into Persia. The people of Iran took a long time to accept the new faith of Islam but rejected Arabism. The famous Persian poet, Abdul Qasim Firdausi (935-1020 AD) who wrote *Shahnaama*, dealing with 3874 years of Persian history, hatefully described the Arabs as uncivilized. He taunts them as lizard eaters who, ironically, now show such courage in vying the Persian empire of Great Cyrus [6].

Many of the contemporary national conflicts have their roots in history and culture. Thus, the ancient hatred traveled generations to surface in an armed conflict between two countries professing the same faith but representing contrasting national self-interests. A similar pattern can be discerned in all national conflicts in recent history, where national pride works to motivate the people and guide their national policies towards others. We can see a nationalistic pride in the Shah of Iran keeping close links with Israel, quite in line with the policies of Cyrus, who treated the Jews with sympathy after conquering Babylonia. Egypt's treatment of the Israelites at the time of

Moses; Prophet Muhammad's treatment of the Jews at Madina or the subsequent attitude of Muslims toward the Israelites cannot easily be erased from the memory of that people.

National consciousness often arose due to foreign conquests. European colonization in Latin America, Asia, and Africa aroused feelings of nationalism not only among the natives but in effect also among the colonists, who refused to mingle with the indigenous population. Historically, all the victorious peoples initially avoided closer social relations with the natives, whom they treated as inferiors. In other parts of the world especially the Indian sub-continent, the Aryans did not mix up with the indigenous population for a long time. When the Arabs conquered Sindh, they too refrained from matrimonial relations with Sindhis. The empires in India created by invaders from Central Asia and the Middle East, for the most part, provide a grave example of racial and religious prejudices.

The history of nationalism and the complex reasons behind its acceptance is chequered and somewhat controversial. But one of the logical factors contributing to the rise of national sentiment is the fact than men have always reacted sharply to foreign domination. The groups of humans speaking the same tongue living in a geographically compact area and having a common past have usually united against the alien aggressor, ultimately developing some common bonds to be remembered and a common hero to be revered. In Asia and Africa, the contemporary wave of nationalism was generally prompted firstly by the ruthless domination of the people by the European colonialists and secondly by the rulers of multinational states created unjustifiably by the colonial powers after the collapse of colonialism.

3- Socio-cultural Elements in Nationalism

Cultural cohesion has always been an unattainable ideal in multinational states. The government usually announces the adoption of one tongue, often of the ruling aristocracy, as the official language, while the linguistic minorities demand that their speech should also be given official status. To satisfy national demands in many European countries, often more than one speech has been declared an official language. In Pakistan, Urdu, which is spoken by a tiny minority of the immigrants, is the official language. The Pakistani rulers are allergic to the demands of linguistic and socio-cultural autonomy from the country's nationalities.

Language as a means of expressing nationalistic ideals has always been considered as the main factor in the evolution of national sentiments. While opposition to assigning any importance to the languages of the ethnic minorities has become the state strategy, the language issue has marred harmonious relations between various ethnic entities in the multi-national states in Asia and Africa.

Language has characteristics that fit into nationalistic notions. It undoubtedly is the main carrier of ideas, sentiments, traditions, customs and religious dogma from one generation to another. In many instances, people speaking the same language usually profess the same faith and often belong to the same stock racially. Many religions, to adopt a very rough generalization, are sometimes distinguished by the language of their adherents. Islam, for instance, is congruent mainly with the Arabic language: even in countries like Pakistan their leaders very often declare their intention to have Arabic as the language of education and official communication. Similarly, Judaism has been closely linked with Hebrew and consequently with the Jewish people. Latin has been identified with Roman Catholicism; Sanskrit with Hindu creeds; Avesta with Zoroastrianism; Germanic languages with Protestantism and Slavonic with eastern orthodoxy.

In early history, political allegiances were usually determined on the basis of territorial states while civilizations were identified religiously. During the 18th and 19th centuries, in the European political theatre, the emphasis was laid on national languages, which resulted in the familiarization of cultural nationalism in political philosophy. Any political claim to independence and self-determination was linked with the national culture and language. After the First World War, the Turkish leaders were fairly quick to perceive the emerging political upheavals. When they lost their European possessions and the Arab lands, the Turks asserted a national identity of their own emphasizing their national culture and historical past as its basis. The state was renamed Turkey and Turkish speech became the basis of Turkish nationalism. In many of the Russian republics, the language was regarded as the basis of nationality. The Ukrainian nationality was the result of the standardization of Ukrainian speech. But among many people, national consciousness grew slowly and became a force regardless of the diversity of speech among the people. In such cases, the national tongue evolved through a historical process and ultimately became the basis of national consciousness. The French, Spanish and English languages were slowly identified with national sentiments.

According to Renan, language is not the only criterion of nationhood. What constitutes a nation is not speaking the same tongue or belonging to the same ethnic group but having accomplished great things in common in the past and the wish to accomplish them in futures [7]. Whatever may be the theoretical definition, it is clear that the main bond is the language, because it is the language that transmits the customs, traditions and religious-theological expressions to the next generations. It is the main link among its people and a powerful instrument of socialization. Therefore, culture and language are interlinked and interdependent. Language is a part of the culture, which will be stagnant if not transmitted through language.

Language has proved to be a strong vehicle for creating national sentiments. In Europe, Slovak nationalism arose on the basis of language. The Slovaks, who previously spoke various dialects with a single root, standardized their tongue and asserted their nationality on that basis. Although they professed the same religion the Hungarians pressed their demand for national identity was obviously based on the linguistic and racial affinity of their people.

Religion is sometimes used by rulers as an instrument of oppression. Religious dogmas are disseminated in the speech of the conquerors. Native tongues freely take borrowings from the religious language of their masters which ultimately become part of the native tongue.

In the countries where the national identity and consciousness was based upon religion instead of language and culture, the people have begun to reconsider their political and national association. Religious factors, nevertheless, cannot be discarded altogether. National consciousness can be aroused on the basis of creed when the rulers profess another faith than that of the subject people.

The cultural nationalism has its peculiarities and must never be underrated. It is untenable to say, however, that any national culture owes nothing to any other culture. But cultural similarity should by no means stand in the way of national rights of the communities on a linguistic and cultural basis. There is much cultural affinity among the people of the historical Sindh and Balochistan, but they are different people with distinct cultural personalities, each aspiring to the national identity of their own.

4- The State

Generally identified with the nation, but in legal terminology, the state is the organization which acts under the law. In Greek political terminology the mention was of the polis, meaning a city-state. In Latin, the equivalent words used were res publica, meaning commonwealth, and civitas, the community of citizens. The Greek polis inevitably differs from the modern state, but it may be mentioned that the polis not only included a city government but also the religious and cultural solidarity of the state's people. The Roman res publica covered a larger region comprising the Roman provinces.

In modern usage, the state is a political organization with a government to manage society. The state is differentiated from other social organizations in many respects. It has distinctions of having a territorial limit. Two different definitions can be proposed here: the territorial or geographical state and the national state. As a nation has a common language, common culture, historical past and moreover an intense desire to live together under the apparatus of the state, the national state is the symbol for national solidarity and consciousness and the deep penetrating pride in the past achievement of a people speaking a common tongue, belonging to a similar racial origin and living under a common law. But the territorial state is devoid of most of the attributes of the national state. It is a union of many peoples speaking a variety of languages, who may have no cultural, religious or racial affinity at all, and is by and large maintained by the coercive force of the state.

The Greek polis was a miniature form of the modern national state. There was absolutely no difference of speech or interests on the part of the citizens of the polis. Even in Roman res publica, the Greek spirit of the city-state can be discerned. Conceptually, in the national state, the feelings of loyalty and patriotism and the readiness to accept the will of the state are overwhelming while in the territorial state many consider themselves unequal citizens and loyalty to their own people will ride high and the general will for the state is apparently absent.

The ancient empires can be regarded as forerunners of the multinational states of today. Those empires were never based on equality and justice but on loyalty to some individual rulers usually believed to be destined to rule. The greatest empires of Asia, Europe, and the Middle East were not national states. While Europe after the great wars of the 20th century, achieved national states of a sort, most of the Asian and African countries which were under European colonialism have been reshaped in a form of the ancient monarchies, embracing multinational populations with contrasting interests. These countries are welded together by the coercive state machinery inherited from their colonial masters. Pakistan stands out as a similar union of peoples where the people have been restive ever since the creation of the country as there is no racial or cultural harmony among the constituent national entities.

The concept of nationalism as originally perceived or at least in vogue during previous centuries is poorly compatible with the political and territorial realities of the modern age. In fact, 'the one-nation one-language theory' stands repudiated by the political pattern the world has taken in the second half of the twentieth century, particularly in the Afro-Asian countries. In Asia and the Middle East, with a few exceptions, the states of today fall into the category of multinational states. Even countries like China cannot be regarded as national in the purely academic sense of the term. China is a union of Huns, Manchu, Mongols, Tibetans and Turkish-speaking peoples. India and its neighbors, Pakistan, Afghanistan, and Iran, are clearly multinational states.

In essence, nationalism stands for the national state. In modern political thought, however, the principle that each nationality should form a state which should include all its members has been recognized with considerable reluctance. In a world of deep schism, it is the most progressive notion, and not only attracts the common folk but gives them a sense of direction and purpose in governing themselves. The spirit of nationalism during the height of imperialism aroused the consciousness of the people to resist alien rule. The smaller nationalities, whose rights had been denied by nations better organized and equipped, started a relentless struggle against the domineering authorities. In the case of Greece, Serbia, Romania, Bulgaria, and in the Arab provinces of the Middle East, national sentiments were aroused to gain independence from Ottoman rule. Nationalism sometimes served as a unifying force. It was taken as the basis of a federation of states in the case of the United States, the Soviet Union and most of the modern territorial states establish after the two world wars.

The present territorial states which erroneously claim nationhood are mostly reminiscent of primitive imperialism and the dynasties of the ancient world. Europe, the Middle East, and Asia were ruled by large empires annexing many peoples and nations into one territorial state to be run by kings and aristocrats. The Roman Empire included a vast and diverse territory with many different peoples. There was neither any geographical contiguity within the empire nor linguistic nor cultural affinity among the peoples. The Persian and Mesopotamian Kingdoms, the Mughal empire in the subcontinent and the Ottoman in Turkey were not nation-states. The cardinal characteristics of these empires were that they were devoid of any national consciousness on the basis of ethnic, linguistic, cultural or religious unity but were mostly administrative units governed by one emperor or monarch. Such states had nothing in common except the will of the monarch to rule his peoples.

In the contemporary world, the emergence of the territorial states has created manifold problems. Everywhere in Asia, Africa or Latin America where ethnic entities are divided by international boundaries, there is considerable pressure for territorial revision with the object of uniting the people and creating new national states. But such ethnic issues or national problems obviously require compromises and accommodation between different points of view. To the rulers of such states, however, the nationalist claims are the gravest threat to the political and territorial integrity of the state concerned, and many arguments are advanced in favor of the present dispensation. It is said that territorial states provide efficiency and pride through a constant struggle with others. This is the primitive concept of empire states and monarchies vying for better resources and commercial benefits in the face of tough competition from equally strong nations.

The competitive theory has other dimensions. The tendency to weld together many nationalities into an empire and inculcate a sense of competition among them in the face of equally strong territorial states, while it served to strengthen the bond among the subject peoples, also resulted in dissatisfaction among the smaller nations within such a union of sates. The struggle of Polish, Irish, Finns, Hungarian, Sindhis, Pakhtun, Baloch, Czechs, Arabs, Kurds, Tamils and a host of other peoples was the outcome of strong centralized governance upon them, which ultimately aroused feelings of ill-will for the ruling factions on the one hand and a sense of national unity on the other. During the 18th and 19th centuries, Europe was the best example of restless nationalities striving for freedom. Factors contributing to resistance against Napoleon were diverse, but it was clear that many people loathed the concept of territorial unions under one ruler, which facilitated the idea of nationalism in a more logical fashion than originally conceived.

Territorial states or ancient empires have often facilitated harmonious relations among people of divergent socio-cultural and racial backgrounds within the empire. In England, there were distinct linguistic groups such as Cornishmen, Norman French, Saxons, and Welsh. But a Norman Saxon synthesis created the English language, which ultimately became the basis of the British national identity. In France, there were more than eight linguistic communities including Bretons, Normans, Germans, and Basques. These groups produced the French language and nation. In the Indian subcontinent, the ancient Dravidian speakers mingled with the invading Aryans perfecting the Hindu religion, their respective languages and to a great extent, the Indian nation, if it can be so-called. The ancient peoples inhabiting Sistaan, Kirmaan, Makkuraan and central and eastern Balochistan, amalgamated with the newcomers to produce the present stock of the Baloch people. Similarly, the Iranians took a long time to attain separate nationhood. But such an analysis cannot be generalized to achieve any scientific conclusion regarding the role of language and race in the formation of national sentiments and solidarity.

The empire or geographical states gave way to national states only because of the immense desire of the particular racial and linguistic entities to have their separate identity. Such sentiments are expressed mostly by the educated or aristocratic elite among the group, influenced ostensibly by theories of national sovereignty. In Europe and Asia, the greatest empires were opposed only on the basis of this popular theory. Territorial states did not concede the rights of nationalities, thus inviting opposition from various ethnic minorities within these states, where previously the sense of belonging was towards the composite unity of the different peoples inhabiting a geographical area. The Austro- Hungarian empire in Europe and the Mughal empire in the Indian subcontinent fell apart because they did not correspond with the rising feelings of national self-identity.

To deal with the national questions, the territorial states often employed coercive power of the state. The contemporary political scene in many regions of Asia and Africa is therefore marred with violence and unrest, mostly, characterized by the resentment of the nations forcibly integrated with other nationalities against their will. The existing territorial states have given rise to many complex issues. The majority of the ruling national entity became the guardian of state nationalism and has become oppressive, assuming a wide dimension with cultural, political, physical and economic oppression of minority national entities.

The geographical states of the modern age can never be seen as national states or states maintained through the free will of their citizens. The supreme loyalty to the collective will is never witnessed in countries that were created after the demise of colonialism in Asia and Africa because the cardinal characteristic of the nation, the very soul is missing. The nations, observed Spengler, are 'neither linguistic nor political nor biological, but spiritual entities [8]. A nation can sustain and prosper as long as its creative spirit is boosted by its members, who must possess a will to power that is a creative spirit. Therefore, nationalism is the first and foremost state of mind, an act of consciousness [9] in the case of Pakistan and may developing countries such a spiritual unity or consciousness is clearly absent. In such countries, nationalistic claims by ethnic groups are generally regarded as separatist and the question of their sovereign existence is dubbed a divisive tendency. This has created tension among the constituent national entities resulting in political, economic and social chaos.

Reactionary nationalism of the state is frequently put forward as the only remedy for economic, political and social chaos in many Asian and African states after their independence. Such an approach may damage the true nationalistic ideology and social solidarity among the group of peoples. Pakistan is a fit case for the study where the security establishment has helped inculcate a reactionary ideology, which implies a dual role for itself. Its political role is emphasized as a pre-requisite for checking the rising tendency towards nationalism on the one hand and social reforms on the other. The armed forces openly espouse anti-populist ideas, justifying them on ideological and social grounds. Even the progressive and truly nationalist army officers, after becoming part of the administration are reduced to rank conformists and swept away by the pervasive military cult.

Modern territorial states, which bank entirely on coercive power to withstand divisive force, consider nationalism a dangerous foe. Pakistan is facing the same problem. Since its rulers do not allow its nationalities to exercise the right to self-rule, they ideologize their monopoly of power on the basis of religion. 'Pakistani nationalism', a misnomer will understandably take a long time to gain any ground. Instead, extreme nationalist sentiments are getting impetus among the Baloch and Sindhis. Mistakenly, the rulers try to identity Pakistani nationality, which has never existed, with a religious ideology. This ideology is fabricated by those on power to manipulate and mobilize the disenchanted people in an already fragmented society. Surprisingly, this ideology has little room for free discussion. It frequently uses the option of political and intellectual suppression of the masses. Pakistan is progressing on the lines of an ideological empire where the ruler is vested with divine authority. The distinction between the national and an ideological state in the Pakistani context is very clear. While the former upholds individual freedom and strives to attain the highest ideals for man's welfare, the ideological state denies that opportunity to its members for reasons inconceivable in modern political philosophy. In every multinational state, the question of national self-determination agitates the mind of the smaller nations. Lawrence Ziring, writing on the Pakistani context, observed that the struggle for national self-determination is traceable to nationalistic motivations brought on by feelings of alienation, fear of personal loss, systematic abuse and outright persecution. The stage has been reached in Pakistani politics where the people, especially the ethnic minorities, see no alternative but to demand the right of self-determination and national emancipation.

5- Nationalism and Contemporary Nation-states

Nationalism, indeed, is an affirmation of love and oneness towards one's group. Deep love and greatest regard for the objectives of the group is the lasting bond uniting the people. A strong urge for self-rule and a common desire for struggle, ignoring all ideological differences within the group, is the spirit of nationalism. The common struggle while strengthening the common bond has ostensible nationalistic overtures. Coming down to the community level or on the level of tribes or larger groups, nationalism had a tremendous role to play. In the contemporary world, nationalism has understandably posed the greatest challenge to countries who have failed to evolve an agreed political dispensation with the ethnic minorities and constantly deny them their rights. It has been considered one of the greatest threats to the existing political set-up in the world. Most of the Afro-Asian and Latin American countries gained their freedom after the world wars when keeping physical control over colonies became untenable for various reasons. The possessions of European nations in Africa and Asia were never demarcated on linguistic or cultural lines or on the basis of nationalities. National entitles were divided into different administrative divisions to suit the alien masters, regardless of the natives' feelings. Although the United States solved the problem of political integration after an internal conflict years ago, most other advanced countries are still living with internal ethnic problems. Canada has the Quebec Issue; Spain has the Basque national entity striving for independence, and in Britain the Scots and Irish are restless. Pakistan, Sri Lanka, Iran, Afghanistan, Iraq, Turkey, and many other Asian and African countries are facing existential crises because of the national resistance movements of the minority national entities within these countries.

There is general agreement among the sociologist that a modern state is inconceivable without nationalism. A land that is not the home of a nation is like a public Kitchen where everyone merely feeds himself. Devoid of nationalism, a state cannot be more than a common source of sustenance [10]. With the creation of artificial states by the colonial powers before their withdrawal from Asia and Africa, the propagation of "state nationalism" became imperative for such states. The state nationalism places more importance on the state than any other theory. It gives unreserved loyalty to the state and rejects groups on the fringe of the mainstream of state nationalism. It invokes the images of state and the official nationhood above all.

Many of the newly liberated countries did not conform with the notions of national states and have problems of theoretical identity and national cohesion. Such countries could eventually become cohesive national states if their political administration were to be based on the principle of recognizing the rights of national minorities within those countries. Reorganizing and regrouping the areas within such countries by giving the national units sufficient autonomy could ultimately strengthen solidarity among the people and make such states strong enough to resist internal dissent and external threats. In order to make the world safer from violence and terrorism, nationalism can be used for the benefit of such states if the rights of the nationalities are respected. The territorial countries in many instances claim to stretch their frontiers by incorporating other peoples and nationalities on the basis of geographical contiguity or racial affinity or the historical precedent of a period when such states or regions were larger in size. Recognizing the national sentiments of constituent nationalities in many multi-national states in Asia and Africa is the only panacea in resolving the contrasting interests of many peoples. The multi-national and multi-lingual states should give way to national states on the basis of language and culture. The solution obviously lies in the further disintegration of the present political structure and the creation of states on the basis of cultural nationalism.

Material wants and their realization may not appear to have any obvious impact in arousing feelings of nationality, but most peoples, especially the subjugated peoples living in a territorial state dominated by the majority, feel a strong resentment against what they regard as the denial of their economic rights. Such thinking usually leads to nationalist sentiments. In Pakistan, one of the main contributing elements to Baloch nationalism is the exploitation of the Baloch and its resources by the Panjab. Seen in a wider perspective, however, the economic cause is not separable from other equally strong factors such as language, religion, geographical unity, ethnicity, historical past and not least the desire to live in solidarity within the nationality. But nationalistic motives can never be attributed wholly to a single cause. There are instances when such movements started among people who were well off economically. The Israelites cherished the concept of a national homeland not because of any impoverishment but because they wanted a state where they could pursue a life on the basis of their cultural tradition. The Pakhtun in Pakistan is better off than many of their compatriots in the country, but they have not given up the idea of a separate Pakhtun identity. The Sikhs in India are one of the most prosperous communities, controlling business and trade in the Panjab and also represented in national institutions but many among them want a separate national status for themselves. Moreover, polish or Czech nationalist movements in Europe never resulted from the greater poverty of these peoples compared to those who were ruling them. The Greeks and the Armenians who fought the Turks for independence were wealthier than their Turkish masters.

The desire to be united and accomplish great deeds in the future is the true manifestation of the great soul of the people, which needs grandeur and glory, prestige and power. These nationalistic impulses sometimes expand to give the idea of superior nationality or master race to many peoples. Such notions lead to the misconceived idea of the rule of the weaker by the stronger. Similar ideas were perhaps the founding principles leading the European colonizers to ruthlessly oppress the Afro-Asian nations for so long. The same premises guide the behavior of most territorial states and their rulers in a post-colonial world. Pakistani rulers are obsessed with the same notions regarding the national minorities like Baloch and the Sindhis.

The alien rule or cultural particularistic of the Asian and African countries is the main cause of anguish for the minorities demanding self-determination. If they are given their right to self-rule within those countries, the separatist demands for sovereign existence can be kept subdued for a long time to come. The smaller nationalities in the multi-national and multi-lingual states are little convinced with the change of masters from the Europeans to an indigenous majority. The forces of nationalism will continue to operate and find fresh grounds in Pakistan and other Afro-Asian and Latin American countries if the ethnic entities are refused any share of political authority.

Pakistan from the very beginning never claimed to be a national state because its creation was based on religion. One of the earlier supporters of Pakistan, Choudhry Rahmath Ali, gave the name Pakistan to the new state, which he called the land of the pure. The word was interpreted as standing for the territories of Punjab, Kashmir, Iran, Sindh, Afghania, and Balochistan. To give it a geographical reality, he said the new country is the land which lies in the northwest of the continent of India. Mindful of the urges for nationalism he maintained that it constitutes the age-old national struggle of the people who represent the original core and content of the "Millath" living in the orbit of Pakistan. This assertion was historically incorrect, because the peoples of the area never formed one people and never socially, culturally, ethnically, and historically remained under one state. The Persian empire dominated some areas, while the various Indian monarchies ruled portions of the land in the ancient and medieval epochs. To give the area a compact territorial reality drawing it closer to nationalistic impulses of the time was intellectual dishonesty.

The Pakistani rulers are mistaken in seeing themselves as different from the colonial rulers. The army ruler, General Zia ul Haq, while announcing his plans for the return of democracy, has objected to newspaper references to his earlier speeches concerning the transfer of power from the military to a civil government. In a press conference, he declared that the term "transfer of power" had a bad smell because it denotes that the power was being transferred from some alien authority to the people. It gave the impression of usurpation of power. He asked the media to discard the expression. Whatever may be the impression, it is clear that alien rule over the minority nationalities will arouse feelings of solidarity among the ethnic groups on the one hand and sentiments of bitter hatred on the other.

The principle of national sovereignty on a racial, cultural, linguistic and religious basis will effect changes in the political and geographical frontiers of many nations. The spirit of nationalism transcends state frontiers. The Baloch never gives any importance to boundaries and for them, the objective of independent Balochistan can only be achieved if all the Baloch, regardless of their present citizenship, work in unison for that cause. However, the case of Pakistan, in the context of Baloch aspirations, cannot be seen in isolation. The Baloch and the Kurds are the most striking examples. Any independent Kurdistan means the breakup of Iran, Turkey, and Iraq, while a greater sovereign Balochistan as aspired to by the Baloch will reshape the boundaries of Iran, Afghanistan, and Pakistan. These states, in spite of their differences, would ultimately cooperate with each other to lessen the Baloch and Kurdish menace to their territorial solidarity. Pakistan has always been willing to offer such cooperation to Iran on the Baloch Issue. During the unrest in Kurdistan and the Baloch insurgency in Pakistan in the Sixties, Pakistan Iran and Turkey signed an agreement establishing the RCD, (the Regional Cooperation for Development) in 1964. It had its rationale, not on economic cooperation but their mutual desire to work in unison to resist the ethnic pressure on these countries. Turkey and Iran had a common Kurdish problem, while Iran and Pakistan had their Baloch people striving for national rights. The RCD, which had become dormant after the fall of the Shah in 1979, was revived and renamed ECO, the Economic Cooperation Organization. This new organization, formed in January 1985, is also more political than economic.

Alien hegemony, whether it may be the rule of the foreigners or of the indigenous majority, is never approved of by the smaller nationalities. Discontent in Afro-Asian countries is the result of rule by a class of rulers from the dominant nationality without any participation by the minority national entities. In Pakistan it has always been the Panjabi majority and their protégés who have dominated the country, creating bitterness among various sections of society. The Pakistani authorities think it inappropriate to allow the people of minority nations any say in the state affairs. They apparently believe in the spirit of an old Chinese saying that there should be a proper distance between the ruler and the ruled. When a Chinese King was informed that his subjects have sacrificed animals for his recovery from an illness the monarch became enraged and punished those responsible because he believed that such acts showed a love-bond between the king and his people and such affection would spoil the governance and had to be nipped in the bud.

References

1. Renan, quoted in Hans Kohn: Nationalism. It's Meaning and History. Princeton,1965, p 139.

2. Johann Gottlieb Herder, quoted in Errol E. Harris: Annihilation and Utopia- The principles of International Politics. Georg Allen & Unwin, London, 1966. p 166.

3. Ernest Barker: National Character and Factors of formation. London, 1948, p 247.

4. Anthony D. Smith: Theories of Nationalism. Duckworth, London, 1971, p 17.

5. Lawrence Ziring: Pakistan= Enigma of Political Development. Dawson Publishing, Kent, 1968, p146.

6. The Shahnama describes the Arabs thus:
   Zi sheer-e-shutter khurdan-o-sussomar
   Arab ra raseed asth jahe bakaar
   Ke thakht e Kayan ra kunad aarzoo
   Thufoo bar thou ay charkh-e- gardoun thufoo

7. Renan quoted in R.M MacIver: Op Cit.

8. Spengler, quoted in R. M. MacIver: The modern state. Oxford University Press, London, 1955, p 123.

9. Lawrence Ziring; Op cit.p 41

10. Quoted in Elias Kedourie (ed): Op Cit. p 34.

CHAPTER III

THE IDEOLOGY OF PAKISTAN AND THE QUESTION OF SUBJECT NATIONALITIES

Ideology appears to be a magical word creating thoughts and temptations, including religious, mythological and socio-political notions. It is generally used for some broad philosophical position whether social, religious or cultural; and usually defined as ideas or concepts accepted by the individuals or group without any regard to their origin and often without question as to their usefulness. It is essentially the product of history or past traditions. Sometimes, there will be serious doubts regarding its suitability. But still, ideologies hold considerable sway in all fields of human behavior, becoming part of social norms and rationalized by individuals or groups after they enter their social thoughts and habits. Pakistan is supposed to be an ideological state and its ideological foundations are based on the "Two-Nation" theory. This ideology has created the never-ending conflicts and hatred among the constituent national entities that comprised the religious state.

1- The Two-National Theory

Political ideologies must have cogitative roots, providing a meeting ground for the sciences of politics and philosophy. Ideologies must also have a system of values. Religions lay emphasis on particular notions and religious ideas have served at times as weapons of theoretical oppression when they no longer had any utility for the people. Religious ideologies are absolute in nature because they seek complete destruction of prevalent notions. Religious ideologies often advocate violence, which is regarded as for the benefit of society. Islam by nature is an aggressive religion and commands the faithful to engage in a perpetual war with the unfaithful. The Arabs, inspired by Islam, carried fire and sword throughout the Middle East and beyond. In Central Asia, they destroyed wonderful cultural treasures as well as other magnificent monuments. Al-Beruni described with great indignation that the Arab Commander Ibn-Muslim had killed all scholars and intellectuals in Khorezm during the Arab invasion of Central Asian principalities. He regretted that no one was left who could know the history and language of Khorezm after the Arab conquest [1].

The ideology of Pakistan could be discussed in the above-mentioned context. Based on the "two-nation theory", it aims to reshape an entire society arbitrarily on some new footing unknown to the people. This is perhaps the totalitarian nature of religious ideology which corresponds best to the concept as applied to Pakistan. The British colonial leaders, who conceived the idea of Pakistan also provided the intellectual base it required in the form of the two-nation theory which became the "Islamic ideology" of Pakistan. The two-nation theory was based firstly on the assumption that the Indian Muslims constitute a nation by virtue of being the followers of Islam, and secondly, being Muslims they can not live together with the followers of other faiths in India after the British withdrawal from the region. But it lacked the criteria of ideology in the conventional sense of the term. It was also self-contradictory in the sense that the followers of other faiths in India were not declared nations by virtue of their religious beliefs. An ideology requires the acceptance of the people. It requires institutions that could advance certain ideas. Any notion put forward must get the approval of the groups it is aimed at: but Pakistan's ideology was self-contradictory. After the creation of Pakistan, it came into conflict with the socio-cultural and regional aspirations of the people of the new state. In spite of tremendous propaganda effort, backed by the coercive power of the state, it could not gain any acceptance among the people because it is irrational on more than one count. It opposed the firmly held notions of nationalism, identified itself with state authority and denied the peoples their social-political and economic rights in the country. Therefore, the "Pakistan ideology" could not gain acceptance among the peoples and as it is without a sustaining personality or 'soul'.

The concept of the nation is more pervasive and sentimental than any religious ideology based on some abstract thought. Ideologies signify philosophical notions but Pakistan's ideology is claimed to be related to Islam, which is based on well-argued ideas at least in the cultural and social context, but religious ideologies as such have nothing to fear because they are not tested on a rational plan. When it is claimed that Pakistan's ideology is based on Islam, all kinds of cogitative discussions are closed once and for all. It becomes arbitrary and totalitarian in its approach and style.

Ideologies always suggest some kind of collectivity of thought. Since the ideology of Pakistan could not attract the people and could not overcome in thought and inspiration its arch-rival, the concept of nation and nationality, the ruling civil-military aristocracy started a campaign against the concept of nationalism. The Pakistani leaders emphasized the inviolability of the two-nation theory in the preservation of the country's integrity and promptly dubbed un-Islamic any advocacy of a social-political system based on equality and justice and branded those favoring progressive reforms as traitors disloyal to the cause of Pakistan and Islam. An ideology cannot get approval unless it is based on some acceptable political myths, but in the case of the ideology of Pakistan, it has never been accepted by many of the people as a socio-political doctrine.

Surprisingly, in Pakistan, anything which appeals to the people is immediately and in a planned manner attached to Islam and Pakistan. Islamic socialism, Islamic democracy, Islamic or un- Islamic Martial Law and Referendum, Islamic or un-Islamic fine arts, Islamic culture, and even Islamic nationalism are usually referred to with few if any qualms with the objective of making Islam more plausible as a political dogma to the recalcitrant masses. The Pakistani leaders and state-sponsored intelligentsia are very quick in picking up ideas and Islamizing them in their attempt to hoodwink the people. Islamic socialism must have been derived from another deluded dogma, such as Arab socialism, which was vogue among the Arab nationalists during the presidency of Jamal Nasser in Egypt, or the Indonesian socialism promoted during Sukarno's reign. The aim is to provide

Islam a well-argued hypothetical foundation, so as to present it to the people as a credible alternative to nationalism, Western democracy, Eastern communism or Afro-Asian State socialism. The efforts by the Pakistani rulers to Islamize each and every concept is undoubtedly a clumsy attempt in irrationality.

Pakistani rule has never been in accordance with Islamic beliefs, but the successive regimes have tried to justify their actions on any possible pretext. There was a time when Pakistan was an active partner in various Western military alliances. Apart from national security considerations, such alliances were thought to be close to Islamic teachings and fully correspond to the spirit of the 'Pakistani nation', because these pacts were against the Godless communism of China and the USSR. But sometime afterward, when Pakistan started developing closer links with Communist China, this Islamic aspect never proved a constraint. Moreover, the entire foreign policy direction became superfluous under the changing geo-strategic realities and Pakistan reverted to neutralism, in which it has little faith. The country's ideologies are now seeking some clue in Islamic teachings to justify neutralism, which was never advised as state policy in Islam, though Islam may not be essentially anti-neutralism.

In Pakistan, the discussions of foreign policy have also been marred with the labeling of non-conformist elements as traitors. While the foreign policies of other Muslim countries have never been discussed in Islamic or un-Islamic terms and have been guided mostly in terms of national self-interest, Pakistan, true to its traditions of infatuated hypocrisy, frequently finds some Islamic aspect in its foreign policy motives. Its support of the British-French-Israeli invasion of Egypt in 1956 over the Suez Crisis and its active role in the crushing of Palestinian uprising in Jordan in 1969 were also justified on the same premises. Ironically, Pakistani leaders always tend to consider all the prevailing notions, democracy, socialism, neutralism, nationalism, or even monarchism in terms of what is Islamic and what is not. They offer Islamic choices for their positions in international affairs. The Pakistani leaders mistakenly perceived Islam to be the only slogan under which they could prolong their repressive rule on the masses and govern the country without sharing power with the people.

Despite the propagation of Islamic ideology by state institutions, closer to the peoples' mentality, however, is nationalism, with its insatiable urge for establishing the identity and rights of national minorities, as witnessed in eighteenth-century Europe: and no amount of religious obscurantism can possibly block its way to ultimate success.

Most interesting is the fact that Muslim nationhood as such was absent in the initial stages of Islam. The people who accepted the faith were usually termed Umma, a term in ancient Arab denoting a group of people who follows some leader. The real nature of Islam for Indian Muslims appears to somehow different from the Islam of people who populated the regions which now comprised Pakistan. It is because of the character of the Indian Muslims, who have been influenced by the powerful socio-political and cultural traditions of India. The Indian Muslims laid emphasis on faith, and in the process developed fanaticism and religious intolerance, while the peoples of Pakistan, especially the Baloch and Sindhis, remained by comparison secular. This is why the refugees who were brought to Pakistan in a planned manner and settled in Sindh in order to give credence to the two-nation theory regarded themselves as superior Muslims to their compatriots in Pakistan.

The ruling elite which comprised of Military, Mullahs (religious leaders) and refugees from north India, soon after independence began to centralize power in their own hands to the complete exclusion of the people. They treated the national state as the focal point of identity, denying the rights of the subject nationalities. The main issue in Pakistani politics was building and sustaining an integrated national consciousness. The rulers have nothing in common with the people of the newly created state. They were to an extent alien. They had no right to rule except on the basis of theoretical notions they attached to the new state. Pakistan's ideology or the two-nation theory was the slogan which they raised in order to consolidate their own position on the one hand and to create an atmosphere of hatred and mistrust between India and Pakistan on the other. The Pakistani ideology aimed at creating a society that is hardboiled, doctrinal, and guided largely by self-imposed ignorance. This was directed at combating regional feelings caused by political and economic deprivation. A peoples' behavior is always guided by custom and an intense pride in their traditions. Pakistan's leaders failed to comprehend that their integration into the system of a newborn country required considerable political acumen, matched by conceding every nationality the right to national existence in an overall political arrangement within the new state.

The country's philosophical foundations were traced in the existence of Hindus and Muslims as two separate nations. This was without any historical truth. The people who invaded and ruled India and who profess the Islamic creed never constituted a nation. The Islamic faith, in fact, was introduced into India at various times and places by different groups in different forms. It has proliferated into a great variety of faiths and creeds, many of which are important events today. The harbingers of Islam were of different racial origins and they brought with them far more than the Prophet's original faith and proclamations [2]. The political expression of Islam has been almost as varied as its theology. It is a misconception to suppose that Islam is the only significant thing about Indian Muslims. Various racial elements colored their religion with tribal and national characteristics. Turkish Islam was very different from Arabic Islam and Afghan Islam was something else again. Further, Muslims were influenced by their cultural surroundings. In particular, Persian culture and Hindu traditions from within India have modified and variegated the Islamic complex.

The only thing common among the Indian Muslims was their political desire to rule the alien land conquered by them. The initial invasions of India in the 8th century was motivated by the desire to loot the Indian riches. Later invaders like Mahmud of Chazna or Muhammad of Ghur were no more than predatory dacoits who during their forays into India plundered the Indian cities and returned to Central Asia with immeasurable wealth. The rulers of Delhi Sultanate never ruled through any pride of nationality. Their aristocracy and military elite came from different areas of Central Asia with different languages and cultural backgrounds. The Mughals, except for the bigoted Aurangzeb, founded their empire on secular lines. There was absolutely no Muslim nation in any sense of the term whatsoever. Muslim social behavior in India was never guided by Islamic instinct alone. The Punjabis, divided into their various castes and creeds, were, Punjabis; and their allegiance to the Mughal rulers or the Afghan, Ahmad Shah Durrani, was never on the basis of their faith. The Baloch and the Sindhis, were early Muslims but did not regard Islam as a basis of their nationality and were not guided by such sentiments at all. Similar was the case of the other Indians who belonged to a variety of racial and ethnic stock with different religious backgrounds.

In India, there are followers of all major cults of the Middle East and Asia. To divide the entire people of the sub-continent into two religious groups, therefore, is an absolute falsehood. However, some theoretical base was needed not only for the creation of Pakistan and the division of India but was also imperative for its continued existence and to give people some cardinal point to ponder over as the basis for their new political reality. In the beginning, the colonial administration's propaganda of the two-nation theory was considered by many as a hoax as there were many nations in India and the followers of the Hindu religion who never claimed to be a nation. Moreover, there is no Muslim nation as such referred to either in the Muslim holy book, the Quran or in later Muslim political philosophy. So, the two-nation theory was just a coercive plan to give some kind of face-saving to the colonial administration which was bent upon creating a client state out of India at all cost [3].

It is obvious that the so-called Pakistan ideology is being interpreted in a variety of ways to suit the socio-political exigencies of different occasions. The military ruler, General Ayub Khan used to consider the whole concept to be entirely centered in his own person. By implication, he was himself the ideology of Pakistan. Chaudhry Nazir Ahmad, a former Federal Minister, in justifying the creation of One Unit in West Pakistan, declared that One Unit was the concept of Islamic ideology and any opposition to it would be tantamount to working against the ideology and integrity of Pakistan and the glory of Islam [4]. Baloch leader, Mir Ghous Bakhsh Bizenjo, was arrested and sentenced to rigorous imprisonment because he was found with a currency note on which a slogan against One Unit was written. Pakistani military president, General Zia-ul-Haq warned the people that while voting to elect him in the referendum of 19 December 1984 would mean a contribution to the cause of Islam, a negative vote would be taken as an act of treachery to Islam and Pakistan.

While Ayub Khan considered himself the inspired savior, Zia ul Haq believes that he is destined by the Almighty to rule the country. On more than one occasion, he has declared that as he is not an elected ruler, he is not answerable before the people but directly to Allah for his actions as the ruler of the country. In an interview with the BBC Television correspondent, Brian Barron, in April 1978, he said: "There is one thing which I can tell you. Sometimes things happen which you cannot foresee and your sixth sense tells you that there is some hand supporting you.... The hand of Providence perhaps which is helping me out. If I am the man whom, perhaps, Allah has chosen to do something for Pakistan and if he gives me strength, by God, I will do it" [5] Several decades ago, the British Viceroy of India John Lawrence (1864-69), advanced a similar notion to justify the British rule in India. He declared: "We have not been elected or placed in power by the people, but we are here through our moral superiority, by force of circumstances, by the will of Providence. This alone constitutes our charter to govern India". General Zia can also boast a superior moral position because of his being in military uniform. He has not infrequently shown his deep contempt for the people and their representatives. His charter to rule is primarily the will of Providence, the 'Hidden Hand', which is always helping him out. He is responsible before neither the people nor his own conscience but directly before Allah alone.

Both General Ayub and General Zia assumed that they really had been ordained by Allah to rule. Ayub was called the "Saladin Saani", after his disastrous war with India over Kashmir in 1965, a reference to the famous crusader, Salahuddin Ayubi, several hundred years ago. Drunk with such eulogies, he promoted himself to the rank of Field Marshal. General Zia has been urged to assume the title of the Caliph [6], the political as well as spiritual authority in Islam.

Muhajir (the refugees or immigrants from north India who became a partner of the alliance ruling the country since its creation in 1947) scholars and writers, perceiving a growing hatred against them in the country, began strengthening various aspects of the country's theoretical foundation. Dr. I H Qureshi, a former Vice-Chancellor of Karachi University, writes that: "if we let go the Ideology of Islam we cannot hold together as a nation by any other means...If the Arabs, the Turks, the Iranians, God forbid, give up Islam the Arabs yet remain Arabs, the Turks remain Turks the Iranians remain Iranians but what do we remain if we give up Islam?"[7] He is right. Immigrants or refugees from India have no identity of their own. If the Ideology of Pakistan or the two-nation theory were to be done away with, the only losers would have been the Muhajirs in the post-independence era. Without the ideology of Pakistan, the peoples of Pakistan will retain their identity and continue to be Muslims as they were before the creation of Pakistan. They have distinct cultures, glorious traditions and a past history of many thousand years. The reality is that it was not the people of Balochistan, Panjab, Sindh, Bengal and the frontier province (NWFP) who struggled for a separate country outside India. For them, Pakistan was neither desirable nor an absolute political necessity. The people of these areas were running their administration smoothly and without any impediment under the aegis of imperial Britain decades before the establishment of Pakistan. It was only the Muslims of United and Central provinces of India and other regions who were used in the division of India and the propagation of the two-nation theory.

Giving a truthful account of the creation of Pakistan and providing a real justification for strengthening the religious state is not in the interest of the ruling alliance. If the group of Muhajirs who are giving the intellectual support to the ruling alliance of Pakistan wishes to perpetuate the "Pakistan ideology", it will be in their interest. They are still a privileged minority and playing a major role in the ideological front. If the right of self-rule is recognized for the people of minority nationalities in a genuine federal framework, the peoples of Pakistan will be the winner while the minority manipulators and the ruling military–mullah-muhajir aristocracy will surely be the losers. Muhajir intellectuals are right in their assertions that if the people of Pakistan achieve their rights, society will witness a transformation to the disadvantage of the rulers. As far as the Muhajirs, they will surely be treated not as superiors but as equal citizens of the country. This is what they fear most and aim to forestall in the name of the ideology of Islam and Pakistan.

Understandably, the majority in the provinces of Panjab, Sindh, and Frontier have never given credence to what a handful of landlords and intelligentsia picked up by the British from the Indian Muslims were promoting in demanding Pakistan. But the partition brought tremendous social anarchy, not simply due to outrageous riots and lootings, but because the imported rulers of the newly created country prevailed over the traditional socio-cultural values of the peoples. The majority of the peoples and their local leaders had opposed the Muslim League in their demand for Pakistan. The creation of the new country was a shock to them, while the new rulers found this a proper excuse to exclude the peoples and their leaders from power. A campaign of mistrust and hatred continued to contaminate Pakistani society until today.

Balochistan, which was never a part of the subcontinent, merged into the new state through a historical misfortune. The Pakistani leaders compelled the impercipient Khan of Kalat to accede to Pakistan. The Baloch leaders are still regarded as anti-Pakistan and anti-Islam because of their political stand at the time of partition of India. After many decades, the behavior of the state elite towards the Baloch and their leaders remains unchanged. It appears that now it became impossible to correct the wrongs done during the initial years of the country's existence. Every government in Pakistan is finding it increasingly difficult to deviate from the fundamental course evolved during the formation years of the state. It is also becoming nearly impossible to bring the country's political-ideological footings in accord with the grim geostrategic realities and the socio-political and national requirements of the peoples of Pakistan.

From the very beginning, the rulers faced the task of creating and maintaining Pakistan's national identity. But a foundation for national identity based essentially on common race, common language, common traditions, and contiguous territory, was altogether absent in the case of Pakistan. The separation of Bangladesh further deepened the crisis of identity and raised serious doubts regarding the existence of any Pakistani nationhood. However, state intelligensia soon began to reinterpret Pakistani nationhood. They began to give new meanings to the Lahore Resolution passed by the Muslim League Party in 1940 which was the basis for demanding Pakistan. They began to assert that the resolution demanded units to be composed of the Panjab, the NWFP (Afghania), Sindh, Kashmir, and Balochistan. Thus, according to them with the independence of Bangladesh in 1971, Pakistan has found its true identity as originally envisaged. It is further declared that most areas of present Pakistan have never been part of the subcontinent and thus the country stands as a historic entity. The Pakistani state has a very confusing and contradictory set of socio-political values drawn from various sources, ranging from the Islamic faith, and the anti-imperialism of pre-independence India, the pseudo-nationalism of the Pakistan movement, democracy, neutralism, and the regional pride of the suppressed peoples of the country. It is proving difficult to integrate these conceptions to suit the ruling elite in their exploitation of the people in general and the denial of the rights of the smaller nationalities in particular.

With the exponential rise of national sentiment for an independent India in the early 20th century, the colonial administration was successful in uniting the Muslim minority by creating a sense of insecurity among them. The colonial establishment successfully portrayed the political movement built for national liberation as Hindu dominated. However, after the creation of Pakistan, the establishment of the new country miserably failed to recognize the altogether different character of the society and feeling of national pride among the people which were quite different from the hate and fear or the Hindu hysteria of the immigrants of north India. They continued the same theme of fear-India-hate India as the Islamic character of the new state and the Islamic basis of its nationhood. This drew sharp controversy among the people. This also caused intellectual anarchy as many among them began to feel that the two-nation theory has lost its charm and new progressive and realistic ideas should replace the ones of the past. Many began to feel that the separation of religion from politics is now inevitable and that Islam must ultimately evolve a proper relationship with the state. They also emphasized that in internal and external matters, the state should decide to choose either socialist or capitalist doctrine or adopt the finer point of both systems especially those which may not contradict the fundamentals of the faith.

Nevertheless, the state-sponsored intelligentsia has never played an appreciable role, but have only magnified the growing confusion. In this context, it may not be irrelevant to point out that the intelligentsia in Afro-Asian countries has always identified themselves with the rulers and not with the common people. In all colonial countries, the intelligentsia, which can be defined as upper-middle-class people of modest attainment and above the level of the common man, have never grown organically with the society but have been created and groomed by the rulers. This elite group always finds itself isolated from the common people and their cause. By associating themselves with the alien masters, the intelligentsia of the oppressed nations cause deep frustration and schism among the people. They have always trumpeted their advocacy of social justice within the framework of the prevailing political and social system run by the rulers, while the masses and their representatives demand national rights on equal footings.

The so-called "Muslim intelligentsia" played into the hands of the British by creating obstacles in the way of the freedom struggle of India. The intelligentsia and Muslim nobility and aristocracy were united in their support of the British to the last. When they compromised with them to achieve a separate state, they replaced the masters not in attitude and behavior but in faces. The ruling civil-military aristocracy has been consistent in its refusal to recognize the multi-racial character of the society, but rather stress the unity and integrity of the country on the basis of its Islamic character and the perception of an overwhelming threat from India.

The regional feelings continued to grow, with a deep sense of nationalism taking firm roots among the various peoples, especially the Baloch, the Pakhtun and to a great extent the Sindhis. Every attempt by Pakistani rulers towards a uniformity based on an Islamic state was severely rejected by the nationalities, who wanted diversity of culture within a federal framework. In East Pakistan, now Bangladesh, which was geographically separated from the rest of the country, the reaction was sharp and penetrating. From the very beginning, the Pakistani national identity was based on a common faith, ignoring national differences among the peoples professing the same faith. Such an approach intensified the conflict, which resulted in the separation of East Bengal on the one hand and discontent among the other nationalities, especially the Baloch, on the other.

By all accounts, the demand for Pakistan was an irredentist one to weaken the struggle for Indian freedom. The British rulers succeeded in giving the demand a religious form, bringing it into total conflict with Indian thinking towards secularism and democracy. The Indian Muslims were arrogant and had little regard for their fellow countrymen. Throughout their centuries of rule by tribes originating from Central Asia, the attitude of Muslims towards the Indian people has been one of contempt and insolence: while other religious groups were living in peace with the Hindus and have respect for their beliefs, the Muslims always openly despised the Hindu creed and ridiculed their leaders [8]. Notwithstanding the doctrinal impurity of the two-nation theory, it helped create the false illusion among a large number of people.

Pakistan came into being overnight. No one believed the existence of such a country was possible: neither the post-partition leaders nor their mentors before them had ever thought that the need for such a country existed or that there was any such thing as separate Muslim nationhood. Even after the passing of the Lahore Resolution of 1940, the Muslim League leader, Muhammad Ali Jinnah, was hesitant to support a separate state and reportedly remarked that he had nothing to do with Pakistan [9].

The claim that Sir Syed Ahmad Khan, a servant of East India Company, had postulated the idea of a nation on the basis of religion is either a clear misunderstanding or a deliberate miss-statement [10]. It is a clear distortion of history to maintain that Sir Ahmad or any such person is given any thought that separates Muslims from other Indians. The word Qoum or nation occurs in the writings of Sir Ahmad in different meanings. Most of his writings at that time were confusing. Qoum was mostly identified with a rather small cultural group within a religious community. Syed Ahmad Khan also used the word Qoum in the meaning of a religious or cultural community. He used the English word nation explicitly connoting a political entity living in a geographical territory regardless of differences among its various communities in religious, linguistic and cultural backgrounds [11].

It is simply inconceivable that Syed Ahmad Khan, a clerk of East India Company, could moot such an idea without the approval and encouragement of its employers. Painting a person of such caliber as being the architect of the hypothesis of separate Muslim nationhood by implication means that it was the British who gave urgency to the idea of Muslim separatism. It may not be irrelevant to note that of all the leaders who supported the Pakistan demands, none was ever convinced of the nobleness of the cause. Many leaders including Muhammad Ali Jinnah, knew very little of the fundamentals of Islam or its doctrine, much to the annoyance of the Muslim clergy. Abul Ala Maududi, whose jamaat Islami now champions the cause of Islam and Pakistan, not only challenged the very bonafide of the secular Jinnah leading the Muslims but was bitterly against the very concept of Pakistan.

It was not Syed Ahmad or any other Muslim Leader who thought up the idea of Pakistan, but the British who originated the two-nation theory in India. Sir Theodore Morrison, a British author gave Muslim communalism its philosophical support in an essay in 1932. Hindus and Muslims, he suggested, were two distinct nations as different from each other as any two European nations. Muslim civilization could not survive under an alien government especially a democratic government which tended towards the standardization of its citizens; the Muslims should rest assured that they were not alone in their concern for the preservation of their characteristic civilization [12].

Such concern from the British was not out of love for the Muslims. It was part of an imperialistic conspiracy with which a handful of Muslim feudal lords were associated. The Indian two-nation theory was created with the shedding of human blood and the cruel frenzy of loot, murder, and indignities. The British were not ignorant of the possible human tragedy. Nor were they unaware that Pakistan could by no means solve the Muslim question in India, nor were they so naïve as not to recognize the Two-nation theory as a mischievous deception. It is now well-established that the British above all wanted to divide India in order to punish the Indian leaders for their opposition to the British war efforts during two world wars and for their intransigence. A then Muslim League leader of Sindh, G.M Syed has alleged that prime minister of Britain, Winston Churchill, had assured a Panjabi politician, Sir Sikandar, in Egypt in 1940 that a separate Muslim state would be created out of India in recognition of the military services rendered by the Muslim and Sikh Panjabis during the war. The Muslims would be rewarded for their loyalties to Britain; Churchill had told Sikandar [13] apart from this the British had other sound reasons for encouraging the Muslim separatists.

Whatever may be put up for its ideological basis or whatever flimsy historical evidence could be dug out to justify its state idea, Pakistan is neither rationally nor ideologically an ideal society. By its very formation, it is among one of the few countries provided with a fictitious air of inevitability. It does not have the appearance of a country that was meant to be [14]. The existence of the country is still questionable, merely because it has no logical foundation to sustain and inspire the people. Even years after its creation, Pakistani nationhood is a matter open to the gravest doubts [15]. These doubts were expressed by no less a person than its founder, Muhammad Ali Jinnah, only three days before its birth. Addressing the Pakistan Constituent Assembly on August 11, 1947, he said "any idea of a united India could never have worked, and in my judgment, it would have led to a terrific disaster. Maybe that view is correct; maybe it is not; that remains to be seen". Jinnah was not sure of the rationale of the new state and let history to be the proper judge, and history showed in 1971 that both the two-nation theory and the religious nationhood were frivolous misconceptions.

After the separation of East Bengal from Pakistan in 1971, many people in the ruling Punjabi nationality have realized the futility of the two-nation theory and continued emphasis on Islam in political affairs. A former commander of Pakistan's air force and leader of the Tehrik-e-Istaqlal party, Muhammad Asghar Khan, advocates a more reasonable attitude towards the country's problems. In his book, Generals in Politics, he favors a more enlightened approach towards the peoples of the federating units. He emphasized that it will be a mistake to think that using Islam as a slogan can be a binding force unless mutual confidence and respect is restored. This can only happen when the people of all regions feel that they are in all respect equal citizens of this country [16].

Autocratic rule, coupled with a growing unitary form of government and denial of the autonomy to the provinces, has created a bitter sense of deprecation which has once again focused the attention of the people on the viability and rationality of the country's continued existence. The rulers are not unaware of the rising trend of political frustration. The military's organ, The Defense Journal, writes apprehensively that the only thing disturbingly peculiar about Pakistan is the persisting uncertainty about its continued existence. This is both highly irksome and terrifying and after the earthshaking events of 1971—even sinister [17].

The demand for Pakistan failed to attract the people to the last. When the Muslim League decided to demand a separate homeland on the basis of its resolution of 1940 nothing materially changed in the political atmosphere in the provinces which now constitute the country. The League had never been accepted as a representative political party of the Indian people. In the elections of 1937, the League secured one out of 86 seats in the Panjab and 37 out of 119 seats in Bengal. In the Frontier and Sindh, the League failed to win a single seat. Even in the early 1940s, the political situation continued unchanged, as the influential sections of society in Panjab and Sindh remained aloof from the League and its policies. The idea of Pakistan was logically so absurd [18] that it took a long time for the people to grasp it.

As far as the common people were concerned, it was only when it became unmistakably clear that India was going to be divided and that the British had deep interests in the cause of the Muslim League and its leaders that the feudal lords in the Panjab and Sindh tilted towards the League and its objectives. Pakistan was not created because of any consensus of opinion among the peoples now forming part of that country, nor was there any spiritual determination which its magnitude deserved [19]; it was because the British rulers and their protégés wanted it to be. They instigated the forces of religious communalism in a constant endeavor to weaken the Indian freedom movement. While many factors, including socio-cultural and economic conditions, mostly in urban areas and the hardening attitude of the Indian National Congress on some issues, tended to strengthen sectional hatred, the British for their part inspired and encouraged communal feelings masterfully through both ideological and constitutional means.

During the initial years of independence, the emphasis was laid on religion, which has provided the *raison deter* for the establishment of the country. The socio-cultural, linguistic and regional character of the peoples of the areas constituting Pakistan was completely disregarded. The concentration on religion gave the ruling class some respite to consolidate their power. Since the intellectual support for the ruling alliance was coming from the immigrants from northern India, it was logical for them to conceive the glorification of Islam because they had nothing in common with the local people. It was also imperative in order to counter the growing dissent from smaller nationalities. It was also because Islam was the only way to appeal to the masses. However, this had its reactionary aspect. Regionalism slowly became a dominating political force and ultimately resulted in the country's disintegration. Bengali nationalism was the result of too much stress on Islam at the cost of the genuine national aspirations of people. Bengali nationalism within united Pakistan was the product of conflicting ideas and aspirations [20].

The continued political discontent and eventual break-up of the country in 1971 could not, however, shake the political power base in Pakistan, but shifted the emphasis for a while from Islam to economic and social reform. During the rule of the civilian Prime Minister Zulfikar Ali Bhutto, for a brief time, stress was also laid on regional autonomy, self-government, and social justice. Efforts were made to create a national outlook not merely on the basis of religion but on the basis of economic interests and shared political goals to be achieved. Nevertheless, the ideology of Pakistan and the two-nation theory continued to be regarded as the only basis for nationhood. A number of the Pakistani ruling elite had by then realized the futility of adhering to a concept that had no reality whatsoever in the prevailing political circumstances. In a television program by the state-run Pakistan Television Corporation, some eminent intellectuals maintained in the discussion that Pakistan should evolve a separate culture unrelated to those of the Arabs, Iranians, Turks, and the Indian Muslims. The historical past of the people living in Pakistan could provide sufficient material to establish the identity of a culture and furnish ample guidance for its future development [21]. This was perhaps the first direct, though discreet, hint through the mass media on the ideology of Pakistan. However, such views were never allowed to gain acceptance among the people because it would nullify notions already held and would weaken the power base of the ruling elite. Such views, it is feared by the ruling alliance, encourage racial tension, accelerates regional differences and could throw the country into an insoluble ideological conflict.

Despite the strong opposition from the establishment, of late, some of the leaders who were prominent during the Pakistan phenomenon have tried to put the record straight by explaining the objectives of the Pakistan movement. Addressing journalists at the Lahore Press Club during a Face-the-press programmed, Mian Mumtaz Ahmad Khan Daultana, an eminent Muslim League leader closely attached to the Pakistan movement, categorically stated that the basis for the creation of Pakistan was not religious fanaticism. Without democracy, he said, there would be no sense of nationalism and without nationalism, it is illogical to think of a nation. Daultana defined the ideology of Pakistan, as the aim for independence for the country in which they were living and being Muslims was a separate issue against the historical background. He maintained that Pakistan was not established to set up a laboratory for the survival of Islam, but to provide a free and separate homeland for the Muslims to save them from multifarious problems and threats to their lives [22]. Another Muslim League leader, Sardar Shoukat Hayat, also emphasized the view that Pakistan was not demanded merely on the basis of Islam. Addressing newsmen in Islamabad, he said that economic considerations motivated the movement for a separate country [23]. A Muhajir leader, Mahmud-ul-Haq Usmani, went a step further ridiculing Pakistani nationality as superfluous and extremely unrealistic. He advised the Urdu speaking immigrants to amalgamate themselves into the cultural environment of the peoples of Pakistan [24].

But it appears that it is now too late to avoid the prevalent doctrinaire irrationality who has crept deeply in the existential doctrine of the state.

After the creation of the state, democratic and liberal institutions were never allowed to flourish. Democratic norms continued to be eroded, while authoritarianism became strong. The country remained under a mindless bureaucratic regime. But it must not be forgotten that the Muslim League and its leader, Muhammad Ali Jinnah, never acted democratically. Jinnah operated undemocratically within the Muslim League and never conceded the right on the part of any party leader to differ with their position. Dissidents were considered traitors, a term that is still frequently invoked in political discourses in the country. Moreover, in the chaos that surrounded partition both Jinnah and the League turned to the viceregal tradition of autocratic rule [25].

Despite its cultural and linguistic heterogeneity and the professed political aim to set up a federal structure in the country, all powers were concentrated in the center with unitary authoritarianism. Public representation in the government was never allowed, and the role of the political parties was minimized. All the democratic institutions and opinion-forming organizations such as the press and mass-communications media were controlled by the government. The successive constitutions were manipulated or re-written at will. In such political indecency and intellectual stagnation, the country steadily drifted towards political instability.

Fear of democracy was intrinsic in the body politic of post-independence. They inherited it from India, where the Muslim League vehemently opposed democratic development. Democratic norms were rejected because the Muslim elite considered it against their interests. In October 1906, a deputation of Muslims mostly comprising Zamindars and Jagirdars met the Viceroy, Lord Minto, at Simla, where they deplored the introduction of institutions of the European type in the social, religious and political context of India. The adoption of European institutions, they argued, was likely among other evils, to place our national interests at the mercy of an unsympathetic majority. The newly created state faced its gravest hours when the same elite from India began to rule the country in the name of Islam and the ideology of Pakistan. The same attitude precisely guided the political behavior of the ruling alliance in Pakistan. One partner in the ruling alliance, the Muhajirs, was especially fearful of any democratic dispensation. Any representative government in the country would have ended their manipulation of power because they were an altogether tiny minority, totally alien to the peoples of Pakistan.

The leaders, who assumed power in the new state, were totally alien to the country's people. Neither of their top leaders. Muhammad Ali Jinnah and Liaqat Ali Khan could even speak any of the languages of the peoples of Pakistan. Urdu, the language of the refugees from north India, was promptly declared to be the official language to the utter dismay of the other nationalities, particularly the Bengalis, who were numerically in majority in the country. In the wake of Bengali protests over the question of the national language in March 1948, Prime Minister Liaqat Ali Khan gave the first official explanation, which was fully indicative of the policies of the new government. He said: "Pakistan is a Muslim state and it must have its lingua franca, the language of the Muslim nation...it is necessary for a nation to have one language and that language can only be Urdu and no other language" [26].

Urdu, the language of the refugees and immigrants was identified with the Muslim nation of Pakistan and subsequently also became a component of Pakistan's ideology and Islam [27]. Earlier, soon after taking office as Prime Minister, Liaqat Ali Khan had issued a statement of policy in which he had warned the country's nationalities that his government would take stern measures to "curb the spirit of narrow provincialism, should it manifest itself in any department or section of the government [28]. The rulers were now unmasking their real faces. They were by all practical means nurturing the theory of a master race. They believed that the Muslims from the Hindu majority provinces in undivided India, who were at the forefront of the Pakistan movement, had the inherent right to rule the newborn state. All the high offices in the new country should go to them. This attitude is evident from one occurrence mentioned by Mir Ahmad Yar Khan, the last Khan of the Baloch. In his autobiography, Inside Balochistan, he mentioned that in the months preceding the introduction of Martial Law in 1958, President Iskandar Mirza had invited the Nawab of Bhopal from India to take the Premiership of Pakistan. No one in Pakistan was considered qualified for such a high office [29]. Gunnar K. Myrdal in his work "Asian Drama", has quoted a Muhajir leader as saying that Pakistan was a conquered country. we have given them the administration, the industrial leadership, the culture, and the language [30].

70

The influence of the refugees and immigrants from northern India brought a traumatic change to society in many ways. Although it could not cement political solidarity among the peoples, between the rulers and the ruled, the immigrants (some eight million in the initial years) took over the country's administration, business, and economy. The economy was taken over mostly by the trading classes from Bombay, Kathiawar, and Burma, while the administration was controlled by civil servants from the north and central Indian states. In this way, the peoples of Pakistan were kept out of the government and policy-making institutions.

The imported leaders had no easy task. They were facing the problem of establishing and structuring the socio-political institutions of the county in accordance with their requirements, ensuring the continuity of their hold on power. They introduced their language as the national language and started to assert their cultural values [31]. Acting like true conquerors, they tried to reform the entire society. The shaky socio-political institutions they founded ultimately failed to integrate the people and resulted in the breakaway of the eastern wing of the country, Bangladesh, which sowed the seed of permanent discord among other peoples in what remained of Pakistan. The Urdu speaking immigrants came primarily from urban India and settled in the big cities. They had brought a set of values with them which were totally alien to the people, particularly the rural masses who constituted at least ninety percent of the population. They had a firm grip on power and the lives of indigenous peoples, who were mainly unaware of the peculiarities of the new political realities. It was the beginning of the polarization of Pakistani society.

2- The Guardian of the Islamic Ideology

The chaotic conditions in the newborn state were ideal for the army to organize itself and sharpen its teeth for political power. The officer corps of the armed forces emerged as the largest single-interest group and immensely benefitted from the ensuing instability. They also considered themselves the just inheritors of political authority in the country on the basis of the prevailing tendency of a largely traditional Muslim society to equate armed strength with national prestige, power, and progress [32]. The Pakistan army, trained, organized and fully armed by the colonial power, had the nature of a mercenary army of the highest order. Its character remains unchanged. The whole army, like the civil administration which Pakistan inherited, was a band of mercenary men. But some were more mercenary than others [33].

The role of the army in Pakistani politics was not unexpected. Whenever a developing country borders on socio-economic and political chaos and the businessmen, feudalists, and aristocracy fail to control the situation, the military will step in to fill the vacuum. Such action by the army is always backed by the business community, landlords and bureaucracy. The army interferes to strengthen the weakening grip of the exploiters. The army's meddling in politics is always referred to as a military revolution or a coup d'état. Another situation that could likewise invite the army to the political rescue of the bourgeoisie is when any government starts implementing progressive policies for the general good but against the interest groups: the armed forces then move in to check the course of political events. In most cases the army's physical intervention may not be necessary; it can pull the strings from behind the scenes. It is generally believed that within the armed forces, the sense of national mission appears to transcend parochial, regional or group interests. But this cohesiveness, in societies which are affected by communal dissent, has not always stood the test of performance. In the majority of cases, the army has miserably failed to perform the function of a national adhesive when the nation is threatened by strife incited by parochial forces. Indeed, the army has very often vitiated the conflict by adopting a partisan posture.

Pakistan provides an interesting example regarding army rule. The predominantly Panjabi army took a keen interest in quelling riots in East Bengal and also fought a cruel civil war there during the 1970 Bengali war of independence, it also crushed the Baloch rebellion during the 1960s and 1970s and Sindhi agitation in 1977 and 1983: but it was reluctant to take a similar attitude in the Panjab during 1977 when there was a general breakdown of law and order during the agitation against Bhutto regime. Many resignations among army officers were reported at the time when they were directed to shoot the Panjabi demonstrators in the streets of Lahore. This behavior of the armed forces created a clear perception among the minority nationalities that Pakistani armed forces serve only the interests of ruling Punjabi nationality. The military leaders are not unaware of this phenomenon. Writing in the army's mouthpiece Defense Journal, Brig (retd.) Abdur Rehman Siddique admitted that every time the military intervenes to shoulder the responsibility of the state ideology, the regionalist elements seem to regard this military option as yet another case of the hegemony of one or two provinces over the others [34]. Similar fears were expressed by the retired air force chief, Muhammad Asghar Khan. He wrote that the use of the army in the minority provinces of NWFP and Balochistan has created an impression in the minds of the people that they cannot expect justice from a Panjabi-dominated central government which controls a predominantly Panjabi Army [35].

The army intervened in 1958 and again in 1977 to wipe out what they then described as widespread corruption, administrative inefficiency, rising regional feelings, deteriorating law and order, and internal security situations, and the blatantly unconstitutional means adopted by the politicians to gain political advantage over their opponents. The army grabbed power to remedy the wrongs done by the politicians; but instead of restoring democracy, removing disparity, conceding regional autonomy, or rooting out corruption and maladministration, the military rulers consider it their duty to hold on to power, justifying it under one pretext or another. Those who may rise against the injustices of the military dictatorship are quickly branded as traitors, the definition of which varies with slight differences in emphasis from one regime to another. 'I am the state' is the mentality of the army generals ruling the country. Moreover, the army is a privileged class by virtue of its training and upbringing. It has an effective structure and cultural homogeneity compared to the other political organizations of the developing countries. It is an enormous social force apparently independent of the government, always ready to take action at the call of its commander. Since its leaders are always in touch with various leading economic and pressure groups in the country, they will get prompt political support from these groups on the assumption of power. The army, in turn, ensures the interests of these groups at the cost of the large majority of the people. In Pakistan, the military dictatorship has always been considered the stabilizing factor in the region by the West. As the protector of its political and strategic interests in the region, the

Western propaganda painted the army's role as the most modernizing element in Pakistan.

The striking characteristic of the role of the military in developing states is its advocacy of law and order and socio-economic reforms. Contrarily, army rule has always resulted in political instability, economic stagnation, and deep mistrust among the various ethnic and linguistic groups. The often-held view of the army as the stabilizing and modernizing factor has been nullified by practical examples. The notion of the armed forces as the champion of internal security has given them the necessary confidence to manipulate political power in times of chaos and uncertainty. To give their action an air of credibility, the military leaders give proper emphasis to an ideological commitment to the country's traditional values. The Pakistani military brass, who are somewhat conscious of their retrogressive record, further stress the army's responsibility in safeguarding the country's ideological frontiers, which they perceived to be always in danger. The army paper, 'Defense Journal', commented that unlike a professional and standing military establishment as the British Indian army, an outfit highly- rated for its professionalism, loyalty, and devotion to duty in peace and war, the armed forces in an ideologically oriented state like Pakistan become the custodians of the state ideology as much as that of its territory [36]. However, by virtue of their organization and their internal security role, by being the unilateral champion of national security, the armed forces always consider themselves superior to any other state organization.

3- Secular versus Religious

Since 1947 the Baloch and the leadership of other nationalities have constantly been demanding greater autonomy within a federal structure. The Baloch leaders wanted a decent political atmosphere, with national democratic institutions taking roots in the country. They were totally opposed to any sectarian or religious system, and striving to have the principle of secularism recognized as the only basis to govern the relations between the state and the people and between the federation and its component units.

Theoretically, individuals or groups are treated as equal citizens of the state irrespective of their creed. The state neither promotes nor opposes any creed nor does it meddle in the religious thinking of any individual or group as long as they do not interfere with human dignity or public morale. In such states, religion is never allowed to assume the right of coercion or intimidation and religious groups are free to organize themselves and preach their creed provided they do not violate other peoples' religious sentiments and deny others the same rights which they enjoy. In short, the individual as an equal citizen of the state is never identified by his religious affiliations. While the state does not allow the individual to interfere in state affaire by virtue of his being related to a particular religious group, it is always mindful of the individual personal relationship with the religion. In a secular society, state and religion operate separately within different fields of operations. While political power is outside the spheres of religion and beyond its direct intervention, the state never organizes or regulates the religious beliefs of the people. Under the principle of non-interference, religion and the state both have tremendous scope to develop and organize themselves without any opposition from each other.

On the face of it, Muhammad Ali Jinnah most probably wanted a secular and bourgeois-democratic state in Pakistan. His speech before the Constituent Assembly of the newly created state of Pakistan on 11th August 1947 gives some clue of his thinking. 'In course of time, he declared, Hindus would cease to be Hindus and Muslims cease to be Muslims, not in the religious sense, because that is the personal faith of each individual, but in the political sense as citizens of the state'. Nevertheless, the speech had tremendous religious and theoretical inconsistencies, which he helped to develop during the last few years of his life. Moreover, his subsequent behavior does not show that he was really able to progress beyond the communal politics of pre-partition India.

Encouraged by Jinnah's openly declared stand, the Pakhtun leader, Abdul Ghaffar Khan approached him and tried to prevail upon him to make the Muslim League a non-communal party. But he failed to convince Jinnah and formed a separate organization, the Peoples Party of Pakistan on 8th May 1948 [37], Ghaffar Khan became the president and the Sindhi leader, G. M. Syed, was elected the party's General Secretary. Besides the secular stance, the Party demanded full autonomy for linguistic groups in the country and the recognition of the inalienable rights of the people to rule. The party leadership also criticized the role of newly arrived refugees and immigrants in the power circle of the state. Ghaffar Khan was arrested on June 15, 1948, on the charge of creating sectarian hatred and the charge of calling Muhammad Ali Jinnah a British agent [38]. The façade of a secular state as portrayed by Jinnah was immediately became obvious as both the Peoples' Party of Pakistan and its affiliated volunteer organizations in the Frontier province, the Redshirts, and Khudai Khidmathgaar declared illegal.

Of late, some feeble voices were also raised even by persons belonging to the ruling alliance of Pakistan against the manipulation of religion in the state affairs. Some of the immigrant intellectuals have expressed their doubts about the continued religious polity in the country. Sabthe Hasan, a well-known writer, has summed up the controversy of the Islamic state and politics in a most logical manner. He argues that most of the prevalent ideas about Islam have been coined by the rulers to suit the emerging socio-cultural and political exigencies and have nothing to do with that faith. Islam, he noted, does prescribe a rudimentary state structure as practiced at the time of Prophet Muhammad, but it is silent on many relevant issues. It is not provident in the Quran that the faithful must establish any state nor there is any mention of any law or political philosophy to be followed in such a state. The Prophet did establish a state, but it appears not to be the aim of his prophetic mission but was merely a historical coincidence. He emphasized that Islamic political thinking is not derived from the Quran but based primarily on the procedures and actions of the Caliphs. Such actions resulted from historical circumstances and have no religious sanctity. The state, he observed, is not the goal of Islam. Muslims were there in Mecca before the Hijrath but there was no Muslim state. In many countries of the modern world, there are a large number of Muslim populations without a Muslim government, but this has by no means affected their creed. Sabthe Hasan maintained that the Islamic state is not traceable in Muslim literature before the twentieth century and that the theory that Islam is the amalgamation of religion and state is a totally new idea coined only recently [39].

With a fixed dogma, the religion left no room for any flexibility. It has caused wars and miseries and has been the most retarding factor in the socio-economic development of any given society. All organized religions, Judaism, Christianity, and Islam, have been the major factors contributing to wars throughout the ages. Religions produced followers who showed intolerance towards peoples of other faiths and cults. History, ancient and modern, is full of tales of cruelty against the people in the name of Jewish or Christian gods. Islam virtually divided the world into two regions: *Dar-al-Islam*, where Muslims prevail and Dar-al-Harb, actually meaning the land of infidels, to be conquered and brought under Islam. This brings in its wake the injunction *amr-bil-marouf wa nahi an al munkar*, which makes it binding upon the Muslims to ensure that righteousness prevails and evil is defeated throughout the world. The Quran declares: *'And let there be among a body of men who should invite to goodness and enjoin equality and forbid evil. And further, you are the best people raise for the good of mankind; you enjoin what is good and forbid evil and believe in Allah'* [40]. For Muslims war is a part of the faith. The Quran says: *'warfare is ordained for you'* [41]. Another injunction from the Holy Book exhorts: *'Fight those who believe not in God and the last day and do not forbid what God and his messenger have forbidden-such men as practice not the religion of truth, being of those who have given the Book- until they pay tribute out of their hand and have been humbled'* [42]. Resistance to evil other than using absolute force is, however, considered the weakest approach to faith. Prophet Muhammad declared: *'Any of you who sees evil should change it by his hand if he can, by his word if he can, by his heart if he can; and this is the least in faith'*. A true Muslim must never believe in peaceful co-existence with the non-believer. This doctrinal foundation of Islam was clearly explained by Ayatollah Khomeini of Iran exhorted the faithful to rise up and conquer their fear of death so that they can conquer the whole world [43].

According to the Quran and the sayings of the Prophet, the conflict with the non-believers is perpetual and total until such time as all the people are brought into the fold of Islam. Millions and millions of people have been killed in wars in the name of the Almighty, in a misguided and vain attempt to uphold what are thought to be the wishes of Allah. Islam mixed the spiritual message with the need to use naked force to transform the people into the spirit of high order ordained by Allah for mankind. The Prophet Muhammad drew his inspiration primarily from Judaism [44]. Islam, in a true sense, tried to use Arabian coarseness to modify Judaea-Christian beliefs in order to bring them in accord with the requirements of the time. It borrowed a lot from the Byzantine and Hellenic socio-cultural thoughts and practices and significantly from Iranian religious beliefs [45]. Politically, Prophet Muhammad gave the Arabs an immense pride and sense of historical consciousness, for which Islam appears to be basically intended. By symbolizing Mecca, as the house of Allah in preference to the religiopolitical city of Jerusalem, Islam clearly bore the marks of its Arabian origin [46]. Initially, Islam played the role of an ideological foundation to unify the separate Arabian tribes into a single centralized state [47]. Islam in originality as far as its religious purity was concerned, mostly remained unchanged when it vied for world domination. The spread of Islam beyond the Arabian Peninsula was perhaps the most unexpected and astonishing historical event in recent history.

The Islamic attitude towards those who may not profess faith is one of contempt and inequality. There is little consistency in Islamic teachings regarding religious minorities. The peoples of the books, Jews and Christians, have been included among those who go to paradise. But sometimes they are classed together with pagans and the Muslims are commanded to fight against those who do not accept Islam and pay religious tribute. Theoretically, the very existence of other communities is inappreciable in Islam. Islam gives rights to religion but never accords the people equal rights as citizens of the state. Even in the contemporary world, theoretically, Christians and Jews were given religious liberty in Islamic countries but practically not equal rights as citizens of the state [48]. This can be judged from one incident in Egypt in early 1980s when a clergy belonging to the Gama 'at el-Islami, issued a '*fatwa*', a religious edict, to the effect that if any of the Muslim groups found themselves short of the necessary resources and could expect no help from the government, it was permissible for them to take what they needed from the shops of the Christians [49]. The Pakistan government's reducing a religious group called Qadianis or Lahoris to the second rank can be seen in this context of intolerance and fanaticism. By executing the members of the Baha sect, the Iranians were perhaps implementing the spirit of Islam in the modern world [50].

Although Islam appears to have become reconciled to the idea of co-existing with other religions including Christianity after the first hundred years of Islamic conquests, its doctrinal rejection of Christianity has been further confirmed and greatly intensified by an abiding political hostility [51] which has resulted in many crusades, between the believers of two religions. Islam and for that matter other religions, may not necessarily be anti-progressive, retarding the path of socio-political and technological advancement; however, emendatory interpretations of these creeds, particularly of Islam vary from time to time and from country to country and from sect to sect and have greatly influenced the essence of its teachings. The interpretations of Quranic injunctions often contradict ideas believed to be progressive and justified under the given circumstances.

As mentioned earlier, Islam never provides peaceful relations with its neighbors. But the monarchs and rulers have usually ignored aggressive teaching of the faith and preferred peaceful coexistence with other peoples when they saw that there was no other choice. After the initial zeal of the Arabs, the *jihad* or the holy war against the unholy or godless peoples ceased to be operative as the only political choice with the Muslim rulers, who even attempted treaty relations with other countries and the *jihad* was never adopted as state policy, as it was during the time of the Prophet and the four Rightly-guided Caliphs. For political exigencies, sometimes, the *jihad* was kept in the backburner for a while by many monarchs and rulers of the Islamic world [52].

From the above discussion, it is not surprising that the leaders of Pakistan based their policies on Islam became intolerant and autocratic. The intolerance of the Pakistani state towards the followers of other faiths and any talk of a secular state they believe is strictly based on the true essence of Islam.

The Pakistani elite always takes pride in Arab-Islamic values as the main basis for Pakistani nationalism. But they forget that even the Arabs themselves gave more importance to Arab nationalism than their faith, which was nevertheless the main inspiring force in their recent history. Many Arab intellectuals put Arab nationalism before their religion, considering Islam a buttress of 'Arabism'. Michael Aflaq, the well-known ideologue of the Iraqi Ba'th Party has maintained that Prophet Muhammad was the epitome of the Arabs and that Islam represented the essence of Arabism towards unity, power, and progress [53]. Abd al Rahman Bazzaz also signifies the role of Islam in Arabism. He argued that Islam, which revived the Arab nation in its entirety and resurrected it, is the manifestation of the Arab genius [54]. During the 19th century, it has been Arab nationalism, Arab pride and Arab consciousness which have united the Arabs against foreign rule, and not the spirit of Islam. If the religion would have been the base then the Arabs would have lost their intellectual and social backing for demanding independence from the Turks, who were also Muslims. 'Before Muhammad, there were the Arabs and before Christ, there were the Arabs' was the slogan which was adopted by Amir Faysal when he led his armies into Syria at the end of the World War I.

In view of modern geopolitical realities and cultural diversity, the role of Islam is increasingly diminished in the political arena as a potent and inevitable force. Arab leaders are not unaware of this fact but Pakistan which derives inspiration from the Arabs and their cultural values, still finds itself intellectually bogged down in an impassable quagmire of religious doctrine periodically reshaped to suit the county's internal political exigencies.

The Baloch are neither irreligious nor atheists. The majority of them are as good Muslims as any of their compatriots in the country. The issue lies elsewhere. They are opposed to any denial of their socio-cultural, economic and political rights in the name of religion. They have had bitter experiences for the last many decades. Firstly, they lost their country in the name of religion. If they accept the misconceived and superfluous notion of two-nations for the entire sub-continent, of which they never formed part, they would automatically become a component of that non-existent Muslim nation and would lose their identity. Secondly, the new state brought with it an alien language, an alien culture, a set of alien social values, and above all alien masters to rule. They lost everything. A Baloch politician, Akbar Bugti, a former governor of Balochistan, has hypothetically suggested that the Baloch tribal leaders, Mir Chaakar and Mir Gwahraam were prudent by hindsight, not to attempt capturing a vast portion of Indian territory and settling in cities as a conqueror during the Baloch tribal sway in eastern Balochistan in the early 16th century. He said many conquerors lost their identity and were Indianized in the course of time. The Baloch would have met a similar fate. They would have lost themselves and everything they held dear; their home base, their Baloch-deh and would be completely extinct as a people without any identity [55]. This proposition is the crux of the matter, shaping the Baloch attitude towards Pakistani politics. For Baloch to accept the British conceived two-nation theory for the Indian Muslims, would mean losing their Baloch identity in the process. The same would be true for the peoples of other provinces, the Sindhis, the Pakhtun and the Panjabis.

The Baloch political elite was always skeptical about the two-nation theory. Mir Ghous Bakhsh Bizenjo, a former governor of Baluchistan, rebuked any such notion in Islam and termed any attempt to associate the Pakistani state with the concept of Muslim nation a crude attempt to deny the socio-political rights of the smaller nationalities in Pakistan. In an interview with Urdu monthly, "Pakistan Forum" reproduced in Pakistan Progressive in 1980, Mir Bizenjo argued that the concept of a Muslim nation, in reality, was nothing at all. He said the Quran nowhere refers to the Muslims as a nation. Whenever the Muslims are mentioned, they are referred to as Ummah, believer or Millath coreligionists. He maintained that the Muslim nation which does not exist in reality is at the same time impracticable as a concept. For example, he pointed out that we do not give any Iranian, Afghan, or Arab the right to vote in our country nor can we appoint them to any high office here. On the other hand, we do give the right to vote to Pakistani Hindus, Christians, Parsis and they often can be appointed to high positions. So, it is obvious that this is an imaginary concept that has no practical existence. If the hypothesis of Muslims as a nation is accepted, then not only the political development and formation of a Pakistani nation will no longer be possible but it will also negate the spirit of the Quran, which stresses the universality and internationalism of Islam by using the Word Ummath and Millath to have a multinational and international connotation [56].

References

1. Al Beruni, quoted in Davendra Kaushik: Central Asia in modern times- A History from the 19th Century, Progress Publishers, Moscow,1970, p 16.
2. In spite of Muslim rule and domination for many hundred years, Islam, could not transform Indian society. Even among the early Arabs, Islam could not change aspects of the cultural ethos such as slavery, and polygamy. The Arab nobility was hardly reconciled to the idea and the command of their Prophet that there was no place for genealogy in Islam.
3. Leonard Binder: Religion and politics in Pakistan, California, 1963, p,4.
4. Quoted in Muhammad Said Khan: What is the Ideology of Pakistan? Peshawar Times, 4th April 1970.
5. Morning News, Karachi,14th April 1978.
6. Daud Kahn, the elder son of Ahman Yar Khan, the Khan of Kalat (r.1933-1948), who now considers himself the Khan after his father's death, suggested that General Zia ul Haq should be called Caliph, not president, because of his glorious services to the cause of Islam and Pakistan. Jang, Quetta, 20th December 1984.
7. Quoted in Waheed-uz-Zaman (ed) The Quest of Identity, University of Islamabad, Islamabad,1974, P 5.
8. The Time of India, 21st March 1924.
9. G.M Syed: Interview for the Indian Newspaper, Sunday, reproduced in Jang (Karachi), 19th June 1985.
10. S. Abid Husain: The Destiny of the Indian Muslim, London 1965, p 24.
11. M.U Haq: Muslim Politics in Modern India. Book Traders, Lahore, PP 30-32.
12. John Cunning: ed. Political India, quoted in Tariq Ali: Can Pakistan survive? Death of a state, Penguin books,1983.
13. G.M Syed's Interview: Op Cit.
14. Lawrence Ziring: Op. Cit, p 59.
15. Rupert Emerson: From Empire to Nation, Harvard University press Massachusetts, 1960,163.
16. Muhammad Asghar Khan: Generals in Politics – Pakistan 1958-82 Vikas Publishing House, Delhi,1982, P 72.
17. Brig, (Retd) Abdur Rahman Siddiqui: The Afghanistan Crisis and sub-continental Security, Defence Journal, vol, IX No 8,1983, P.1.
18. Kenneth Cragg: Counsels in Contemporary Islam. Islamic survey No.3, University Press, Edinburgh, 1965, p 19.
   Ibid. p 28.
19. G.W. Choudhary: The Last Days of United Pakistan. C. Hurst & Company, London, 1974, P.1.
20. Ahmad Abdullah: The Clash over the identity of Pakistani Culture, Dawn,3rd March 1975.
21. MAG(Karachi),1-7 September 1983, p 9.
22. Jang, Quetta, 10th January 1985.

23. Ibid. 24th December 1983.

24. Stanley A. Kochanek: interest Groups and Development Business and politics in Pakistan Oxford University Press, Karachi,1983, p 42.

25. Liaqat Ali Khan, quoted in Tariq Ali: Op Cit, p 45.

26. Urdu as the language of Islam, as referred to by Liaqat Ali Khan, contradicts some old notion among the Arabs and the Jews regarding the religious sanctity of their respective speech, Arabic and Hebrew. Both peoples claim that their languages are the parent tongue of making in which God addressed Adam, and will also choose to communicate to the peoples in the life after death. Where Urdu stands in importance as the language of Islam is yet to be defined.

27. Dawn, 17th August 1947.

28. Ahmad Yar Khan: Inside Balochistan. Royal Book Company, Karach,1975, pp,175-177.

29. Gunnar K. Myradal: Asian Drama. Vol 1 pelican Books Massachusetts, 1968, 310.

30. There are many instances where people, especially in a tribal society have adopted the Language of the powerful neighbor, or the ruling factions mostly to attain the desired social status. Many conquered people have learned the speech of their conquerors. In the case of Pakistan, Urdu has been imposed on the Absolute majority against their wishes and at the cost of tongues older and richer than Urdu.

31. Kalim Siddique: Conflict, Crisis, and War in Pakistan, Macmillan, London,1972, p 96.

32. Mercenaries are hired soldiers; Nubian slaves served the Egyptian Pharaohs while the Philistinian freebooters were also engaged in various middle-eastern conflicts. The Mercenaries played an important role in European wars from the fourteenth to the seventieth centuries, including the Hundred Years War (133-1453). Throughout history, mercenaries have produced heroes, murderers, freebooters, and hired agents. The Indian invaders from Central Asia from time immemorial were formed mostly of the freebooter. In modern political terminology, a state army that comprises only a particular section of society is not regarded as being national. The Pakistani army comprises Panjabis and to some extent Pakhtuns from the frontier province. Its behavior has always been parochial. Moreover, it is now serving many Gulf states including Sudi Arabia in return for higher remunerations.

33. Ibid. pp 90-91.

34. Brig (Retd) Abdur Rahman Siddique: The Military option, the Defense journal, vol IV NO,11, November 1978, p 7.

35. Muhammad Asghar Khan: Op Cit. p 71.

36. Marsiglio of Padua was one of the Most influential Writers to contribute to the Idea of secularism. In his famous work defensorPacis of 1324 Ad, he distinguished between temporal and spiritual law. He strongly opposed any punishment on the basis of religious beliefs, maintaining that the rights of citizens are independent of the faith they profess.

37. M. Rafique Afzal: Political Parties in Pakistan. National commission on historical Research, Islamabad, 1976, pp9-91.

38. Ibid.

39. Sabthe Hasan: Naveed-e-Fkir, Makataba Danial, Karachi,1982, p 60-61.

40. Quran: 3: 105,

41. Ibid.3:111

42. Ibid. 2:216

43. Ibid. 9:29

44. Gustave E VonGrunebaum: Op Cit. pp 322-324.

45. Reuben Levy: The social structure of Islam. Cambridge, 1965, p 91.

46. M.I Isayev: Op Cit, pp 31-32.

47. H.A.R. Gibb: Religion and politics in Christianity and Islam J. Harris proctor (ed): Islam and International Relations. Frederick A. Praeger, New York, 1965.p 7.

48. Muhammad Heikal: Autumn of fury-The Assassination of Sadat. Corgi Books, London, 1984, p 231.

49. Some 200 Baha'is have been executed and more than 700 were sentenced to imprisonment in Iran in the first five years of the revolution. Twenty of them were sentenced to death in February 1983 by an Islamic Tribunal in Sheraz on charges of spying. An Iranian government spokesman said were condemned because not only did they not regret what they had done; they were also proud of their religion, the Iranian government has also ordered Bahais formerly employed in the government to pay back their lifetime earnings (Morning News, Karach, 18th February 1983: Dawn, 3rd February 1985, and Fergus M. Bordewich; Their crime is faith, Readers Digest, February 1985, pp 92-96).

50. H. A.R. Gibb: Op Cit.

51. Majid Khaduri: Islamic theory of international Relations: Islam and international relations. Op, Cit. P.34, After prolonged conflict and war between the protestants and the Catholics, peace was restored by the Augsburg Agreement of 1555. The Principle of peaceful co-existence was further augmented by the Treaty of Westphalia in 1648. The Christian rulers agreed to accept the principle governing the relationships among European states and later among states of different faiths throughout the world.

52. Ibid.

53. Machael Aflaq: quoted in Elies Kedeurie's Introduction to Nationalism in Asia and Africa. New American Library. New York, 1970, pp 68-69.

54. Ibid.

55. Akbar Bugti: in his foreword to Aziz Bugti's work, Tehrkh-e- Balochistan– Shakhsiyat ke Ainey Mien. Sales& Services, Quetta 1984, p 12.

56. Pakistan Progressive Vol 3, Nos,3& 4, New York, December 1980, p 70.

CHAPTER IV

THE SOCIAL ORIGINS OF THE BALOCH NATIONAL STRUGGLE

The Baloch national struggle has its genesis in history and culture. Fiercely independent, the Baloch has never assented hegemony and domination either by other tribes or by organized states in any stage of history. His periodic movements, apart from many other reasons came about because he never had to contend with a subordinate status. Tribal wars and jealousies, although had their roots in economic competition, were also due to efforts by one tribe to gain supremacy over another, which were actively resisted. The Baloch was unsettled and preferred a nomadic life because in that he felt truly emancipated. During the Khanate era, for a while, although Balochistan theoretically was supposed to be under Afghan hegemony, for all practical purposes, various Khans of Kalat never assented the afghan overlordship. The war between Ahmad Shah Durrani and Mir Naseer Khan was primarily a contest on the question of Afghan sovereignty over Balochistan.

1- Baloch Sense of Independence

Socio-culturally and traditionally, when the Baloch feels that his liberty is threatened from any quarter, he will become restive. In individual acts of vengeance or in the collective removal of curbs on freedom, the Baloch always resorted to wars and hostilities. In many such cases, peace or arbitration with the enemy would be impossible.

'Conciliation can be achieved when palms can grow hair; the jackal becomes the guard of the chickens or the fowl; lions are grazed together with the camels; cotton becomes non- inflammatory; elephants have reduced to millet in size, and fish can live out of water' [1]. 'He will forego vengeance when tamarisks grow spikes and snakes' feet; lions are domesticated and boats are run through sands; sardars start the menial jobs of slaves and shepherds graze wolves' [2]. An enmity once started never easily subsided. Blood had to be paid in blood. 'If stone could melt away in waters then the spirit of revenge can be subdued. But neither can stones melt away nor can the spirit of revenge be extinguished in a Baloch heart. For two centuries it persists and remains smart like a young deer of tender age' [3]. His way of revenge is fierce and ruthless. 'He will treat the enemy in a manner a falcon does the pigeons; as hot winds dry up small ponds; as swine devastate millet crops: as goats swallow up the branches of prosodies spicier: as the wolf does with lambs and fisherman with river fishes' [4].

Such cultural traits show a peculiar trend, a collective intellect. The role assigned for a Baloch in society is one of honor and freedom, not of subjugation and dependence; therefore, he places his loyalty in no one but himself and his people. Individual liberty and honor are above everything. However, the honor of the tribe as part of his identity is also important. He is always ready to defend his freedom as well as that of the tribe. The wish of a mother in her lullaby to her baby-son is that he should grow in the true tradition of freedom so that he should be called for war by the tribal Chief. Her advice to his son is to show exceptional courage: *"make use of your sword and bow and prove yourself a true Baloch, because the people await your feats of war as a sister has confidence in her brother or hopes for reunion with her remote family, and as a girl in love trusts her lover"* [5]. This is the proper manifestation of the cultural personality that evolved out of his independent nature. He believes in a constant battle with the forces of evil. The fight is perpetual and this socio-cultural approach has clearly been shaped by the Zoroastrian outlook, which is still deep-rooted among the Baloch personal and collective behavior.

The Baloch never accepted alien domination. He was engaged in a constant struggle for tribal supremacy which usually resulted in wars and migration. He had a deep sense of national independence and a restive spirit of resistance to dominating forces. His extreme love for his homeland had been phenomenal. Once settled in a place, he never gave it up without fighting, and after migration from the area, the remembrance continued for centuries. *"Waah e Wathaan o Hushkien Daar"*-the fatherland even barren is worth anything-so goes the saying. Many features of this creep into folk stories and literature. Folk traditions refer to the finest things of a place once inhabited by the Baloch.

Baloch poets and scholars never lagged behind in arousing social consciousness. The epic poetry of the Rind-Lashaarera or poetic references to previous tribal conflicts gives a penetrating insight into national pride and an uncompromising attitude towards national freedom. Tribes settled in an area always made it a safe abode for themselves. It became their land, love, and regard for which had the first priority. In tribal conflicts, the main cause had been economic interests, ultimately identified with the area itself, and the love of the country was the prime objective. The Baloch who had moved out from Kirmaan and Sistaan always kept the memory of the area fresh in their folk tales. We come across many stories that indicate sentimental regard for those regions where the Baloch once lived. Even mountains and rivers enjoyed lasting affections. Koh e Kaaf, the KafKaf Mountains, where the Baloch might have lived in ancient times are mentioned in their folk stories with a feeling of profound love that even a casual observer can feel.

2- The Baloch Sense of a Dignified life

The British suzerainty over Balochistan affected a tremendous change in the social outlook. We find an element of scholarly warning against political inactivity and expression of sorrow over the loss of national sovereignty and respect. Mullah Fazul, a nineteenth-century poet, chastises the Rind, the tribe to which he belonged, for giving up the traditional role of conquerors. In a famous poem in which he narrates with some exaggeration, the exploits of the Rind in support of the Mughal emperors, Babar and Humayun, he calls upon them to fight and conquer vast lands and mountains and keep for the independence of the Baloch country.

The Baloch concept of protracted war against evil forces sets the ground for enlightenment where fighting for a just cause becomes synonymous with nobility and honors. The same idea remained an influencing factor and was recapitulated in subsequent decades in Baloch poetry. While foreign domination had a considerable impact on the socio-political institutions, it intensified social consciousness in an unheard-of way in the Baloch annals. The martyrdom of Mir Mehraab Khan became a guiding spirit which in many ways helped to foster a spirit of resistance against foreign domination.

The year 1839 marks the beginning of far-reaching changes in Baloch political history but its social imperatives proved to be of greater magnitude. Among some of the Baloch who elected to side with the new dominant power of the British empire, the social attitude was gradually being changed from the traditional independence to one of passive subservience. The self-respecting Baloch, however, was gaining a perceptive awareness of political upheavals which conceptually shaped their social outlook in the years to come.

The new rulers of Balochistan attempted to create a socio-political set up with the help of the Baloch notables who detached themselves from the common folk to create a new class of aristocracy and feudal lords. The Baloch poets and opinion leaders soon discovered this new dimension. The Indian freedom movement also had a tremendous fallout. Many prominent personalities and tribal elders influenced by the Indian national movement formed the Kalat state National Party to struggle for an independent Balochistan. The capitulation of the Khan of Kalat to join Pakistan in 1948 came as the greatest shock to the patriotic elements and has been regarded as an ignoble act of the highest betrayal. From there, a sense of agonizing frustration and profound sadness can be witnessed among the intelligentsia. Baloch poetry was completely reoriented. Mir Gul Khan Naseer (1914-1983), the poet-politician, gave a new meaning and form to Balochi poetry. The concept of freedom and sovereignty was beautifully portrayed. He lamented the tragic event of Balochistan losing its independence. The degrading poverty of the Baloch masses, he thought, was due to the betrayal and treachery of the Khan. His poetry is the greatest manifestation and the most profound expression of the Baloch political and social approach since the early thirties. His exhortation to the Baloch to uphold their tradition is a clear sign of the deep-rooted hatred felt toward the new rulers and strong disapproval of the new political dispensation. His poems soon turned to popular slogans and were the subject of discussions by the elite.

Mir Gul Khan Naseer was a revolutionary poet in Baloch's literary history. His work embraced some fifty years of his life. He participated in the Baloch struggle for national independence and remained behind bars for several years. He was a socialist by inclination and opposed the tribal system and its attendant injustices. His contribution to Baloch political awareness is overwhelming. Mir Gul Khan Naseer considered himself destined to guide the people towards social awareness and the achievement of their political rights. He assigned himself the task of educating the youth for the great cause for which he suffered immensely during his lifetime. He was uncompromising, honest and respectable. As far back as November 1936, he composed a poem praying that he might have the courage and strength to awaken the people from ignorance so that they would be able to find a proper place among the community of nations once again. The poem, which is in Urdu, shows his determination for a lifelong struggle in a cause that was very close to his heart [6].

Naseer's message is impressive. It circles around the Baloch and their history. His works portray a deep hatred for Pakistan and its institution, which he regarded as corrupting and degenerating in substance and nature. The new generation of revolutionary poets has been greatly influenced by his philosophy. I have not attempted any translation of his work for the simple reason that none of his poems can be singled out for omission for the purposes of this chapter. A separate treatment would be required if Mir Gul Khan Naseer's poetry were to be analyzed in the context of the Baloch national struggle and its impact on youth.

Mir Gul Khan Naseer is the author of many books on Baloch history and traditions. He had a prolific pen and a philosophical mind. His treatment of the Baloch social and traditional ethos depicts a high sense of history and culture. His poems describe the Baloch and their country in a true historical perspective. Mir Gul Khan was the product of agonizing socio-political conditions. He saw the British rule in Balochistan, a brief period of Baloch sovereignty and ultimately Balochistan losing its independence and merging into a newborn state. British rule perfected a tribal system molded to the requirements of an alien rule, with the tribal chiefs, appointed by the colonial administration for exploiting the Baloch masses. The pre-independence era was also the period of Khan's oppressive rule with the connivance of his British masters. The short period of

Baloch independence from August 1947 to March 1948 witnessed conspirational maneuvers against the Baloch, culminating in the annexation of their state into Pakistan. For the Baloch political and social elite, the post-1948 years are the time of constant struggle to gain some sort of political and social rights. Mir Gul Khan Naseer participated actively in the process and his attitude was clearly shaped by these events.

3- The Literature: A Medium of Nationalistic Sentiments

The periodic uprisings and deep discontent among the Baloch after 1948 are by no means an isolated phenomenon. It is fairly widespread in Balochi literature and folk traditions. Disapproval of the accession to Pakistan was a common literary expression. The Khan is greatly hated. This hatred is widely depicted in folk literature as well as in poetry. To quote a single instance, a cartoon was carried by the Balochi magazine, in December 1957 showing the Khan of Kalat prostrate before the Pakistani authorities, asking for privileges. The cartoon was captioned: *'Dream, this is your destiny. Our Khan–e–Muazim, do not dream for power (and glories) of past days".*

Since the great betrayal of 1948, the Baloch poet watches every event with distaste and expresses his resentment for the socio-political set-up. The opposition to the accession of the Khanate to Pakistan was upheld and Abdul Kareem Khan, the brother of the Khan of Kalat, Ahmad Yar Khan, is regarded as one of the great patriots. In 1958, came the first major encounter of the Baloch with the Pakistan army, when Mir Norouz Khan and a few others revolted and took to the mountains. Apparently, they were aggrieved because of the arrest of the Khan of Kalat by Pakistan army in a pre-dawn attack on his residence in Kalat on 6th October 1958, but the causes were deep down. Mir Norouz Khan and his followers were clearly against the Khan's decision to accede to Pakistan, and when the Khan showed a semblance of resistance by demanding certain rights for Balochistan, they readily pledged their support.

The insurgency had, however, wider repercussions. The leadership of that uprising was in the hands of tribal notables, and in some cases, they behaved in a manner prejudicial to their professed aims; still, they were regarded as heroes by the masses. In certain places, many people were harassed by elements claiming contacts with the *yaagis*, the rebels, and sometimes alienating people in the Makkuraan region; but as a whole, the people considered them the upholders of their pride and self–respect. Baloch literature, during and after this period, is full of praise for them.

In the later years, the nature and pattern of the Baloch national resistance transformed when the educated class played a greater role in the 1973-77 uprising. This event has been regarded as the beginning of the broad-based Baloch liberation movement. The Baloch from all walks of life supported the movement which was so popular with the masses that the Pakistan government decided not to trust the local people and brought in on a massive scale, army officers seconded to the civil services, to hold the administrative assignments in Balochistan. By 1975-76, almost every district head was an army officer or a civil servant from the Punjab and North-West Frontier Province.

The revolt of Prince Abdul Kareem in May 1948 did not gain much momentum. Along with some of his followers, he had entered Afghanistan with the hope of getting assistance from the Afghan rulers. He harbored such hope primarily because of the Afghan attitude towards Pakistan, and secondly, the traditional support the two peoples had given each other in time of distress. But the prince received no aid from his host, and feeling extremely disappointed, he returned and surrendered to the Pakistani army. Detained and subsequently released, he helped form the *Usthumaan Gal* and its successor, the National Awami Party.

Prince Kareem's revolt was given the highest praise by the minstrels. He was made the symbol of courage and velour. A poem composed after his return from Afghanistan narrates the entire episode, lauding the prince and his valiant comrades who are determined to uphold the Baloch cause. A poem by Azaad Jamaldini appeared in Balochi magazine (January 1957) captioned *Paigaam* (message) to Aagha Abdul Kareem Khan, beautifully composed, it mentions the Baloch determination to fight for the great objective of achieving national independence. The poem condemns 'the three' (meaning Afghanistan, Iran, and Pakistan), for dividing the Baloch land among themselves. It criticizes the sardars (tribal chiefs) for bartering away the people and expresses the hope that the Baloch will continue to offer sacrifices in blood for the noble cause.

Mir Norouz got the highest tributes. Poems and sonnets composed after the tragic event are still sung as lullabies and as traditional "*haallo*" in many parts of Jahlawaan during social ceremonies. He is depicted as a hero and placed amongst the greatest in Baloch history. He is accorded a place next only to Mir Chaakar, Mir Gwahraam and Mir Mehraab Khan in velour and righteousness. The treachery of Pakistani rulers in executing the colleagues of Mir Norouz Khan and going back on their promises is regarded as the mean tactic of a contemptible enemy. The Baloch are exhorted to follow Mir Norouz and his brave comrades, who fought for a cause as glorious as that of Mir Mehraab Khan. Mir Gul Khan Naseer's poem before and after the executions of Mir Norouz's comrades are the most marvelous pieces of literature ever composed on various aspects of a struggling people. In the suffocating milieu of 1963, a poem published in Monthly Ulus, expressed deep resentment over the continued political subjugation of the Baloch. Although it did not refer to the rebellion of Mir Norouz, one can infer that the poet is not unaware of the happening. The poet says he wants to be the master of his own land and guide his own destiny. He has no chauvinistic claims and wants the restoration of the honor of his motherland.

Sayad Zahoor Shah (1926-1977) was a renowned poet and writer. A few excerpts from his book of prose, *Sisthagein Dasthunk*, show that he was deeply shocked to see the Baloch losing their national sovereignty:

> My heart bleeds
> To wet the barren land for my miserable people
> In the hope that one day these lands will turn
> green and there will grow red flowers.
> Gather the seeds of those flowers
> because these are from my blood [9]

> After subjugation for a thousand years
> The Baloch is still oppressed by the merciless,
> (But) He is a people who can hardly be crushed [10]

> I am like those brave youths,
> ambushed by the enemy,
> Injured by the sword, lying hopelessly in a
> vast desert, without water.

Hungry wolves are waiting for the flesh.
But I tell them {the enemy} not to be off guard:
Revered mothers will bear
Such invincible sons again [11]

Referring to the powers and states that are responsible for the miseries of the Baloch, he said:

The one whose hands are red
with my blood, says he is pure;
The other, like a jackal who has stolen my pouch,
boasts of being a tiger;
The third that has snatched a portion of my shawl,
and has an eye on my shirt,
says, I am your brother';
The fourth one is so courteous
that I am frightful [12].

We (the Baloch) do not want your palaces
do not set our huts on fire;
We do not require your forts,
do not encircle our mountains;
We do not eye your abundance,
do not ravage our fields;
We do not demand your ships,
do not destroy our boats;
We do not desire your aircrafts
do not snatch our camels;
We do not aspire your amours,
do not break our arms;
Do not oppress us
lest you may be oppressed by a superior spirit [13].

We are still unarmed
And living under the shadow of swords.
But we are not hopeless
A day will come
when we will be shadowing the swords.
If you are not imperceptive, than
you are desperately miserable [14].

Sayad Zahoor Shah, in a poem, *Biyadiga suhrien maadene*, expresses in a very lucid language, the Baloch determination to fight his way through for emancipation and freedom. 'The Baloch will crush the enemy, shedding blood and drinking it in revenge', the poem says [15]. In his poem, *hazaar ganjien napaan thaawaan kanien*, he exhorts the Baloch not to hesitate to withstand the difficulties which may come in the way of achieving their great objective. He reminds the Baloch of their glorious past and asks for sacrifices to secure a position of honor and respect [16]. In the poem, *Sarjam Bothaganth*, he tells the Baloch that the enemy wishes their oblivion. Weakness is the last link between strength and miserableness. Wake up and do something for your survival, he exhorts them [17]. In *Shamushkaar Naaban*, Sayad Zahoor Shah says, he cannot forget the Baloch country, the vast barren land, its valleys, mountains, and rivers which are unforgettable. The people and their history, their bravery and courage and the hardship they suffer cannot be erased from his memory [18]. In *Saankalaan Sindien*, he urges to find a way to break the chains of slavery. He calls upon the Baloch to follow the footsteps of their forefathers, who resisted the enemy and never let themselves be dominated by others. Unless the enemy is defeated there will be no peace for the Baloch in their country, he says. In another poem, *Gehien Shahsawaraan*, the poet exhorts the people to fight the enemy who has occupied his land. He is optimistic that the enemy will be defeated. The Baloch will surely carry the day. In *Mangihien Baloch*, the poet takes pride in the idea that the Baloch are determined to give battle to the enemy. He hopes that the Baloch will crush the enemy and avenge the wrong done to them.

Ghulam Rasool Mulla believes in his destiny as the poet of a subjugated people whose rights have been snatched and whose vast land has been under alien hegemony. The establishment of Pakistan and the accession into it of the Baloch country was the greatest shock to Mullah; whose poetry depicts a revolutionary trend with an optimistic overture under agonizing socio-political conditions. He is influenced by the movement for self-determination. The general frustration after the events of 1948 shaped Mulla's poetry to a great extent. G.R. Mulla has a deep possessive affection for his homeland. His style and poetic genus placed him among the few revolutionary poets.

The first compilation of Mulla's poems appeared in 1981 entitled Bazhn. A few excerpts condensed and rendered freely are produced below:

> Balochistan is my heart, my soul,
> a panacea for all conceivable pains of life.
> Why should I not sacrifice,
> or hesitate to suffer indignities of confinement,
> when my motherland is facing the poisonous bullets [19].

> You will face the consequences of your evils,
> You will suffer from trickery and sweet talks,
> and hateful taunting.
> You instill fear like tigers,
> You boast as a superior,
> But I have never seen signs of bravery or respect for you,
> in the pages of history,
> Do not consider me helpless.
> Do not see my condition as miserable.
> You are prosperous, strong,
> I am weak, resourceless.
> But do not be off guard,
> The day will come when you will be accounted,
> for all your evil doings [20].

> The Baloch are miserable,
> Their youth appears aged, unclothed, and unfortunate
> There is no remedy for them,
> They cry and cry at night,
> For help and succor,
> I wonder why all the ills aim at the Baloch
> Listen to me the great youth,
> Let us commit ourselves
> To struggle and retake our land,
> Unite and lead our people to happiness and respect [21].

> Listen to me the honorless devil,
> You never regret the oppression, cruelties,
> you perpetuated on me,
> You have caused misery everywhere,
> Children and newborn are crying,

Bleeding in tears.
A fire may destroy you
I will take revenge.
Can you see the wrong you have done, O despicable!
Looted our land, our dwellings,
Traces of evil and destruction everywhere.
I am witness to all this,
But I am patient, hopeful,
That you will also be burnt and destroyed
The way you are destroying me [22].

O the grown-up youth of my people,
Let me narrate a pathetic tale,
Give you happy news.
If you see the sun red,
bright moon, and stars,
Any redness in flowers,
These must be the blood of your people.
You are the son of a great people,
Hailing from Baloch Khan, Mir Chaakar and
Gwahraam.
You are the son of Kambar,
You belong to Aali and Beebagr,
You are my only hope,
The spirit of a great people
you will do the impossible.
If you want my advice,
Have the courage to face the bitterness,
Embrace the revolution and destroy the enemy [23]

O, my comrade!
Your motherland has been captured,
The enemy has spread over your land
Like the pigs in multitude.
They have pillaged a vast land,
Ravaged our dwelling,
The bullets are coming like rainfall.
Why are you at ease?
Your motherland has been subjugated,
You have been made a slave,
Thugs and cowards are ruling you,

Your national rights snatched and
The beautiful country is being looted.
Your brothers have been killed,
Sons are hungry, thirsty,
It is your people who are being destroyed,
It is your land which is being devastated,
By the worthless, contemptible,
Why do you consider yourselves weak?
Take up your guns,
Check your strength [24].

Muraad Saahir's compilation of poems, *Bahaar*, (Fazul Academy, Karachi, (1970) is an appreciable contribution to Balochi literature. He has a grieving heart but a healthy mind. Balochistan occupies the highest place in his thoughts. His poetry circles around the beauties of the land and his people. He believes in total revolution and awaits the day when 'a tirade from the east' sweeps the entire world. Baloch subjugation is referred to in several of his poems. Muraad is proud to be a Baloch and expresses his determination to continue the fight against national oppression. He is not direct and aggressive like G.R Mulla or philosophical like Sayad Zahoor Shah but his poetry reflects a constant endeavor to send his message of revolution to Baloch youth.

The event portraying the upheavals in the 1960s is expressed in a forceful style in Balochi literature. No Baloch has ever been truly reconciled to the idea of the Baloch losing his independence. The firing in Quetta in 1968 when Zareef Khan, a college student, was killed and many others injured remained fresh in peoples' memory for many years. It was regarded as the greatest provocation. To forestall the agitation by students and political activists, the government clamped down with a dawn to dusk curfew in Quetta. Atha Shaad, in his poem, *Sah Kandan*, composed in June 1968, regrets the martyrdom of the student and says efforts to put a curb on the peoples' consciousness is an exercise in futility. The poem refers to the death of a son of this great land (Balochistan), and considers it a defeat for the oppressive rulers, declaring that conscience and thoughts cannot be snatched away by death; it is everlasting, ever vigorous, like overwhelming love and affection. The poem chastises the rulers for their victory over helplessness and their control over the forcibly snatched land about which the poet maintains, we are its true inheritors and upholder of its pride. Peoples' spirit cannot be destroyed by killing. It is restless, ever resentful and leads the people to their ultimate goal, *Ajoi*, the emancipation [25].

Malik Touki's poem Reta, written in the context of western Balochistan, gives a glimpse of the poet's political preferences. He wishes that oppression may stop and an atmosphere of freedom prevails upon his land. He desires that imperial Iran be destroyed. In *Shier O Roche Waajae Bundar Suchaath*, the poet gives an account of a deeply conscientious individual who is treated as insane because the freedom he conceives is beyond his reach. This madness is, therefore, without any remedy as long as the beautiful land continued to be dominated and oppressed [26].

Zuraaki, by Bashir Bedaar, draws a parallel between the situation in Balochistan and that in Vietnam, Kampuchea, Laos, Rhodesia, and Palestine. It hates the continued exploitation of the people. The poem says that inactivity can never bring self-rule [27]. In *Biya ke Goun Kanien Marga Madaahe*, Bedaar says that national rights can be achieved through sacrifices in blood. He exhorts the youth to give up inactivity and fight for the great cause [28]. In *Hambalaan*, the poet urges the people to take up arms to fight for their national glory. The poem portrays the miserable conditions in which the Baloch are living and calls upon the people to change their lives through an armed struggle [30]. In the poem *Gwaank*, he says it is time to free the motherland from the clutches of the enemy. The poem expresses contempt for those who act as agents of the enemy. It says a motherland mortgaged with the enemy can be restituted only through blood [31].

Muneer Shahwani, in his poem *Wathan*, pledges every sacrifice for Balochistan. Expressing deep love for the motherland, he declares that the enemy will not succeed in its ignoble tactics [32]. M. H Khalil Aapsari is more candid when he defines the Baloch, Balochi, and Balochistan. He is proud of the land and its great but innocent and simple people [33].

The military operations in Balochistan of that period had a tremendous impact on the people. The intelligentsia deeply resented the atrocities perpetrated by the operating army. In *Bohe Bohe Adami*, Surath Mari fictionalizes a painful situation when a blind nine-year-old girl is shot by the army because she cannot understand their command to stop when she is passing near their camp. She was proceeding in the direction of roaring engines she guesses is the village bus which periodically comes to the area to bring ration to the people. She wanders around the bus every week when it comes to the village [34]. A fiction, *Cape pul,* by the same author narrates the story of a simple man who goes into town to fetch toffee for his two children. Since everybody traveling at night is searched by the security forces, he was also searched, but without any fault of his, he is abused and detained for many days. His children waited for his return in vain. The story depicts the nature and style of military operations and the helplessness of the people who are subjected to humiliation [35].

In another fiction written by Niamatullah Gichki, which appeared in monthly Ulus, entitled *Be Waakien Zinde Hudunaaki,* the character in a dream sees a hungry youth with shabby clothing who looks to his new masters for food. He sees an old laborer oppressed and pauperized. He sees a proud mother also poverty-ridden. The story is an intellectual inference to Baloch helplessness and an attack on the socio-political dispensation. It also reflects a deep hatred for the rulers [36].

Amazingly, the government publications have often discreetly been used by nationalist writers to further the cause of Baloch nationalism. The reason being that the officers who manage such publications are either non-Baloch or have no knowledge of the Baloch language, giving a chance to the Balochi writers to publish their work unnoticed. The Tribal Publicity Organization of the Government of Pakistan, which was entrusted with the task of propagating the official point of view, in an attempt to present an alternative to the Baloch nationalist political choices, published a booklet entitled *Perband* in 1970. The Baloch poets were invited to contribute patriotic poems reflecting Pakistan's national objectives. Although, the poems were duly vetted before publication, yet the compilation still contains poems and songs of patriotism exhorting the Baloch to be conscious of their rights and mindful of their misfortune. Balochistan has been symbolized as their only hope and aspiration. It was published during the Indo-Pakistan conflict of the 1970s and officially aimed to whip up war hysterias. The idea was frustrated by default with the inclusion of poems pertaining to the Baloch and Balochistan.

Ghous Bakhsh Saabir, attached to the Pakistan Broadcasting Corporation, contributed two poems, *Ajueay Sogind* and *Zamin Hamrang Biet.* In the former, he vows to preserve Balochistan from the clutches of the enemy through sacrifices in blood. In the second, the poet refers to the Baloch traditional military and political insight by mentioning the feats of Baloch heroes and warning the enemy that war with the Baloch will prove disastrous for them [37]. Atha Shaad's *Yalien Sarmachaar* and *Deh Makkahien* speak of a people and its invincible fighters who give their lives to uphold national pride. *Yalien Sarmaachar* referred to degrading dependence and asked the Baloch to change the course of events through force and determination [38]. *In Deh Makkahien*, the poet eulogizes the Baloch motherland and vows to fight for its honor [39].

Ulus, a monthly magazine, has been a prominent literary publication primarily intended publicizing government versions of events, however, quite a few articles appeared in the paper either because the management did not know what had been written in those articles or poems or they committed a deliberate oversight to further the cause of Baloch nationalism. A striking example is a poem contributed by one Muraad Awaraani for the 1976 anniversary celebration of Muhammad Ali Jinnah. In the poem titled Quaid–e-Azam, the poet wishes the name (of this great leader of Pakistan) to achieve notoriety and ill-repute throughout the world. The composition appears to be in line with the usual eulogy, but the phraseology used in the repetitive stanza, *Per Kapaath Thai Naam o Quaid Per Kapaath: Man Jahaana Thai Naam Naamo Dap Bebaath,* has extremely bad connotations, giving an impression of deep hatred for Jinnah [40]. Another poem in Ulus also appears to be against official policy. In a clear reference to Balochistan, *Sogind* by Muhammad Beg Begul avows to sacrifice lives for the motherland [41].

Publications arranged by students contain articles and poem which clearly give the impression of the inner-thinking and socio-political choices for the youth. The interpretation of events in newsletter form issued by the students, such as *Baam, Pajjar,* and *Sangath,* have been regarded as anti-government, or to be precise, advocating a separate socio-economic and political identity for the Baloch. These papers are usually banned by the provincial or federal government under press and publication laws.

The student's literary circle, *Balochi Labzaanki Diwaan,* the Balochi Literary Forum, published a booklet comprising poems and articles, some of which are on patriotic lines. A poem, *Granien Gamaan Aasaan Kanth,* by Barkatullah, counsels the Baloch to be ready to shoulder greater responsibility. The poet believes that deprivation and servitude are due to lack of determination and inactivity. The poem declares that if the Baloch really wants a change and a bright future, he must realize that without war and sacrifice, a guarantee of a better future is absolutely out of the question [42]. The same booklet contains two poems by Mubarak Kazi entitled *Chushen Sar Man Kanaan Kurbaan Hazaraan* and *Junz o Ashopaani Hazzaam Bebaath*. In the first poem, he pays tributes to Balochistan. The poet imagines that the motherland is to be watered in the blood to make it green and get it out from the drought of centuries [43]. In the second poem, he wishes a drastic change through war and revolution. The Baloch can get their freedom only through war. He visualizes the clashes of sword and singing of war music which should bring the defeat of the oppressors and freedom and emancipation for the masses [44]. Two issues of *Labzaank* were published in 1976. Peer Bakhsh Zahid in his poem counsels that the Baloch should fight his way through dependence and servility. The poem also outlines the social contradictions in society [45].

Ghani Parwaz, in the poem *Kassi Nahen Maathien Wathan*, says those who perpetrated the atrocities and those who are instrumental in selling out the people can no longer be trusted [46]. Barkatullah, asks the Baloch to ponder over his position and maintains that the days of slavery should end. He says the other nations have achieved unimaginable progress but the Baloch are still impoverished and in chains. The poet believes that the degrading condition of the Baloch is due to the socio-political set-up which must be changed [47]. Peer Bakhsh Zahid's poem welcomes the eventual revolution [48] A poem in Urdu, *Baloch Sarmachaarun ka Tharana* by Saleem Kurd, was published in *Sangath*. The poem narrates conditions where the Baloch are facing oppression and the heavy arms of the enemy. Balochistan is under fire. The armed struggle which is the only way towards an honorable future is carried by youth with renewed determination and courage [49]. *Roch Bieth*, an article contributed by Abdur Rahman deals with the socio-economic conditions prevalent among the Baloch. Dissatisfied, he favors a new approach worked out through renewed struggle. The author maintains that the Baloch are facing very pathetic conditions and there seems to be no way out of it. Therefore, any movement should guarantee a promising dispensation. Mentioning the hardship suffered and setbacks received, a reference to recent political upheavals and the suspension of armed resistance, he proposes that no one should be frustrated. A lesson is to be learned from other peoples' struggles [50]. The Literary Circle, another student forum, published a booklet which contains a poem by Mubark Kazi entitled *Akebath*. The poet is determined to go through every hardship. He will not be grieved even if hanged. He will be content if his blood may help bring a change for the poor and downtrodden [51].

Three poems that appeared in the first issue of the monthly *Makkuraan*, published from Thehraan soon after the fall of the Shah of Iran, merit consideration. It should be noted that during the Shah's reign no Balochi publication was allowed. The change of government encouraged the Baloch literary elite to bring out the paper. But the Khomeini Government immediately revived the previous policy towards the Baloch and *Makkuraan* ceased to appear after two editions. *Uf Passao Nadanth Kass*, by Siddique Azaath, describes the grinding poverty and hopelessness of beloved personified as Balochistan. As the lover of her motherland, he promises to better her life and fight for her cause [52].

The first important publication in Balochi, *Ouman*, a literary monthly from Karachi, started in February 1951 under the joint editorship of Moulvi Muhammad Husain and Hakim Ahmad. It ceased publication in November 1959 mainly due to financial problems. The paper was brought out by the Baloch Educational Society (BES). BES, formed in Karachi in 1948 to promote Balochi language and culture and also voice Baloch political and social grievances. Apart from publishing *Ouman*, The BES started a school in Liari which was later upgraded to a high standard. The school, the Baloch Secondary School, was nationalized during the time of Prime Minister Bhutto in 1973. *Ouman* carried many articles and poems depicting the Baloch national aspirations. In one of its early issues (June 1951), the paper carried a poem by Qazi Abdur Rahim Saabir, who calls upon the people to behave like true Baloch, the great decedents of Mir Chaakar and Mir Gwahraam, and be conscious of their national rights. In the article, *Aey Koum*, O nation, Abdul Ghafoor Baloch lists the glorious deeds of the Baloch throughout history and asks the youth to launch a struggle to help them out of confusing inactivity. The article maintains that without sacrifices the Baloch cannot attain its objectives [53]. Asko Jamaldini's poem regrets that the motherland has been sold out to the aliens, a reference to the Khanate of Kalat's accession to Pakistan in 1948. The poet laments that the entire people have been reduced to slavery [54]. Muhammad Husain Unqa, a political activist and poet, in *Azaathi* says that freedom is the highest ideal of mankind. In a clear reference to Baloch's desire for independence, Unqa exhorts the people to fight for their liberty [55]. In another poem, Unqa refers figuratively to the Baloch, who are in slavery and their country under alien domination. The poem which is one of Unqa's masterpieces reflects a deep sense of frustration [56]. Shoukath Nadeem, in a poem that praises the Baloch as a brave and gracious nation, regrets the agonizing poverty and helplessness of the people. The poem calls upon the Baloch to act true to his traditions, defeat the enemy and acquire a place of respect for them [57]. A fiction, *Waabe*, meaning a dream, by Jumma Khan, reflects the Baloch miserableness. The character in the dream sees a lady and her husband who died of hunger, their infant son, Chaakar, left unprotected. Chaakar is also the legendary figure in Baloch history. The story figuratively compares the Baloch with the future of the infant Chaakar who is left without any hope for the future [58].

Another monthly magazine, *Balochi*, was published from Karachi under the editorship of Azaad Jamaldini in 1956. It stopped publication in 1958. It reappeared from Quetta after more than two decades and dies its natural death after its editor Azaad passed away in 1981. Balochi greatly contributed to the national cause. Quite a few poems and articles appeared in the magazine from 1956-1958 on the Baloch national movement. Hasrat Baloch in a poem says that Balochistan has produced so many brave sons that they will not let the motherland be kept in alien hands. He was hopeful that the time will come when the Baloch will stand in revolt [59]. Malik Saeed regrets that the Baloch are unarmed and helpless and that the enemy has ravaged their country. The poem says it appears that the Almighty has turned indifferent towards the Baloch, otherwise such a great people could not be dominated by others [60]. Adam Hakkani taunts the Baloch for inactivity. He says the Baloch has been deprived of his land, his sovereignty, and his honor. He exhorts him to fight until the country is restored to him [61]. Ambar Panjguri, in the *Ahthagen waar*, says it is time to start the great struggle for the achievement of national rights. Passive indifference, he says will be disastrous [62]. Azaad Jamaldini expresses determination to achieve the independence of Balochistan. He says a great change will be brought about in which everyone in the nation will fight for the freedom of his country [63].

In *Balochistan Gwaank*, Jazmi hails the Baloch for his resolve to fight for his emancipation. He expresses the hope that Balochistan will be recreated through the warm blood of his people [64]. *Nawa-e-Wathan*, an Urdu fortnightly published from Quetta, also contributed many poems and national songs. A poem by Kasar Kandi, *Wathane Gwaank*, appeared in the paper on April 1, 1958, saying that a nation cannot achieve freedom without a struggle. The poem says the motherland is asking for sacrifices. In a poem *Shaheedani Kulao Pa Padrecha*, Azaad asks the youth to follow the footsteps of their heroes and contribute to a struggle for which innumerable lives have been laid down and untold cruelties suffered by their ancestors. The poem reminds the Baloch that only through sacrifices can the spirits of the martyrs rest in peace [65]. Malik Touki's *Mushkilien Rochaan pad Makenzaathe Bach Mani* is a piece of advice by an aging father to his young son. Narrating his misfortune and vulnerability in the face of grave circumstances, he advises his son to carry his dying declaration to every youth: persuade them to preserve their identity and shoulder greater responsibilities towards Balochistan. In a derogatory reference to all those who collaborate with the establishment in Iran and Pakistan against the interest of the Baloch people, the father confesses that he passed his life as a mercenary and served against the dictates of his inner-self. He admonishes his son not to sell his conscience or to be hoodwinked or ever intimidated. He should be an enemy of the oppressor and a friend of the oppressed, he advises [66].

Various publications by student organizations indicated the political trend among the youth. In an article published in Baam, *Jee Pa Wathan*, M. Kareem expresses deep love for Balochistan and determination to sacrifice to vindicate its honor and destroy the enemy [67]. In the same issue, a few boxed lines from Gaagiyaan Baloch say the enemy wants to subjugate us through superior strength and modern equipment which we lack. But he warns that times have changed. The Baloch will make the enemy accountable for its brutalities [68]. *Baam* carries two poems from Anwar Saahib khan and M.H. Khalil Apsari. Anwar's poem *Man Baloch*, says that the Baloch have given blood for their freedom, which is now not far away. He warns that the Baloch cannot be intimidated. He will surely attain his goal [69]. In *warnae Naama*, Khalil asks the Baloch to follow their traditions of bravery and courage and to give a new meaning to their struggle [70]. Ibrahim Abid, in *Dier Naenth Rozhnaaen Roch*, advises the people to work for a brighter future. Inactivity, he says leads them nowhere and will surely bring further miseries [71].

The BSO national convention, the council session, held in Quetta in 1983, was followed by a poetry evening, or Mushaira. The young poets, who participated were mostly students save G.R. Mulla, who read two poems depicting the national aspirations of the Baloch people and their continued struggle for freedom and emancipation. Two poems read by Mubarak Kazi, a university student ridiculed Pakistan, its ideology and regime in a language full of humorous scorn. One poem is titled Pakistan + Islam=Tobacco-jar (Hookah). The other entitled, Islam+ Pakistan = Mullah. All the poem read before the gathering of several hundred youths reflected the national mood by eulogizing the Baloch heroes and expressing the determination to offer sacrifices for the glory of the Baloch fatherland.

An article in Balochi titled *Granwaab Sarouk Benag Dah*, by Mulla Rodi, the pen-name of Azaad Jamaldini, expresses remorse that Balochistan is full of riches and vast resources but its sons and daughters are hungry and poverty-ridden and are denied all facilities. The fatherland is in the hands of usurpers. He blames the leadership and alleges that they have sold out the country in return for privileges for themselves. The author reminds the Baloch to follow the path of those people who have snatched their rights through the sword [72]. Monthly *Balochi* published a poetic dialogue between Balochistan and a dove, *Kapoth*. This bird is a symbolic messenger between lovers and has a unique place in Balochi literature. It is titled *Teeki*, Gift, poetic imagery of what Balochistan desires, it addresses the bird to carry to its barren lands, gifts of tears of pain and frustration; to flood the land so that it produces in abundance. In return, Balochistan promises that when its vast barren land is irrigated through its painful tears, it will guarantee a safe carefree life for the bird where there will be no fear for it to be hunted. This dialogue reflects a situation where the land is asking its sons to take pity on her slavery and shed blood for her [73].

The Baloch Sardar (tribal chief), identified as an agent of the enemy, has been much criticized in the literature of national resistance. The literary elite has little regard for them due to their alleged collaboration with the government. In his poem Baloch Sardar, *Ajo Blaoch* condemns their role. He terms them cruel agents who sell out the people for their own petty ends [74]. Akhirdad Husain Borr in *Maathien Wathan Balochistan* maintains that the day is not far off when our beloved land will get its independence [75]. Shahdaad Chahsari expresses a firm determination in *Raji Sarmacharaan* to uphold Baloch tradition and declares that the Baloch will fight to the last for their rights. The poem says the Baloch are awakened and can never be kept in chains [76]. In *Suhr Dapien Baam*, Mubarak Kazi says the Baloch are a brave and courageous people, a freedom-loving nation, but now they are jeered at for their inactivity and lethargy. Their daughters and sisters are mourning their degrading conditions. The poem, however, expresses hope that the situation will give way to revolutionary dawn and a brighter future [77]. W. B Iraki, in a poem captioned Balochistan, vows to fight for the liberation of the country. The poem says war and conflict is the only solution to the issue [78]. Ghani Parwaz, in *Santien Shap*, hopes for a bright morning after a long dark night of servitude [79]. Amirul Mulk Mengal, in *Hech Nazanake Chia*, expresses disappointment over prevailing conditions. He wonders why the Baloch are always in trouble; why there appears to be no way out. He ponders on whether or not such conditions prevail as a matter of ill fate [80]. In *Guptar*, Bahraam Mengal addresses Balochistan symbolized as the mother and says that her sons have forgotten her. No one appears to be aware of her condition. Balochistan mournfully replies that her sons were those glorious Baloch of the past epochs who fought to uphold her honor, she advises the Baloch to struggle for a better future [81]. *Gwaank* by Ulfath Naseem says that although the Baloch is oppressed, nevertheless, he will follow his proud traditions. He exhorts him to carry the banner of freedom and fight the enemy with renewed determination because freedom only is purchased in blood and a huge toll in lives [82]. Wahid Bakhsh Rahi's poem, *Baloch* advises people to uphold their traditional pride by fighting for national freedom. The poem asks the people to break the chain of slavery. It says everywhere people are enjoying their sovereignty and freedom while Balochistan is under alien rule [83]. Muhammad Ashraf Mulazai, in *Perband*, asks the Baloch to be united as only through unity can they get their rights [84]. Ajiz Panjguri in *Ham Karawaan* urges the youth to destroy the remnants of barbarity and oppression. The poem reminds them that as the sons of glorious people they have a great responsibility to lead the way to victory [85]. Inayatullah Qoumi's poem *Maathien Wathan* praises everything attached with motherland: it's vast landmass, its mountains, its rivers; and vows to offer sacrifices for its glory and well being [86]. Ibrahim Abid, in *Zura Gulien Baaskaan Bedie*, asks why grinding poverty and ill-fate has betaken the Baloch. Come out, he exhorts, ready to lay down your life for your rights. This is the only way to get a place of honor among the nations [87]. Anwar Saahib khan, in *Zubana Aahenien Saankal Nadaraan*, says the people will fight for their national cause and oppressive exploitation will no longer be tolerated [88]. Another poem by the same poet, *Shubenag*, expresses the determination to offer sacrifices and get freedom through the force of the sword. The poem says difficulties cannot retard progress toward the goal of national independence [89]. Shahdaad Chahsari in his poem says wishful thinking cannot bear results unless backed by intense efforts. The glorious past cannot repeat itself unless the people act and behave like those in the past. He advises a more active role in achieving national objectives [90]. Ghani Parwaz in the poem *Jah Janeth* expresses the hope that the struggle will achieve its goal. The poem points out the difficulties to be overcome and that after the goal is achieved, there will be happiness all over the motherland [91]. Din Muhammad Borr's *Zrumbeshthe Thawaar*, asks for the unity of the people. The poem says we are treading in the dark without anybody to lead. The miseries and hunger can be countered through the determined efforts and unity of the masses [92]. Peeral Baloch in *Than Kadien Maeg o Thai Jang Nabienth* pointed out that oppression cannot be endured too long and a peoples' aspiration cannot be kept in check and therefore, war is to be waged. A collision is inevitable, unavoidable [93]. Jan Muhammad Jan Apsari, in Diljami, thought the Baloch will not be deterred any more. Every cruelty and act of oppression will be avenged and the enemy will be paid in the same coin. He cannot withstand our wrath [94]. Muhammad Beg Begul in *Kohan Manieganth*, claims that although the Baloch is now miserably poor and helpless that situation will change because he inherits a great land and he hails from a great and ancient nation [95]. Anwar's *Maathien Wathan* praises the motherland and expresses determination to offer sacrifices to vindicate its honor [96]. Mansoor Baloch, in *Shap Thahaarenth Maah Mahgera Gepthag*, pessimistically paints a picture of miseries and asks for sacrifices in the blood [97]. In another poem, *Yaagi*, he vows to fight for the country. The poet identifies himself as a true Baloch who rejects every comfort and works to achieve the desired objectives [98]. Nabi Bakhsh Buzdar in his poem lamented that we have lost our country, our honor, and our sweet language. He says the Baloch himself is responsible for such subjugation to the aliens [99]. Noor

Ahmad Ouman, in a poem titled Balochistan, eulogizes the Baloch land and expresses confidence that it will get its freedom [100]. In *Wathan*, he expresses the determination to fight for the Baloch, land [101]. Nazeer Sufi, in his poem *Balochistan*, expresses determination to fight for his homeland [102]. Kamaal Baloch, in *Jah Janeth*, urges the people to resist the enemy. The poem says it does not behave the descendants of a great people to be passive while their country is being pillaged [103]. Iqbaal Raaz Shiraani, in his poem *Wath Nazanaan Man Kujahaan*, refers to the political confusion and says that the sense of direction has been lost [104]. Din Muhammad Siddiq in *Hambalaan*, urges the Baloch to rise in revolt against subservience and maintains that a bright future can be guaranteed only through unity and sacrifices [105]. Fida Ahmad Baloch, in his poem *Salam SarbatNamiranan*, pays his tributes to those who are behind bars; the people are oppressed and there is no hope of any change in their painful conditions [106]. Khalid Suhail, in *Belan Mani*, asks the people to take up arms for a change from the black night to bright dawn [107]. Mubarak Kazi, in *Sekien*, believed that the subjugation of a people cannot end without a fight and a firm response to the enemy. The poem counsels youth to take up arms to achieve their objective [108]. Akhirdad Husain Borr, in *Sarmachaar*, exhorts the Baloch to fight for a separate status of their own. The poem says the time has come for the unavoidable battle against the enemy [109]. Abdul Latif Adil, in his poem *Balochistan*, wishes the enemies of his country to be destroyed and the motherland to take its proper place among the free nations. He desires its flag to be unfurled red in the blood [110]. Abdul Sathar Shahzaad in *Parcha Baloch* advocates unity among the people and a fight against the enemy [111]. Wahid Bakhsh Rahi is disappointed because of disunity among the people. He says graceful nations do not rest peacefully unless they get their freedom [112]. Habibullah Amir, in his patriotic song, lauds the motherland and its people. It identifies the country with honor, pride and the glorious past of its people [113]. Gul Jan Gul, in *Jah Janeth Belaan*, regrets that Balochistan is overwhelmed by savages and robbers. He calls upon the people to stand united against tyranny and bring the gift of freedom to the poverty-ridden Baloch [114]. Ghulam Haidar Arman in *May Balochistan* awaits the auspicious day when he can contribute towards the prosperity of his motherland [115]. Mubarak Kazi in *Mani Honaani Thrinzukk*, figuratively addresses Pakistani rulers, asking them to stop the oppression because the bloodshed will stain their hands and make them notorious for their misdeed [116]. Ghani Parwaz's *Roch*, says the day of revolution earnestly waits because it is the only hope in a dark hopeless night. The day will bring happiness to everyone [117].

There has been a strong feeling among the intellectuals that the Baloch cause has been betrayed by those who called off the armed struggle after the collapse of the revolt in the 1970s. The youth, especially the student's organization, BSO, opposed any settlement with Pakistan without acceptance of their minimum demands for autonomy, and self-rule. Mansoor Baloch, in *Justhe Cha Sarouk o Mastheraan*, recounts the killing and miseries during the struggle. The poem clearly implied the failure of the leadership and betrayal of the trust placed in them by the people. The armed uprising was started on the urging of the leaders and was called off by them without any substantial gain. The poem is critical of the policies pursued by the Baloch leaders [118]. Monthly Balochi in an editorial in 1981, was critical of the leadership for inactivity and lack of initiative [119]. Akbar Barakzai, in *Mied o Thupaan*, figuratively mentions the loss of direction of his boat in the stormy waves of high seas. The inference is that the Baloch people are being led astray. The poem wishes for a safe coming ashore which may bring happiness and compensated the pains taken during the trouble [120].

Although disappointed with the collapse of the resistance movement in the 1970s, the Baloch literary elite was hoping for a bright future. Mansoor Baloch, in an article titled *Likoh*, portrays a fisherman named Haibitan who is mistakenly thought to be mad. He weeps for a cause, he weeps because he thinks of Balochistan, its helplessness and servitude, and he imagines everything is weeping including the deep impassable sea which includes his tears of blood. But he has not given up hope, because although he has lost his way, he sees in the dark the way that is lit by martyrs like Safar, Lawang, Rashid, and Asad. He imagines that darkness is eventually replaced by a gleaming light [121]. Abdul Majeed Gwadari, in *Ruzhne Mes*thaag, expresses the hope that the days of frightful tyranny will end and there will emerge happiness and freedom out of a long dark night of slavery. The poem says Baloch youth will surely redeem their pledge to the motherland and get it emancipated from the enemy [122]. In another poem *To Nameraney*, the poet eulogized the youth and the martyrs saying that they are the only hope of a glorious future [123].

Akbar Baloch in *Gulzaminey Pussage Kulao*, a message from the son of the soil, exhorts the youth to continue their struggle against torturous servitude so that it gives way to freedom and fortune [124]. In another poem, he says though the Baloch is weak and helpless, a day will dawn when he will have the strength to face the enemy [125]. Abdul Majeed Sohrabi, in *Baareeg*, addresses the Baloch, saying that the red sun of hope is rising in the east, which will bring comforts all over the motherland. He visualizes the auspicious occasion when freedom is achieved and everyone is jubilant [126]. Saleem Shohaz, in *Hambal o Bel o Yalaan*, paints an agonizing picture of the motherland and asks for a struggle to liberate the land from usurpers [127]. M.H Khalil Apsari in *Man o Thou* compares the Baloch with the enemy, who is powerful, cunning and cruel but unaware of the changing mood of the Baloch. The poem says, he is enduring the malaise because he is born in misery and hardship. He is perfected in grief. He is mature and brave. He warns the enemy that now he cannot sit at ease [128]. Mubarak Kazi in *Wathan*, says he is writing history in the blood to remain as a witness to the truth that the motherland is an indestructible, invigorating, inspiring and ever-lasting reality through which the individual can achieve perfection [129]. Rashid Baloch sees his motherland in bondages, his heart weeps like an orphan and then becomes proud like flooding Nehing river. He regrets that our land has been ravaged and our settlements destroyed because we lack a leader and fighter like Mir Kambar to frighten away the enemy [130]. Bashir Bedaar in *Pandal* regrets that the people are being oppressed. He opines that killing cannot destroy human instincts. Every drop of bloodshed will nourish the tree of freedom and emancipation to grow [131]. Siddiq Azaath, in a poem written in Beirut while in exile titled, *Thou Har Kasi Maathien Wathan*, addresses the motherland as holy and revered, saying: I am staying away from you not for the sake of any personal pleasure but to seek help in order to free you from subjugation. I am in exile because I want to redeem the pledge which I made to you, a promise I want to fulfill. In spite of immense comforts, I am not happy in the alien land. Things, objects and images from you are haunting me in wonderful dreams. I cannot detach myself from your sweet memories, the poet writes [132]. Ashraf Sarbazi, in the poem *O Brixton e Burzien Chinaal*, addresses the *Chinaal* an evergreen tree, a nicely composed poem in dialogues, seeks advice from the tree. He says since you have a long last life of centuries experiencing many upheavals: evergreen and tall, you may be in touch with a high God. The poet asks the tree to inquire from God in confidence why the Baloch are shackled, living a tormented life plagued by outrageous poverty. Why are they being tyrannized? Can they not become sovereign and free? Are these miseries and this ill-fate ordained by God? The tree rejects the notion with dejection and fury that such fate is not ordinate by any God. It remarks tauntingly that unless the Baloch decides to live in liberty and offer sacrifice to achieve that freedom, the conditions will remain unchanged for them [133].

The Baloch writers, while mourning prevailing conditions were mindful that their glorious heroes have not been mentioned in the history books composed by state authorities. They lament that the Baloch themselves have forgotten their heroes. Mir Chaakar, a Baloch hero of the fifteenth century, who migrated to the Punjab where he is buried in Sathgaar, is the subject of a poem by Khan Saabir. The poem paints a shabby picture of his grave. Recalling the events of his time, it says he is not being remembered and his grave is not lit because his sons and daughters are indifferent to the past. Disunity among the Baloch led the great hero to come to an alien land. The poet wishes him to come to life again and defeat the enemies of the Baloch once again [134].

4- The Episode of Hameed Baloch

The execution of Hameed Baloch, an activist of Baloch Students Organization, on 11th June 1981 by the military regime, after a controversial trial in a military tribunal, left a visible mark on Balochi literature. The Baloch intellectuals were quick to react, calling it another vindictive execution of a patriot by the Pakistani rulers. Anwar Shaadman Sajidi, in a poem titled *Dashte Pul (The flower from Dasht)l*, allegorically paints a pleasant picture and a graceful count of Hameed's execution. The poem is beautifully composed with lovely imageries. It says the painful execution has taken place for a cause that never dies [135]. Mansoor Baloch's poem *Yaazda June Naama*, says the dawn of 11th June looks miserable. It has come out with tears, but taunting and jeering. The day demands an end to atrocities once and for all [136]. Mubarak Kazi's *Choun*, says the blood which was shed will not go in vain. It will provide a red light to guide many other [137]. *Biya*

Ke Rawien, a poem by Fazal Khaliq, in an oblique reference to the event, urges the youth to follow the path shown by Hameed in order to vindicate the Baloch honor and avoid taunting for generations. The poem exhorts the people to follow the glorious path which brings the hope of a great win [138]. Before his execution, Hameed had sent a new year greeting to Azaad Jamaldini, the editor of Balochi. In an emotional reply published in his paper, Azad regrets that the Baloch is helpless and this helplessness has lost him one of his glorious sons. He says the Baloch has lost a sense of direction [139]. Muhammad Beg Begul, in *Chaakar e Obadage*, says the national desire for freedom cannot be gagged through oppression and killings. The poem says the Baloch will surely take revenge of Hameed's murder [140] Atha Shaad, a renowned poet, dedicates a poem to the memory of Hameed, saying a cause will never die along with the bodily death. If I am a tree set me on fire: but a mountain cannot be destroyed by mere lightning [141]. Malik Saeed, a poet, and historian, composed a few lines in Persian to be put on record in the deceased village; says those responsible for Hameed's killing have done a tyrannical act comparable to what Yazid did to Husain, the grandson of the prophet Muhammad [142]. In a similar piece, *Kushendahe Naama*, Bashir Bedaar expresses the hope that the enemy will become exhausted and the people will fight through to freedom. The poet thinks that the Baloch will take revenge and the enemy will be brought to account for the cruelties he has perpetuated [143].

Hameed had written his last will and Testament before his execution. Addressed to the Baloch and especially the youth, it is a remarkable document depicting wisdom and foresightedness. It reveals a peculiar intellectual frame of mind which is not uncommon among the youth. The testament of the youth of twenty-one year who had only eight hours to live emotionally charged with frequent quotations from the Baloch tradition and folk poetry, emphasizing the need for supreme sacrifices; is a document which shows a firm and lasting commitment to a national cause, and declaration of an endless struggle against the enemy. It was carried in many student publications. Its English translation under the heading *Testament of Freedom* was published in Azaad Balochistan June 1983 Issue which was dedicated to the memory of Hameed. Some excerpts are produced below:

"He who avenges himself

Says farewell to his beautiful wife
Has no longing for power or wealth"

"It does not worry me a bit if this well and testament of mine reach or not the great people of the glorious Balochistan. As I write these words, there are armed guards all over the place, keeping a watchful eye on every move that I make. I have only eight more hours to live. Eight hours from now I shall be proudly walking to the gallows. I have no feeling of remorse, nor I bothered by the thought that I should have lived longer rather than be dead soon, because to lead a life without any purpose or to live under the yoke of slavery, is a curse.

I am not the first nor the only one to give his blood for Balochistan, hundreds of Baloch have laid down their lives for the fatherland. In my family alone, I shall be the second person to kiss the hangman's noose. And thus, sacrifice my life for the great goal, which, I am certain, the younger generations of the Baloch shall ultimately achieve. One of my ancestors, Sheraan Daad Kareem, was executed by the British in 1901.

I would like to tell my friends that such a priceless boon like freedom cannot be won without the supreme sacrifice. I know of no precedent in history where nations have achieved freedom without rendering the supreme sacrifice. The path to freedom and independence is admittedly a difficult one. However, the goal awaiting us is truly magnificent. I feel happy and consoled to think that though independence may elude us for a long time to come-- my little daughter Bibi Banadi who is now 3 years old may experience it in her lifetime--my grandchildren and those of my brother Beebegr's will surely be blessed with it and that day will be the day when my soul will finally rest in peace and receive true comfort.

Can you, by severing the heads
From the bodies,
Kill the living thoughts
And Ideas?
Can you, by wrenching the flowers from the branches,
Stop their fragrance
From spreading?

I am certain that every member of my family will take my execution with calmness and fortitude. I wish my mother were alive

113

today, for, she must have sung this lullaby in my ears when I was a child:

> If you die a hero's death,
> I shall visit your grave,
> In the best of attire
> And makeup.
> Instead of morning
> And lamenting
> I shall sing you a song
> Of joy;
> And shall proudly
> Give birth
> To another child
> Exactly like you.

I am sure dearest sisters will not weep and go into mourning over my death. I ask my grandmother to recall the lullaby she used to sing for all of us:

> When my flower-like son
> Becomes a youth
> He will arm himself with
> The best of weapons.
> He shall make the traitors
> Bite the dust,
> He shall fight and crush
> His enemies.

The lofty mountains and the vast plains of Balochistan are waiting for those who could embrace them and turn them into castles and battlegrounds.

> Mountains are the fortresses
> Of the Baloch
> Impregnable heights are
> Their treasure-houses
> Flowing springs quench
> Their thirst
> Their children are selected arrows
> Sharp-edged daggers are their son-in-laws

Baloch fathers are
Broad-bladed swords."

Throughout the 1970s and 1980s, strong feelings of Baloch nationalism were evident everywhere. In formal or informal social get-togethers, discussions always turn to the political failures of Baloch people. In all youth conferences since the early sixties, patriotic songs are sung and martial music is played before the start of such a meeting. Exhortations in such gatherings are always on the Baloch identity and separate nationhood. In the council sessions of the Baloch Students Organization, which is traditionally followed by a musical concert, ninety-nine percent of the songs are patriotic songs in praise of the Baloch land and its people and vow to fight for its independence. The students have evolved a national hymn, *Ma Chukkien Balochaani*, which is played in martial music. It was a composition by Abdul Majeed Gwadari in the early sixties. An English rendering of its few lines is given below:

We are sons of the Baloch,
Free and sovereign,
Masters of our own destiny;
The earth panics from our wrath,
Castles shake in fear,
We are tigers,
Fearless defenders (of those who seek our help):
We are an encouragement to our fathers,
The pride and honor of our mothers and sisters,
Support to our brothers;
Our blood one day,
will be required by our nation,
We will prove true to the lullabies given by our mothers;
We have sucked the milk of honor,
In the shadow of swords,
Red blood in our eyes shows descent from martyrs;
We are defenders of the helpless and the poor,
We have destroyed the castle of terror,
The days of oppression have gone forever.

References

1. Hama wahda mani (o) thai suhl o thran bieth, (ke) shagaal murgo kapothani shipaank bieth,
   Shikaraani pulang goun ushtheran bieth,
   Agan pukki gouna aasa ham kanaan bieth,
   Agan maahi redian dannaan shathan bieth,
2. Hama wahda mani (o) thai suhl o thran bieth,
   Ke gazzaan kuntag o maraan paad,
   Boji man hama ranjaan roath,
   Lao banth hama jangi Sheir,
   Sardar diyanth langaaran,
   Gurkana shipaank chaarenanth.
3. Sing agan chaathani buna rezanth,
   Kenag cha mardaani dela kinzanth,
   Na sing rezanth na kinag kinzanth,
   Bier Balochaani than do sad saala,
   Lassaen aahuge do danthanien.
4. Man goun badaan hanchu kanaan,
   Med kanath goun maheyaan,
   Banz goun kapothi walaraan,
   Garmen lewaar goun chuluraan,
   Hukkien ladi goun arzunaan,
   Buz goun kaheeri dangaraan,
   Gurk goun mazan chedien jadaan.
5. Jange saahathan grannenaan,
   Zahma goun watha sasakan,
   Helanth pa thai sharouan,
   Gwahaar pa drawaan durenaan,
   Kaad pa summalaan koulean,
   Koum pa thai Balochi naama,
   Math pa datagien loliaan.
   Leel o leel kaneth bachchara,
   Bachch o sad muraadien laala,
6. Gul Khan Naseer: Dua (composed on 10th November 1936) Balochi Dunya, Multan, December 1984, p 2.
7. Jan Muhammad Baloch: Shaheed Mir Dadshah, Balochi, Quetta, March-April 1979, pp 56-58.
8. Akbar Barakzai: Man Shomay Azmana Nalotaan. Ulus, Quetta, saltak 1963, p. 51.
9. Sayad Zahoor Shah: Sisthagien Dasthunk, Karachi,1962, p 28.
10. Ibid. p 62
11. Ibid. p 63
12. Ibid. p 64
13. Ibid. p 66

14. Ibid. p 67
15. Sayad Zahoor Shah: Thrampkunen thramp. Karachi 1962, pp 33-35.
16. Ibid. p 55-56
17. Ibid. p 63
18. Sayad Zahoor Shah: Angar o Throngal, Karachi, 1962, pp22-20
19. G.R. Mulla: Bazhn, Paazul Academy, Karachi,1981, p,37
20. Ibid. pp 39-40
21. Ibid. pp 52-54
22. Ibid. pp 87-90
23. Ibid. pp 106-109
24. Ibid. pp 116-120
25. Atha Shaad: Sahkandan, subsequently published in many papers including Ulus and in a student leaflet, Suhb (June 1969).
26. Malik Touki: Reta, Geshien, Balochi Academy, Quetta, 1972, pp 83-86
27. Bashsir Bedaar: Zuraaki, Zamana, Quetta, December 1972.
28. Bashir Bedaar: Gwarbaam, Pak news agency, Turbat, 1982, pp 67-68.
29. Ibid. p 50
30. Ibid. pp 51-52.
31. Ibid. pp 71-72.
32. Muneer Shahwani: Wathan, Ulus, Quetta April May 1973, p 23.
33. M.H. Khalil Apsari: Balochistan, zamana, Quetta,1883.
34. Surat Mari: Bohe Bohe Adami, Balochi, Quetta, July-August 1980. pp21-23.
35. Ibid. January,1981, pp72-74
36. Niamatullah Gichki: Bewaankien Zinde Hodunaaki. Ulus, Quetta, June 1968, pp 17-18.
37. Ghous Bakhsh Saabir: Ajueay Sogind and Hona Zamin Hamran Bieth. Perband, Tribal Publicity, Quetta, 1970, pp 94-95.
38. Atha Shaad: Yellien Sarmachaar. Ibid, pp 87-89.
39. Atha Shaad: Deh Makahien, Ibid. p 55-56.
40. Muraad Awaraani: Quid-e-Azam, Ulus, Quetta, April1976, p 28.
41. Muhammad Beg Begul: Sogind, Ibid, July 1979, Reprinted in Balochi, Quetta, September-October 1980, p 38.
42. Barkatullah: Granien Gamaan Asaan Kanth, Nokien Tham, Balochi labzaanki Diwaan, Karachi, pp 140,141.
43. Mubarak Kazi: Chushien Sar man Kanaan Kurban Hazaraan, Ibid.p. 170.
44. Mubarak Kazi: Junz o Azshopani Hazzaame Bebath, Ibid. p 17.
45. Peer Bakhsh Zahid: Gal. Labzaank, June 1976. P 53.
46. Ghani Parwaz: Kassi Nahen Maathen Wathan, Labzaank, Vol 11 December 1979, p 50.
47. Barkatullah: Gaal, Ibid. p 49.
48. Peer Bakhsh Zahid: Gaal, Ibid.
49. Saleem Kurd: Baloch Sarmachaarun Ka Tharana, Sangath, Quetta, p 27-28.
50. Abdur Rehman Baloch: Roch Bieth, Baam, vol, iv, Quetta, pp 44-46.

51. Mubarak Kazi: Akebath. The youth literary Circle, Turbat.
52. Siddiq Azaath: Uf Passa Na Danth Kass, Makkuran, vol I Tehran 1980, pp 18-19.
53. Abdul Ghafoor Baloch: Aey Koum, Ouman August 1952, pp,14-15.
54. Asko Jamaldini: Ouman, February-March, 1954. p 20.
55. Muhammad Hussian Unqa: Azaathi, Ouman, August 1955, p 27.
56. Ibid. March 1956, pp 11-13.
57. Shoukath Nadeem, Ibid. July-August 1958, pp 17-19.
58. Jumma Khan: Waabe, Ibid, January 1959, pp 19,18.
59. Hasrath Baloch: Balochi, Karachi, July 1956, p 14.
60. Malik Saeed: Ibid. February 1957, p 8.
61. Adam Hakkani: Ibid, March 1957, pp, 12-13.
62. Ambar Panjguri: Ibid, July 1956, p 10.
63. Azaad Jamaldini: Koul, Ibid. May 1957, pp 44-45.
64. Jazmi: Balochistane Gwaank. Ibid, September,1957, p 11.
65. Azaad Jamaldini: Shaheedani Kulah Pa Padreecha, Makkuraan op, Cit, pp 3-6.
66. Malik Touki: Muskilien Rochan Pad Makenzaathe Bach Mani, Ibid. pp 15-17.
67. M. Kareem: Jee Pa Wathan. Baam, Quetta, August 1977, pp 21-22.
68. Gaagiyaan Baloch: Ibid, P22.
69. Anwar Saahib khan: Baloch Warnae naama, Ibid, November 1977, p 44.
70. M.H. Khalil Apsari: Baloch Warnae naama, Ibid, pp 30-31.
71. Ibrahim Abid: Dier Nayanth Rozhnae Roch. Ibid, November 1977, p44.
72. Mulla Rodi: Granwaab Sarouk Benag Dah, Balochi, Quetta, July-August 1979, pp 59-61.
73. Mulla Rodi: Teeki, Ibid. June 1979. pp 68-69.
74. Ajo Baloch: Baloch Sardar. Ibid. March-April 1979, p 36.
75. Akhirdad Husain Borr: Maathien Wathan Balochistan, Ibid. p 25.
76. Shahdaad Chahsari: Raji Sarmacharaan. Ibid. May-June 1979. p 28.
77. Mubarak Kazi: Suhr Dapien Baam, Ibid. March-April 1979, p 28.
78. W. B. Iraki: Peoples' Front, London, August 1978, p 2.
79. Ghani Parwaz: Santien Shap. Balochi, Quetta, January-February 1979 p 29.
80. Amirul Mulk Mengal: Hech Nazanaan Ke Chiya, Ibid. p 26.
81. Bahraam Mengal: Gupthaar, Ibid, July-August 1979, p 39.
82. Ulfath Naseem: Gwaank. Ibid, pp 27-28.
83. Wahid Bakhsh Rahi: Baloch, Ibid, May 1982, p 15.
84. Muhammad Ashraf Mullazai: Perband, Zamana, Quetta, February 1982. p 17.
85. Ajiz Panjguri: Ham Karawaan, Sougaath, Karachi, August, 1982, p 50.
86. Inayatullah Qoumi: Mathien Wathan, Ibid. March 1980, pp38-39.
87. Ibrahim Abid: Zura Gulien Baskaan Beday, Balochi, Quetta. May-June 1980, p 14.
88. Anwar Saahib Khan: Zubaana, Ahenen Saankal Nadaraan, Sougaath, Karachi, September 1979, p 32.

89. Anwar, Saahib Khan: Gaal, Shubenag, Vol 111 Pasni P1.
90. Shahdaad Chahsari: Gaal, Balochi, Quetta, January-February, 1080, p 7.
91. Ghani Perwaz: Jah janeth, Ibid, May-June,1980, p 15.
92. Din Muhammad Borr: Zrumbeshth e Thawaar, Ibid, p 15.
93. Peeral Baloch: Than Kadien Maeg o Thai Jang Nabieth. Sougaath, Karachi, November 1978.
94. Jan Muhammad Apsari: Diljami, The youth literary circle Turbat. p 24.
95. Muhammad Beg Begul: Kohan, Maniegant, Sougaath, Karachi, March April. p 71.
96. Anwar Saahib Khan: Maathien Wathan, Ibid, p 72.
97. Mansoor Baloch: Yaagi, Bramsh, Sayad Academy, Karachi, 1984, pp 64
98. Mansoor Baloch, Ibid
99. Nabi Bakhsh Buzdar: Balochi Dunya, Multan October 1984, p 35.
100. Noor Ahmad Ouman: Balochistan, Nidae Balochistan London, March 1981, p 1.
101. Noor Ahmad Ouman: Wathan, Peoples Front, London, February- March 1981, p1.
102. Nazeer Sufi: Balochistan. Sougaath, Karachi, August 1984, p 33.
103. Kamaal Baloch: Jah Janeth, Peoples Front, London, February– March 1980.
104. Iqbal Raz shiraani: Wath Nazanaan Ke Kujahaan. Balochi, Quetta, April 1981, p 23.
105. Din Muhammad Siddiq: Hambalaan. Ibid.
106. Fida Ahmad Baloch: Salaam Sarbaath Namiranan, Ibid February, 1981, pp 47-48.
107. Khalid Sohail: Belaan Mani. Ibid. p 40.
108. Mubarak Kazi: Sekien, Ibid. P 39.
109. Akhirdad Husain Borr: Sarmachaar. Ibid. April 1981, p 24.
110. Abdul Latif Adil: Balochistan, Ibid,
111. Abdul Sathar Shahzaad: Parcha Baloch. Ibid. July-August 1981, p 24.
112. Wahid Bakhsh Rahi: Gaal, Ibid, p 42.
113. Habibullah Amir: Balochistan, Ibid. June, 1981, p 27.
114. Gul Jan Gul: Jah Janeth Belaan, Ibid.
115. Ghulam Hyder Arman: May Balochistan, Ibid. p 31.
116. Mubarak Kazi: Mani Honaani Thrinzzuk, Ibid. p 31.
117. Ghani Parwaz: Roch, Ibid. p 34.
118. Mansoor Baloch: Justhe Cha Sarouk o mastheran, Ibid. September 1981. P 23.
119. Balochi, Quetta, Shun gaal, January, 1981, p 6.
120. Akbar Barakzai: Med o Thupaan, Ibid. 29,
121. Mansoor Baloch: Likkoh, Ibid. February 1981, pp 28,29.
122. Abdul Majeed Gwadari: Ruzhne Mesthaag, Sanj, Sayad Academy, Karachi 1985, p 402.
123. Ibid. p 448.
124. Akbar Baloch: Gulzamine Pussage Kulaho. Ibid. p 403.
125. Ibid.

126. Abdul Majeed Suhraabi: Bareeg. Ibid. p 442.
127. Saleem Shohaaz: Hambal o Belo Yalaan, Ibid. p446.
128. M.H. Khalil Apsari: Man o Thou, Ibid. p 460.
129. Mubarak Kazi, Wathan, Ibid. p 452.
130. Rashid Baloch: Ibid. p 428.
131. Bashir Bedaar: Pandal, Ibid. p 441.
132. Siddiq Azaath: Thou Har Kassi Maathien Wathan, Ibid. p 439-440.
133. Ashraf Sarbazi: O Brixtone Burzien Chinaal, Ibid. p 444-447.
134. Khan Saabir: Chaakar, Ibid. 22.
135. Anwar Shadman Sajidi: Dashthe Pull. Ibid. December, 1981.
136. Mansoor Baloch. Yaazda June e Naama, Ibid. June 1981, p 23.
137. Mubarak Kazi: Choun. Ibid. p 22.
138. Fazal Khaliq: Biya Ke Rawien, Ibid. March 1981, p 40.
139. Azaad Jamaldini: Ibid. January 1981, p91
140. Muhammad Beg Begul: Chaakar e Obaadag, Ibid. p 45.
141. Man Agan Drachkiyaan Dey Aas Mani Baalada.
     Bale Pa Naptheya Kohe Bosochith Chosh Na bieth
142. Aan kas ke qasde khoune Hameed shaheed Kard
     Kaare Yazid ra ba jahaan baare mazeed kard
     Dasthe qavi nabud ke dasthish bedashthien
     Thurse Khuda nadashth ke kare Yazid kard.
143. Bashir Bedaar: Kushindah e Naama, Geroke 1985, p 31.

CHAPTER V

EMERGENCE OF BALOCH NATIONALISM: A REAPPRAISAL

Although we do not have any proper picture of the Baloch administrative set-up in ancient times, keeping in view the geo-social imperatives and the Baloch tribal structure and tribal unions, it did by any definition constitute a pseudo-state by primitive standards. The first mention of the Baloch is made in connection with their support of Cyrus the Great (546-529 BC) against the Medes. Considering the tribal set–up during that era, we can safely draw the conclusion that the Baloch had a tribal union or coalition which extended military assistance to such a powerful monarch. References by the Arabs and Persian chroniclers to *Koch o Baloch* and their hold on major areas of Kirmaan and Sistaan as far as the sea after the collapse of Sassanid empire, signify that these tribes had a political and administrative structure with some centralized authority which forged alliances with other tribes as well as with rulers of Persia and the Indus valley.

1- Tribes and Tribal Unions in Medieval Times

The Baloch was a fierce and warrior people who always resisted foreign domination. The first organized attack on them on a large scale came from Anushervan (the Immortal Soul), around 531 AD. After the Arab invasion of Central Asia and the fall of Sassanid power in the region, some powerful regional rulers of the Iranian plateau and Central Asia had fought frequent battles with the Baloch to keep the trade routes open through their land. Balochistan came under the domination of various rulers but their influence was never felt beyond the plains and settled districts. They could never penetrate into the hilly region of Balochistan. Therefore, it is simply untenable to presume that the Baloch had no state apparatus or administrative structure and were merely a wandering folk. They could never have resisted Iranian might or the invading Arab troops without some kind of an administrative infrastructure or without some central authority or command. Organization of the Baloch in the fifteenth and sixteenth centuries gives us a fair glimpse of their tribal administration. The central and eastern part of present-day Pakistani Balochistan came under the sway of a fresh migratory branch of the Baloch tribes described as Rind–Lashaar and their allies. The Rind Lashaar union and their later conflict and war provide us with the first elaborate account of their tribal set-up as well as the socio-cultural and religious views of these tribes. Even if we discard the Baloch tribal unions who fought the Anushervan and later many other rulers, for which we have sketchy records, the Rind-Lashaar hegemony can be called the first Baloch principality in eastern Balochistan with state machinery reminiscent of similar tribal monarchies in Central Asia of medieval times. Earlier in the 14th century, numerous Baloch tribes who had migrated from the Iranian part of the Baloch land dominated a part of western Balochistan up to the outskirt of Jahlawaan. This tribal union headed by Mir Jalalaan has been called the first Baloch confederacy and lasted till the end of the 15th century [1]. An alliance of the Brahui tribes at Kalat was later replaced by the Rind-Lashaar alliance. Another confederacy in Derajath came into ascendency many decades later under Dodai rulers [2].

The Rind-Lashaar ascendency was an extraordinary event bringing far-reaching cultural and ethnic changes to the region. The migrating Baloch tribes reinforced the existing Baloch settlements in the region, who accepted this fresh influx without any opposition. But after a few decades, the Rind-Lashaar political differences resulted in intermittent wars with disastrous implications. The legendary chiefs of the two tribes, Mir Chaakar Rind and Mir Gwhraram Lashaari, sought help from neighboring rulers. Mir Chaakar brought in Argons from Kandahar while Gwahram had the assistance of many indigenous tribes and moral support from Sindhi Rulers [3]. During their over thirty years of settlement in eastern Balochistan, they fought nearly twenty-five battles including three significant encounters. In the final battle, the Rind, supported by the Argons, defeated the Lashaars but subsequently became too weak to continue their hold in the area. This also resulted in the rapid resurgence of the Brahui tribal alliance in Jahlawaan, who defeated the Rind nominee Mir Mando in Kalat [4]. The Rind and many allied tribes migrated further east to Sindh and Punjab, while the bulk of the defeated Lashaars pushed towards Gujarat in India.

The Rind-Lashaar interregnum diffused the Balochi language and culture over a vast area. At one stage, the entire area was in effect divided: Sivi with Rind, and Kach-Gandhawa with the Lashaar, while a Rind representative ruled Turan. The Tribal affiliation and union were strong and the area was administered by a tribal chief or Sardar with the help of the clan heads. Mir Chaakar and Mir Gwahraam were heads of two powerful tribal confederacies and were a constant deterrent to each other. The internal organization of each confederacy was based on democratic principles. Important decisions were made by the tribal council chaired by the Sardar. The indigenous tribes also had a say in matters concerning war and peace. This is particularly true of the Lashaar tribal union.

Mir Chaakar and Mir Gwahraam often acted and reacted ferociously and as regards political consequences, where Mir Gwahraam was sagacious, pious and revered, Mir Chaakar was viciously shrewd, highly gifted but far from noble. The conflict came to such an impasse that fighting to the last man on each side became inevitable, with grave results, which Mir Chaakar himself felt not long after.

Mir Gwahraam had considerable acumen to mobilize indigenous factions and used them in his war against the Rind. His influence was much greater than that of Mir Chaakar. He had diplomatic harmony with the rulers of Sindh. A critical analysis of the political strategy of both Mir Chaakar and Mir Gwahraam accords a superior status to Mir Gwahraam. He was a better organizer and strategist. He had an acute sense of history. He preferred relations with neighboring Sindh rather than the rulers of Herat. Even after the defeat and migration of the Lashaars, folk stories give him a place of respect and reverence, while Chaakar has been depicted as a man of dual character. His hypocrisy and treachery are shown in folk tales. Mir Gwahraam's policy of peaceful co-existence with the indigenous tribes and neighboring states brought appreciable political dividends and could have established a strong Baloch state in the region if Mir Chaakar had contended within the limits of his territorial authority. His aggressive designs brought the two powerful tribal unions into direct conflict, with attendant miseries and misfortune.

After the end of the Rind-Lashaar era of supremacy in the last quarter of the fifteenth century, the center of activity shifted from Sibi-Gandhava to Kalat. Mir Ahmad (1666-1695 AD) of the Kambrani clan established a tribal union of Brahui tribes based in Kalat when he was declared the Khan of the Baloch. It was structured on the lines of Rind-Lashaar confederacies. The tribal confederacy of the Khanate of Kalat continued until the British invasion of Kalat and the martyrdom of Mir Mehraab Khan in 1839. Khanate affairs were henceforth managed by British political officers, with the Khan of Kalat retaining nominal status. Besides, the Talpurs of Sindh who ruled from 1783-1843 AD, the Khanate was the only centrally organized political entity bordering the Persian Empire. The tribal alliance of the Khanate was broad-based, with tremendous power allowed to the tribal chiefs, who recognized the Khan as the paramount power and contributed nominal revenue to him as well as a fixed contingent of men in time of war. The tribal area of responsibility was fixed and allowed to continue. The Khan was assisted by a council of advisors representing the major tribes and allied people, and a Wazir usually selected from Tajik or Dehwaar immigrants of Kalat. The rights and interests of the principal indigenous tribes were respected and restored. The Khan was the head of the confederacy but he enjoyed no absolute power. All important decisions were taken by the Khan in the council of advisor. The tribal heads of the Sarawaan and the Jahlawaan were the most powerful and policy decision could be taken only with the consent and approval of these two Sardars. The Sarawaan group of tribes was headed by the Raisani chief, and Zehri headed the Jahlawaan tribes. The indigenous tribes in the area were aligned with the respective tribal grouping.

Militarily, every able-bodied tribesman was supposed to take up arms in an emergency. The Khan was supplied with contingents of fighting men by the tribal heads according to their respective strength [5]. There were three main territorial divisions of the Khan's forces, men from Kach-Gandhawa, Kalat, and Noshki were known by their green flag. Sarawaan troops used red and the fighters from Jahlawaan and Las Bela had a yellow banner. This division roughly corresponds with the tribal unions of the Khanate.

The Khan had no standing army beyond a contingent of household servants and bodyguards. During the time of Mahmud Khan, these guards were distinguished by a red jacket. Khudadaad Khan's standing army was the largest. He also had artillery pieces, cavalry, and a considerable infantry, above the requirements of personal security.

The main revenue was from the agriculture tax, collection from the port of Karachi for some times and taxes on the goods passing through the Bolaan Pass. Taxation was unequal and depended on many factors including the distance of the area from the capital. Taxation on sea-borne trade from the Makkuraan coast was also nominal. Generally, the Sarawaan and Jahlawaan tribes who provided the bulk of the Khan's troops and some other important factions in the area were exempted from land revenue. In Makkuraan, one-tenth of land produce was the state share while the Jath of Kach-Gandhawa paid one-half and the indigenous and Dehwaar farmers of Kalat, Mastung, and Shal paid one-third to the Khan.

Land possession as a matter of state policy was allocated to tribes and important clans, which were responsible for its collective cultivation. The land remained tribal property. The grant of land was conditional however on the number of troops provided by every tribe in the time of war. Land could be forfeited if the tribes failed to provide a specified number of men and material. Certain clans were exempted from providing troops but they were sometimes required to work on tasks beneficial to the Khan and his important Sardars. Forts, citadels and war materials were manned by such people without any remuneration paid to them.

The office of the Khan was hereditary in the Ahmad Zai family but the tribal sardars were most often selected through the general consent of the clan headmen [6]. The Khan was a benevolent ruler of a decentralized administration and the Khanate was a loose confederacy. Mir Naseer Khan augmented the union. He succeeded in evolving an effective and strong union of tribes. He never interfered with internal tribal issues. The Rind and Magasis of Kach-Gandhawa and few others in Sistaan had complete independence, without paying any land revenue. With them, the political allegiance was considered sufficient.

When the Khanate was established in 1666 AD by Mir Ahmad, his domain comprised only Sarawaan and Jahlawaan. Three among the long list of Khans during the one hundred and seventy-three years up to 1839, were men of resolute determination and competence. Mir Abdullah Khan (1715-1730 AD) extended the country's borders to far-flung areas. He dominated all the major tribes, compelling them to pay allegiance to Kalat. Mir Naseer Khan (1750-1795 AD) not only further extended the Khanate to the entire region of present-day eastern Balochistan and most parts of the Iranian and Afghan controlled Baloch land, including the port of Karachi (for some years only) but also provided a political structure for the confederacy. Mir Naseer Khan, who was seventh in the line, stands out for being a remarkable general and statesman. Mir Mehraab Khan (1816-1839 AD) had to his credit the uncompromising determination and exemplary courage to uphold Baloch tradition in fighting the British forces. He preferred death rather than come to a degrading compromise. Among others, Mir Mahabat Khan is known for his shortsightedness and cruelty, and Ahmad Yar Khan for his political immaturity and for demonstrating lack of acumen, self-confidence and administrative skills. While Mir Mehraab Khan preferred death rather than surrender, Ahmad Yar Khan was easily intimidated in agreeing in the most abject manner to the accession of his state to Pakistan by accepting a personal payment from the rulers of the newly created country. Such disservice to the Baloch people has no parallel in the three and a half thousand years of Baloch history.

Mir Naseer Khan was a confident ally of Afghan King Ahmad Shah Durrani. He accompanied the Afghan Sovereign in his numerous marauding forays into the Indian Subcontinent and Iran. He extended support to Ahmad Shah but never regarded himself as a tributary to Durrani but rather a junior partner [7]. However, the Afghan attitude toward the Khan provoked Mir Naseer Khan to declare complete independence of Kalat in 1758. The conflict took such an ugly turn that the Afghans decided to invade Kalat. Afghan troops under Shah Wali were defeated at Mastung by Mir Naseer Khan, but the Khan was later compelled to retreat by the forces under the command of Ahmad Shah Durrani. Mir Naseer Khan took up a position in the Kalat fortress, which was besieged for forty days by the Afghan forces. Numerous assaults were made by the Afghan army but met with dismal failure. Ultimately both the former allies came to an amicable agreement, known as the Treaty of Kalat recognizing the sovereign status of Balochistan. The Afghan monarch promised not to interfere in the internal and external affairs of the Baloch confederacy. The Khan, in turn, promised to help Afghanistan in case of external aggression or in its foreign expedition. Both countries agreed not to give asylum to rebels within their states. The agreement provides the basis for the Khanate's subsequent relation with Afghanistan.

The foreign policy of the Khanate was one of peaceful coexistence with all the neighboring states. It had cordial relations with Sindh and the Persian states. Khanate in practical terms was a sort of buffer zone between Sindh, Persia, and Afghanistan.

2- The Occupation and the Baloch National Question

The question of Baloch national sovereignty in a historical perspective dates back to the days of British hegemony in Balochistan in the 19th century. The big-power rivalry in central Asia which resulted in the British invasion of Afghanistan also brought its forces into the Baloch region. The Khanate of Kalat under Mir Mehraab Khan did not want to be involved in foreign aggression against the Afghan people with whom Kalat had had treaty obligation from the time of Mir Naseer Khan. The British supply routes to Afghanistan could not be safeguarded without securing Balochistan, which had by now gathered much importance in British Central Asian policy. Its forces were therefore ordered to subjugate Kalat. A detachment from Quetta attacked Kalat on 13th November 1839. The Khan, Mir Mehraab Khan refused to surrender and fought back against the invaders. He was Killed in the battle. With his martyrdom, Balochistan came under British rule till 11th August 1947, when the Khan, Ahmad Yar Khan declared its independence on the eve of the end of British rule in the subcontinent.

After the martyrdom of Mir Mehraab Khan, the British were facing the dual task of keeping in check tribal sentiments and fury on the one hand and administering a vast territory with a scattered population on the other. The British could not reverse the existing administrative pattern which would have required a huge bureaucratic structure and considerable finances. There was also the possibility of resistance from the people if such an administration was introduced.

Therefore, it was thought prudent to evolve a policy based on minimum interference but maximum efficiency. The system called the Sandeman System after Sir Robert Sandeman who masterminded the political set up of the region. The system recognized the Khan as nominal head of the state. The government was run with the help of tribal chieftains. But the British representative was the supreme arbitrator of conflicts between the Khan and the Sardars and between the Sardars themselves. This system, while it ensured British overlordship and a permanent British presence in the region, reduced the Khan and the Sardars to mere vassals of the British crown. Disputes had always been settled through mutual consent in a *Jirga*, which acted as a court of law. Sandeman introduced a *Shahi Jirga*, unknown in Baloch legal and administrative annals, where only Sardars and aristocrats could sit. The Sandeman system broke up the traditional pattern and accorded immense authority to the Sardar over their subjects and they were made responsible for maintaining law and order. Each of them was allowed to keep a certain number of levies paid by the government. The system was a shrewd mechanism of indirect rule with power vested in a few carefully selected tribal elders loyal to the British and ready to act against their own people. It was legalized through a treaty between the British and the Khan and Sardars in 1876. Under the agreement, Quetta and its adjoining areas including the Bolaan Pass were leased to the British on a permanent no-rent basis. The nominal authority of the Khan of Kalat was accepted over the region but it was to be administered by the British in accordance with local customs. The treaty was formally signed in Delhi where the Khan and Sardars were received with full honors. To give the occasion an air of solemnity, the Viceroy of India awarded heraldic banners to the tribal chiefs and the Khan.

The British occupation of Kalat was perhaps the greatest event in Baloch history for many centuries. The British, in their desire to have peace in the Khanate, installed Mir Naseer khan II, the son of Mir Mehraab Khan, as the Khan of Kalat. But the British were aware of the Baloch feelings and hatred caused by the Khan's killing. Relations between succeeding Khans and the British always remained sour. The climax came during the reign of Mir Khudadaad Khan (1857-93) who was detained in 1893 in Quetta by the British. Mir Mahmud Khan, his elder son was installed as the Khan of Kalat.

After the fall of Kalat in November 1839, many tribes stood in revolt against the alien authorities. The Bugtis gave battle to the British forces in December 1839. The Bugti chief Beebagr was captured in the battle. On 1st October 1847, Bugtis fought a battle on the borders of Sindh against lieutenant Merewether commanding the famous Sindh Horses. Seven hundred Bugtis took part in the attack, all of whom were killed or wounded except 120 persons who were taken, prisoners. Another important battle of Mari, Bugtis and their allied tribe, Kethran, was fought in the Chachar valley near the borders of Dera Ghazi Khan on 26th January 1867. The Baloch troops, 1200 strong were led in the battle by Mir Ghulam Husain Masoori Bugti. He was also killed in the battle, which was lost by the Baloch forces. Hostilities with the Maris were started in August 1840. On 31st August a hotly contested battle was fought at the Naffusak Pass. Kahaan, the Mari capital was taken by the British but was vacated at the end of September 1840 after an agreement with the Mari Chief Mir Doda.

The Zehri tribe revolted under Sardar Mir Gohar Khan, who collected a large *Lashkar* and indulged in harassment in a vast area in Central Jahlawaan. Mir Gohar Khan was a brave leader who defeated the British force under Major Temple and Lieutenant Maurier in Norgam and Salmanjo. The insurrection prevailed for one year until Mir Gohar was killed in a battle in Garmaap in 1894 along with his son Mir Yusuf. During the uprising, Mir Alam Khan and others decided to lay down their arms while Mir Noor Mahmad, known as Noora Mengal, refused to surrender [8].

The unrest was not confined to the Jahlawaan or Mari-Bugti region. In Makkuraan the British political agent was attacked and injured by Shahdaad Gichki. Mehraab Khan, who coveted authority in the Kech valley, detained the British agent and the manager of financial affairs, Undo Das [9]. This infuriated the British, who ordered an attack on the district from Karachi to assert their authority. Resistance was organized by Mehraab Khan and Mir Baloch Khan. A large number of rudimentarily armed people gathered at Gokprosh, a few miles from Turbat, on 27 January 1898 to fight the advancing troops. But when fighting was about to begin, Mehraab Khan decided to withdraw the men under his command and left Mir Baloch Khan and his followers alone on the battlefield. He is believed to have made contact with the British, who had promised amnesty to him. The last-minute betrayal by Mehraab Khan Gichki decided the outcome of the battle and after a brief encounter, the invading forces defeated the remaining Baloch *Lashkar* killing all 250 of them including their leader, Mir Baloch Khan Nosherwani.

The British influence beyond Makkuraan was a source of constant worries in Iranian Balochistan. In 1909, when the Iranian Monarch withdrew his governor from Bampur, Sardar Bahraam Khan Baranzai established his authority in the area, declared himself Shah-e-Balochistan, and assumed the title of 'Shir-e-Jehan'. He also maintained close links with foreign governments, especially with the Germans. In 1915, he attacked British outposts in Makkuraan. Troops under the command of British agents were defeated and Mir Bahraam laid waste a vast region before withdrawing to Bampur [10].

In 1914, an alliance of Mengal, Zehri, and Nosherwaani forces under the leadership of Nawab Muhammad Khan Zarakzai posed a threat to British authority in Balochistan. In a letter to the British government, he demanded inter alia the release and rehabilitation of Sardar Shakar Khan as Sardar of the Mengal tribe and the appointment of Habibullah Khan Nosherwaani as the Nawab of Kharan to replace his murdered father. But the British did not respond to his demands and instead hatched a plan to eliminate Muhammad Khan, who was encamped at Gatt Zehri with the professed aim of attacking Kalat. On 24th August 1915, his younger brother Mir Norouz Khan, who had joined the British in their conspiracy, killed Muhammad Khan in his tent while he was asleep. Subsequently, the Baloch *Lashkar* was dispersed [11].

In December 1916, Sardar Noorudin Mengal and Sardar Shahbaz Khan Gurgnadi revolted. Noora Mengal, Mir Gwahraam, and Suleman joined the rebellion. After some time, Sardar Noorodin and Shahbaz Khan surrendered to the British authorities, but Noora Mengal refused any conciliation with the alien masters and continued his efforts to mobilize the people in an armed struggle. Noora wanted to cross into Afghanistan but was arrested by Habibullah Khan in Kharan and handed over to the government authorities in December 1917 [12]. This was a most unconventional act by the Kharan ruler. Noora was tried and sentenced to life imprisonment. He died in British goal in Hyderabad in November 1921.

The British government was not happy with the rising discontent in Balochistan and wanted a permanent solution to the problem of law and order. It could not afford any disturbances which might take the form of a liberation movement in this sensitive region. In order to secure Baloch loyalties and also to augment the British war efforts, they wanted the Baloch to serve in the British Indian army. A proposal to this effect was first put forward before a meeting of the Baloch sardars in Quetta in October 1916. The sardars rejected the suggestion and refused to provide manpower for such an army. The proposal was again mooted in January 1917. Sardar Khair Bakhsh Mari categorically opposed the idea. Now the British decided to punish the Mari and started preparations for war against the tribe. Mari fought furiously against the invading forces. Two decisive battles were fought at Gunbuz and Hadab in which the Maris were defeated. Seven hundred of them were killed and five hundred received injuries in the battle of Gunbuz. Another three hundred Maris were killed and nearly seven hundred received injuries at Hadab.

The Baloch resistance to British authority continued for more than a century with varying intensity. These were undoubtedly the acts of individual tribal chiefs or a collection of them who were aggrieved by one or another act of the government. Isolated events could not assume the form of a national struggle, firstly because the Baloch tribal leaders lacked proper liaison with each other due primarily to lack of communication between them. Secondly, the sardars had too little confidence in themselves to take the hazardous course of fighting an enemy superior in arms and resources. Thirdly, the Khans could not provide the leadership and inspiration necessary for such a fight. Fourthly, the Baloch had no contacts with the Indian peoples and were unaware of their struggle against the British, and finally, they lacked a political organization to mobilize the masses for such a cause. But in spite of these drawbacks, the Baloch continued their resistance in their own peculiar way throughout the British period of hegemony and never allowed the alien influences to pervade their society.

3- Beginning of Nationalist Politics

After the First world war, the Baloch nationalists began political activities for the liberation of Balochistan and increased their efforts to achieve unity among the masses. The Anjuman-e-Ithihad–e-Balochaan (henceforth referred to as Anjuman), a political organization, started working in the early 1920s. Mir Yousuf Ali Magsi (d.1935) and Mir Abdul Aziz Kurd organized the Anjuman, whose activities remained underground for many years. It was formally launched in 1933.

The Baloch nationalists tried to publicize their agenda by using the media. Mir Abdul Aziz Kurd and Nasim Talwi started publishing a newspaper from Delhi by the name of Balochistan in 1927. The paper stopped publication after a few months. Later Mir Yousuf Ali Magsi helped publish another newspaper, Azaad, from Lahore. Al-Baloch, another newspaper, was brought out by the Baloch intellectuals in Karachi in 1933. These newspapers voiced the demands of the Baloch and worked for an independent Balochistan. Mir Yosuf Ali Magsi wrote an article *Faryad-e-Balochistan*, 'Wailing of Balochistan', in a Lahore newspaper in 1929, which resulted in his arrest and detention for nearly a year. The Anjuman started publishing a weekly magazine, Al Baloch, from Karachi. In its issue of 25th December 1932, the paper published an article by Ghulam Mahmad Baloch titled 'An unfulfilled Dream', in which the author gave a map of grater Balochistan showing the Baloch areas of Iran, the territories of the Khanate of Kalat, the leased areas under British control and the Baloch land in the Punjab and Sindh. In 1933, Magsi brought out a pamphlet, *Balochistan ki Awaz*, 'the voice of Balochistan', aimed at apprising the British Parliament of the socio-political conditions in Balochistan. In another pamphlet in 1933, titled *Shams Gardi*, 'Tyranny of Shams' (Shams was the Prime Minister of the Khanate of Kalat), Mir Yousuf Ali Magsi, bitterly criticized the policies of the Shams government and demanded constitutional rule through elected representatives in Balochistan.

Through the efforts of the Anjuman, the Baloch leaders and tribal elders announced the convening of a 'Balochistan and All India Conference' in Jacobabad. A joint statement on 20th October 1932 signed by Mir Yousuf Ali Magsi, Sardar Jamal Khan Leghari, Nawab Mushtaq Ahmad Gurmani, and Ghulam Rasool Kurai declared that the conference was aimed at achieving greater unity among the Baloch people and evolving means of protecting their national rights [14]. In the three-day convention in Jacobabad, delegates from Balochistan and India participated. The conference adopted several resolutions calling upon the people to be united and work for the unification of the various Baloch regions. The resolutions also demanded socio-political reforms and the formation of a constitutional government in

Balochistan [15]. Another Baloch conference was held a year later in Hyderabad, which also demanded, inter alia, constitutional rule in the Baloch country [16].

The first organized political party in Balochistan was formed at Sibi on 5th February 1937. Political workers from the Kalat State and a few members of Anjuman attended a convention at Sibi and formed the Kalat State National Party which in the years to come played a leading role in shaping many political events in the state [17]. The convention discussed the prevailing situation in Balochistan and views were exchanged regarding the Baloch national identity in the fast-changing political conditions of the region.

The party manifesto issued at the convention maintained that Balochistan had gained immense importance because of its geographical position as a buffer state separating Afghanistan, Iran, and India. It declared its objective of uniting the Baloch people with a representative government that could reflect their tradition. The party manifesto was one of the best documents ever produced on the Balochistan situation. It reflected the deep nationalistic sentiments and conscious expression of the political elite, determined to work for the liberation of the country. The Baloch, the document maintained, were avowed to achieve the goal of national independence. In the meantime, the party expressed its desire to fill the political vacuum in the absence of a sensible and responsible government in the Kalat State.

The Kalat-State National Party declared that it accepted the Kalat government of the Khan as a national government and would cooperate with it on the basis of a nationalistic agenda. The idea behind the party-political support to the Khan lies in the fact that while the party favored a united front which should include the Khan and his loyal sardars, it aspired to identify itself with the Baloch confederacy of Kalat. Although the Party declared its backing for the government of the Khan, it never gave up its progressive stance against the Sardari System which the British, with the Khan's connivance had established in Balochistan, and which was the main instrument of oppression in the state. However, taking into account the limitations of the party, it avoided open confrontation with powerful sardars. The Khan, for his part, though he agreed with certain viewpoints of the party, especially its demand for a sovereign independent Balochistan and its avowed goal of maintaining the traditional norms of the Baloch people, which by implication meant the Khan's continued overlordship, could not go very far in the party's support without compromising his position with the British or annoying the sardars.

The Kalat State National Party wanted an independent and sovereign state for the Baloch people. For this, the party was gathering tremendous support especially from the educated and saner elements of the Baloch society. The party workers and its leaders were not unaware of political movements in India but they wanted a separate identity and were by no means ready to lose their political sovereignty. They were conscious of the fact that Balochistan faced a peculiar geopolitical situation and the Party had a tremendous task to achieve the pre-determined objective of national independence. Balochistan had a status different from other Indian states. The British had certain treaty relations with the Baloch state and the affairs of the Khanate were dealt from White Hall through New Delhi.

The Kalat State National Party vehemently objected to British efforts in early 1939 to acquire the Jiwani port on lease from the Khan. The party's main thrust was its active hostility to the Sardari system and its attendant oppression of the people. This earned many enemies among the sardars, the government and the British authorities', who wanted to curb the party activities through administrative as well as underhand tactic. The party convened a three-day convention in Mastung on 5th July 1939 which was attended by a large number of people. On the second day, the party was expected to explain its stand on various political and administrative issues to renew its commitment to its stand on the Baloch national identity as an independent and sovereign people and to demand social reforms. A tribal *Lashkar* was secretly organized by certain Sardars with the connivance of the government which attacked the Party meeting on 6th July 1939. The Party workers and its sympathizers could have resisted the attack by armed means but the party leaders who were not in favor of any bloodshed and tribal rivalry, asked the workers not to be provoked and the meeting was called off. The next day, the tribal sardars called on the Khan to protest against the policies of the party and demanded a ban on its activities and the internment of its leaders. They also demanded that Darul Uloom, Mastung, a religious institution run by pro-national party clergy, should be closed down and the entry to Kalat of all newspapers published from British Balochistan should be disallowed [18]. The Khan patronizingly assured them that he would consider their demands favorably. He also alleged that the party workers had made some insulting remarks against the sardars which would not be tolerated because they were part of his government [19]. The Khan had little enthusiasm for the activities of the party and its convention at Mastung. He had refused permission to party workers and sympathizers from outside the state to attend the party convention. The president of the party had submitted a list of twenty-one prominent persons on 22nd June 1939 who intended to participate and had sought the government permission. They included important political figures from Sindh and British Balochistan. The prime minister, in communication on 24th June 1939, refused to allow the enlisted persons to attend the convention, maintaining that the party was confined to the state territory, therefore it could not be allowed to extend its activities beyond the state frontiers.

On 20th July 1939, two weeks after its abortive convention the Kalat State national party was declared illegal and its activities banned. Its leading figures, including Malik Abdur Raheem Khawaja Khel, Mir Ghous Baksh Bizenjo, Mir Gul Khan Naseer, and Abdul Kareem Showrish and a large number of workers were interned or banned from entering the state [20].

After the ban and the internment of its leaders, however, the party managed to continue its struggle with remarkable support in the state and remained a strong force on public opinion from its headquarters at Quetta. The party strongly condemned the move by the British government to recognize Kharan as a separate state, independent of Kalat. The Party's General Secretary, Abdul Kareem Showrish, termed the move an attempt to break–up Balochistan. He feared that Kharan's separation would ultimately destroy the Baloch unity and national identity [21]. On 25th August 1939, he warned against attempts at the further disintegration of Balochistan. He said: "at present, the Kalat State means the survival of the Baloch, in whose name we can form a united front of all the Baloch in time to come. If this is broken into pieces today, it will render inevitable the disorganization of the Baloch. Thus, political wisdom demands that we should avoid such shortsightedness, which contains the seed of disintegration and ignominy". He called upon the people to demand the reintegration of Kharan and Lasbela with the Khanate [22].

During the Second World War, the internment orders on many of the party leaders were withdrawn. In the meantime, the party entered into an alliance in 1945 with the all India States Peoples Conference, headed by Jawaharlal Nehru. In a meeting held in Sri Negar on 6th-8th August 1945, the Standing Committee of the All India States Peoples Conference discussed the question of the alliance of the Kalat State National Party with the conference. The committee also expressed concern over the curbs on the activities of the party by the government of Kalat, the internment of party president and others, and the restriction on entry into the state of newspapers from British Balochistan [23].

Relations between the Khan and the Party remained strained from the date of its being declared illegal by the government. The Party's belligerent attitude can be judged from the resolution adopted in its meeting on 26th-28th July 1945. The resolution condemned the decision of the state council held on 25th April 1945, in which it had demanded more power for itself in order to establish effective control of the state administration. The Party opposed the very nature of the state council, in which only nominated Sardars and tribal elders were members. The party maintained that if the power of the council were enhanced it would let loose a reign of terror in the country. The party asked for a representative government through elections on the basis of the universal franchise [24]. However, when the Khan announced his intentions to associate the people with his administration and also to frame a constitution for the state, the party considered the step a progressive one and informed the khan of the party's support. In a letter to the Khan on 14th August 1945, the party president welcomed the decision as a step perfectly in line with the high tradition of three hundred years-old Dynasty and exactly what ought to be expected from a worthy scion of the Mir Naseer Khan. The party also expressed the hope that it would be invited to take part in the discussion concerning the vital changes so as to pave the way for future accord and cooperation between the Khan and the party in the interest of national progress [25]. But the Khan spurned the offer of cooperation and refused to allow the party to take part in the elections, which he called in 1947. The party members contested the polls in their individual capacity and were returned to Balochistan Parliament in a sweeping majority. The party secured thirty-nine out of fifty-two seats in the lower house.

4- The Accession to Pakistan

The Kalat State National party strongly opposed the idea of the accession of the Baloch State to Pakistan. Balochistan's newly adopted constitution provided that only parliament could take such an important decision. The Khan also wanted a decision to be taken with the approval of the Baloch parliament. A meeting of parliament was convened on 12th December 1947 and took up the accession issue on 13 December 1947. Mir Ghous Bakhsh Bizenjo, who was then the leader of the Party in the house of commons, rejected the proposal. In his speech on 14th December 1947, he strongly advocated a sovereign status for Balochistan. The Prime Minister and Foreign Minister of the Khanate also addressed the assembly. On this occasion, Mir Ghous Bakhsh delivered a long and forceful speech against any move that violates the independence of the Baloch State of Kalat. He told the House: "We have a distinct civilization. we have a separate culture like that of Iran and Afghanistan. We are Muslims but it is not necessary that by virtue of our being Muslims we should lose our freedom and merge with others. If the mere fact that we are Muslims requires us to join Pakistan then Afghanistan and Iran, both Muslim countries, should also amalgamate with Pakistan ...The British conquered Asia through the force of the sword. They also subjugated the Baloch homeland. We never accepted their authority. We resisted their rule but being oppressive and cruel they deprived us of our freedom. We were a separate entity. We were never part of India before the British. ...Pakistan's unpleasant and loathsome desire that our national homeland, Balochistan, should merge with it is impossible to concede. It is unimaginable to agree to such a demand... it is no secret that before the creation of Pakistan, our Khan had patronized the Muslim League party. Our homes, Bungalows, and transport were at their disposal. Under Khan's guidance, many Baloch helped the League through every possible means. What was our attitude toward Pakistan and what is its behavior towards us...? Lasbela and Kharan, two constituent units of Balochistan are being snatched away; Kalat's sovereignty over those areas had been accepted by the British. They are our brethren in blood and have been part of Kalat in that capacity. Pakistan has even refused talks and is making any discussions on the subject conditional on the repentance of the Baloch government and its prostration before them...we are ready to have friendship with that country on the basis of sovereign equality but by no means ready to merge with Pakistan. We cannot humiliate the Baloch nation and amalgamate it with others. How we sign the national death warrant of fifteen million Baloch? That is inconceivable. That is impossible. We cannot be a party to such a grave mistake. We cannot commit such a great crime.... We are told that we Baloch cannot defend ourselves in the atomic age. Well, are Afghanistan, Iran and even Pakistan capable of defending themselves? Today, if Russia and America so desire, they can wipe out many such states from the world map. If we cannot defend ourselves a lot of others cannot do so either... As regards the question of statehood, let me emphasize that no Asian country including Pakistan fulfills the criteria of a modern state in true sense... They say we must join Pakistan for economic reasons. That is also absurd. We may not have hard currency but we have numerous means of income: we have minerals, we have petroleum, and we have ports.... We should not be made slaves on the pretext of economic viability. We can survive without Pakistan. We can remain without Pakistan. We can prosper outside Pakistan but the question is what Pakistan would be without us...? I do not propose to create hurdles for the newly created Pakistan in matters of defense and external communication. But we want an honorable relationship, not a humiliating one. If Pakistan wants to treat us as a sovereign people, we are ready to extend the hand of friendship and cooperation. If Pakistan does not agree to do so, flying in the face of democratic principles, such an attitude will be totally unacceptable to us, and if we are forced to accept this fate then every Baloch son will sacrifice his life in defense of his national freedom [26]. The Assembly was adjourned without taking a vote on the issue. Meanwhile, the Governor-General of Pakistan wrote a threatening letter to the Khan of Kalat on 2nd January 1948, asking him to accede to Pakistan without any father delay. The Khan in reply on 15th February suggested that he would inform the government of Pakistan of his decision after convening the Kalat Assembly by the end of February 1948. The Parliament was once again convened in Dhadar on 25th February 1948. The Prime Minister spoke favoring the accession to Pakistan but soon after his speech, Mir Ghous Bakhsh Bizenjo tabled a motion before the house signed by all members of the parliament rejecting any merger with Pakistan. The resolution, however, favored good neighborly relations with Pakistan on the basis of sovereign equality [27]. The Khan summoned a meeting of the

Upper House of the parliament which discussed the issue and passed a resolution on 27th February 1948 maintaining that since the resolution disapproving the accession to Pakistan by the state parliament has been adopted in haste, the matter should, therefore, be taken up by the assembly once again and the Balochistan Government should approach the government of Pakistan to give Kalat another three months to decide on the issue. Earlier, the Upper House of the Parliament had met on 3rd-4th January 1948 and rejected the notion of a merger with Pakistan. All the members unanimously approved a resolution that said: 'This house is not willing to accept the merger with Pakistan which will endanger the separate existence of the Baloch nation' [28].

However, the Khan succumbed to pressures exerted by the British and the Pakistani governments and signed the accession treaty in March 1948. After the Khan's unilateral declaration of unconditional accession to Pakistan, the Kalat State National Party's reaction was one of bitter opposition and deep shock. Soon after the merger, the Party leaders were arrested and banned from entering the state. Those arrested included Mir Ghous Bakhsh Bizenjo and Mir Abdul Aziz Kurd. The Party was banned by the Government of Pakistan in June 1948 for its anti-state activities and for its support for Prince Kareem's rebellion against Pakistan.

The Kalat State National Party has a chequered history. It started in a very unfavorable socio-political environment. The state was being run by a corrupt and inefficient government manipulated by the British agent stationed at Kalat. The people were never allowed to participate in state affairs which were considered the domain of the Khan and his protégés under the direction of foreign rulers. The Party worked in a society that was not acquainted with party politics. It was working in a tribal set-up in which politics circled around the figure of the tribal elders and Sardars. Nevertheless, a large number of conscientious educated people who were in the service of the state were willing to join the party and pursue its program. Some of its very distinguished leaders. like Malik Abdur Raheem Khawaja Khel, Mir Gul Khan Naseer and Abdul Kareem Showrish were serving the state in a very important position, between 1937 and 1948, the party was allowed to operate for less than two years, but it left a tremendous impact on the people. When the Khan held elections, the party was returned to parliament in a comfortable majority in spite of the fact that it was not allowed to contest as a party and its members contested in their individual capacity.

Despite enormous difficulties, the party and its leaders provided an intelligent lead to the people. Although declared illegal after the state's accession to Pakistan, its soul, continued to guide the people. Party stalwarts like Mir Ghous Bakhsh Bizenjo and Mir Gul Khan Naseer have dominated Balochistan politics since then. After the ban on the party, its leaders joined various political groups, but their stand remained unchanged. The political elite in Balochistan could not shrink from the idea of an independent Baloch land put forward forcefully by the Party in 1930. It had such a magnetic influence that its workers and leaders, quite unconsciously and in wholly changed circumstances, could not even detach themselves from its nomenclature. The National Awami Party (NAP), was the extension of the National Party to most workers, because it had national in its title, and for all practical purposes at least in Balochistan, the NAP worked for an independent and sovereign state for the Baloch people. Its successor after the party was banned by the Bhutto regime in 1975, had again the appellative national in its nomenclature: The National Democratic party. The name was suggested by Mir Ghous Bakhsh Bizenjo. And again, after their estrangement with the NDP, the Baloch leaders formed the National Party, the word National, is not involved by coincidence or without any meaning, it recalls the Kalat State National Party which is referred to as National Party among the old stalwarts and nationalists. They could not simply detach themselves from the spirit of a movement that put forward progressive ideas in a time of political stagnation. Mir Ghous Bakhsh Bizenjo told a gathering of the Pakistan National Party. PNP, workers in Quetta in January 1985, some forty-five years after the National Party was founded, that the Party he is heading now was not a new one. In fact, it symbolized a movement and an organization that was launched in 1937 [29]. The National Party was the real harbinger of the freedom movement in Balochistan in the modern era, and its successor organizations out of its debris will continue to guide the people of Balochistan for a long time to come.

5- The Accession: Historical Perspective

After the occupation in 1839, Balochistan had a distinct treaty relationship with the British. In 1854, the British entered into an agreement of friendship with Mir Naseer Khan II, which was subsequently renewed and affirmed in another treaty in 1876, in which the British government once again committed itself to respect the independence of Kalat and to aid the Khan in case of need in the maintenance of a just authority and protection of territories from external attack. During the British reign in India, Nepal and Kalat were the only two states which had such relations with the British government and were allowed to appoint Ambassadors.

The British authorities never considered Balochistan part of the Indian sub-continent. The doctrine of paramountcy was never applicable to its relations with the Khanate of Kalat. The special relationship was manifested in several documents written by colonial officers. In 1872, Sir W. L. Merry weather, who was in charge of British interests in Kalat, wrote that 'there cannot, in my opinion, be the least doubt of the course which should be followed with regard to Kalat, or Balochistan as it should be correctly termed. His Highness the Khan is de facto and de-jure ruler of that country. We have treaty engagements with him under which he is bound to keep his subjects from injuring British territory or people, to protect trade, etc. But the treaty is with him as ruler only, and under none of the engagements are we called upon to enter directly into the manner in which he carries on his government' [30]. The same view was held by Sir Bartle Frère, who wrote in 1876 that 'it was a cardinal rule to attempt no disintegration of the Khan of Kalat's sovereignty, whether nominal or real over the Baloch tribes, but rather by every means in our power to uphold his authority. The Khan was regarded as our independent ally, free to act as he pleased in internal affairs, but externally subordinate to the British government in all that could affect anything beyond his own borders. We deal with Kalat as far as possible as we would with Belgium or Switzerland' [31]. But before the occupation of Kalat on 13 November 1839, on many occasions, due to political expediencies, the Baloch land was variously treated, sometimes as an independent country, while at other times it was considered as a vassal of Afghanistan. After the 1854 treaty, it was duly recognized as an allied state in treaty relations with Britain outside British India. Many of the

Pakistani leaders before the creation of Pakistan were aware of this fact and openly advocated the independence of Balochistan. In 1946, I. I Chandrigar, who was a leader of the Muslim League and became the Prime Minister of Pakistan in 1957, wrote in his memorandum on 'independent Kalat' and its future as follows: *"Kalat which is not an Indian state and which was brought into relation with the British government on account of its geographical position on the borders of India is just like Afghanistan and Persia... The state has no intention of entering into a federal relationship with successive government or governments in British India and I have, therefore, to request Your Excellency to declare the independence of Kalat state"* [32].

However, despite the treaty of eternal friendship between the Khan and the British Crown, during British hegemony, Balochistan was arbitrarily divided into three parts. One portion was given to Iran, a small portion was included in Afghanistan and the north-eastern regions of the Khanate remained with the colonial administration under the lease. The rest of the country was in the Khanate of Kalat State. The province of British Balochistan was created with the inclusion of some Afghan districts and the leased areas of the Khanate of Kalat including Quetta municipality.

In a memorandum submitted to the British Cabinet Mission in march 1946, the Khan of Kalat asserted that Kalat would regain its independence after the British withdrawal and that all the leased areas of Balochistan would revert to its sovereignty. The memorandum maintains that Balochistan will become fully sovereign and independent with respect to both internal and external affairs and will be free to conclude treaties with any other government. The memorandum declares that the government and the people of Balochistan can never agree to their country being included in any form in the Indian Union. The Khan and his government will, however, be glad to enter into an alliance with any government which succeeds the British government in India on the basis of the respect of mutual sovereignty [33].

After the British government decided to divide India and announced the 3rd June Plan, the Viceroy of India entrusted the responsibility of deciding whether British Balochistan should join Pakistan to the members of the Shahi-Jirga and non-official members of the Quetta Municipality. This was against Baloch interests because the Shahi-Jirga also included the members from the leased areas of Sibi, Naseerabad, Quetta and the Mari–Bugti tribal regions. Legally, these areas were to be given back to the Khan after the British withdrawal from India. The Khan of Kalat and leaders of the Kalat State National Party protested to the British government and demanded that the names of the Baloch members from the leased areas should be deleted from the voting list. The British refused but promised that the question of sovereignty over the leased areas would be discussed with the Khan and the representatives of Pakistan. Later, during negotiations between Pakistan, British and the Khanate of Kalat in Delhi, it was decided that the Kalat and government of Pakistan would open talks on the sovereignty of the leased areas and their return to Balochistan.

However, the controversial vote of the Shahi-Jirga, in which the Baloch members of the leased areas participated complicated the matter and Pakistan refused to honor the provisions of the Standstill Treaty of 4th August 1947 on the basis of the Shahi-Jirga vote. Shahi-Jirga was a nominated body of tribal chiefs, both Baloch and Pathan, who acted as a consultative and advisory panel to settle disputes. It was non-elective. A tribal chief became the member by virtue of his becoming the Sardar of his tribe. The date for the referendum was fixed on 30th June 1947 but the issue was declared to be decided a day earlier on 29th June. Advancement of the date resulted in a non-participation of five members of the Quetta Municipality and three members of the Shahi-Jirga. The electoral college consisted of forty-three Shahi-Jirga members and twelve persons of Quetta Municipality. Earlier a meeting of Shahi-Jirga was held on 21st June in which the efforts of pro-Pakistan elements to put through a declaration suggesting the accession of British Balochistan to Pakistan, failed and pandemonium prevailed. The meeting had to be broken up. The majority of the members of the Shahi-Jirga and Quetta Municipality were against accession to Pakistan. A conspiracy was hatched by the British authorities with Jafar Khan Jamali and Nawaab Muhammad Khan Jogezai to manipulate the situation in favor of Pakistan. The meeting of the Shahi-Jirga was called a day earlier than scheduled on 29th June in the Municipal Hall. The AGG, Sir George Prior read out the declaration of the Viceroy of India and asked the members to decide the issue of the accession to Pakistan. Soon after the AGG speech, Nawaab Muhammad Khan Jogezai stood up and announced that the members of the Shahi-Jirga had agreed to vote for Pakistan and that the AGG should take cognizance of that fact. This was followed by a few unheard speeches amongst shouts and noises. Four Baloch Sardar of the leased areas wanted an explanation from the AGG as to whether this vote was to determine between the Khanate of Kalat and Pakistan or between Pakistan and India. They also pointed out that they would side with Kalat if it pertained to the sovereignty of Kalat or if their decisions had any effect on the future status of their country. The AGG maintained that this was a matter between the British government and Pakistan. This incorrect statement led to the impression that the question of the leased areas would be decided separately. The meeting could not decide the matter nor was any vote taken. The meeting was again broken up. But the AGG declared that the matter had been resolved and the members had voted for Pakistan. He sent a message on the same day to Delhi informing the British government that the Shahi-Jirga has unanimously voted to join Pakistan without any debate.

The pro-Pakistan members of Shahi-Jirga were in a minority. The Baloch members, except for Jaffar Khan Jamali were in the camp of the Kalat State National Party and the Khan were not in favor of the Baloch areas participating in the voting. The Pakhtun were being mobilized to vote against Pakistan by the Congress and Abdul Samad Khan Achakzai. The Hindu members of the Quetta Municipality were also expected to give a negative vote. Therefore, no voting was allowed and the matter was decided through the pandemonium.

In the partition plan of 3rd June 1947, both Pakistan and the British had accepted the sovereignty of the Kalat. The Muslim League leader, Muhammad Ali Jinnah, in his policy statement on 30 July 1947, also declared his intentions not to interfere in the affairs of the princely states, including Kalat. The Tripartite Agreement between Balochistan, Pakistan and the British on 4th August 1947, called the Standstill Agreement also accepted the sovereign status of Balochistan. Article I of this agreement says that the government of Pakistan recognized the status of Kalat as a free and independent state which has bilateral relation with the British government and whose rank and position is different from that of other Indian states.

After the signing of the Standstill Agreement, Balochistan was declared independent by the Khan on 11th August 1947, three days before the creation of Pakistan. In a speech on the occasion, he declared his intention to build Balochistan as a prosperous sovereign country, free of foreign influence. The aim of an independent Balochistan, he said, would be to achieve unity of purpose among the Baloch so that they could retain their identity and live in accordance with their traditions [34]. In a proclamation on 11th August 1947, the Khan declared that in future the government of Kalat will exercise the complete rights of an independent government in internal and external matters. It will establish relations through treaties of friendship with its neighboring Muslim governments of Afghanistan, Iran, the Arab countries, and in particular with Pakistan and at the same time it will also establish friendly relations and treaties with India and the outside world [35].

Soon after the declaration of independence, elections were held to Balochistan bicameral legislature and a period of tranquility and independence ensured in the country. However, Pakistan began pressurizing for the merger of the Khanate. The Khan appeared to have firmly decided to face the increasing pressure from Pakistan. The Parliament and the tribal sardars were supporting the Khan in his professed aim of remaining independent. Baloch people from all over the country and outside were jubilant about the creation of an independent homeland for them. When the Khan visited Karachi in October 1947, he was received by a large number of the Baloch. In a reception at Masti Khan lodge, the Khan urged the Baloch to make every effort for the uplift of their country and to raise their educational standard. He appealed to the participants of the gathering to inspire the people with freedom and equality. The Khan, however, refused to comment on the nature of negotiation between Kalat and the government of Pakistan. The meeting was exclusively Baloch, and both the address of welcome and reply was made in the Balochi language [36].

In the meantime, the government of Pakistan started a campaign against the Khan aimed at persuading various rulers of Balochistan Union territories to accede to Pakistan. Local elders and petty chiefs were offered large sums of money to betray the unity and integrity of the Baloch state. A statement of one Muhammad Hasan of Lasbela appeared in the Karachi press. The statement said geographically, culturally and socially Lasbela was linked with neighboring Sindh and suggested its amalgamation with Sindh [37]. Statements of such non-entities were a regular feature in Pakistani newspapers. Such reports have always got front-page coverage. Another news item filed from Quetta appeared on the same day regarding Habibullah Khan Nosherwani, the Nawab of Kharan who according to the report had undertaken a seven-day tour of the Zhob district of British Balochistan to bring the tribesmen closer to Pakistan. In his speeches, the paper reports, he promised that the evil mechanization of the enemies of Pakistan would not be allowed to succeed [38]. A statement of one Muraad Awaraani, claiming to be the secretary of the Baloch Jamait, Karachi, appeared on the front page of the daily, Dawn, favoring the accession of Balochistan to Pakistan. Awaraani was never Known as a political or social figure among the Baloch, as painted by Pakistani press. He wanted Kalat to join Pakistan on the grounds of geographical contiguity as well as the wishes of three million Baloch. In his statement, he asserted that segregated from Pakistan, Balochistan cannot exist. Its accession to Pakistan, therefore, was an absolute necessity in its own interests. The statement criticized the National Party as a group of old nationalists who were advising the Khan to remain aloof from Pakistan [39]. The statement prepared and issued on behalf of such persons always contained an element of threat and coercion towards Balochistan. The ruler of Kharan was persuaded by Pakistani authorities to have negotiations with them. Nawab Habibullah Khan left for Karachi via Quetta. He told a journalist on the eve of his departure that Kharan was an independent state and rightly wished to merge with Pakistan [40]. The statement of another tribal elder, Abdul Qadir Shahwani, was found a place on the front pages of Pakistani media. In his statement, he said there was no power in the Kalat state which could stand in the way of unity between Kalat and Pakistan. He regretted that there was opposition to the question of accession in the Kalat parliament [41].

In the meantime, there appeared to be an uneasy calm in the relation between Kalat and Pakistan. Pakistan was indulging in conspiracies and underhand tactics to force the Khan to announce his decision to join, while the public opinion was overwhelmingly against any such action who wanted an independent Balochistan maintaining relations with Pakistan as an equal and sovereign state. The Khan, after years of British rule and subordination, was also mindful of the consequences of any merger of Kalat with Pakistan but, beguiled and impercipient, he was wavering under pressure and the offer of money and privilege from the government of Pakistan. He was also aware of Pakistan's secret maneuvering with some of the tribal leaders in the state and fearful of Pakistan attacking Balochistan with its military might. The Pakistani papers continued to harp on the theme of the accession of the state with increasing intensity. The daily Dawn published a report circulated by the official news agency, API, on 5th March 1948, saying that while the question of Kalat state accession to Pakistan was still in the balance, optimism in informed circles in Karachi regarding the outcome of the issue surprisingly verged on complacency. The self-imposed time limit, the report says fixed by the ruler of Kalat to inform the Pakistani government of the decision of the state assembly on the issue by the end of February, had expired and the Pakistan government was understood to have received no official intimation. The report further added that it was stressed in political quarters that the question of the merger of Balochistan with Pakistan should be viewed under the various angles resulting from its odd political position vis-a-vis Pakistan after the signing of the Standstill Agreement in August 1947. Under the agreement which was signed for an indefinite period, Pakistan was not only responsible for the transport and communications system of the state but was also charged with the responsibility to defend the state frontiers with Afghanistan and Iran, the report claimed. The declaration of independence made by the Khan on the lapse of British rule, the report said, was subject to the provisions of that treaty.

The government of Pakistan was using coercive methods for a forced merged of the Baloch state. The last British advisor to Khan B.Y. Fell who had also served as Foreign Minister of Kalat in 1947, mentioned Pakistani threats to Kalat in a letter to an American scholar. He called Pakistan policies toward Balochistan inappropriate and unjust. He said 'Pakistan was abandoning a sound conservative attitude based upon years of successful British political experience for an aimless and rather childish excursion into power politics'. 'The Balochis', he maintained, 'can be treated either by repression as in Ireland or by conciliation as in Scotland'. If the Baloch problem cannot be solved in the context of the present world order of national economic units at loggerheads with each other, what Fell suggested was that Baloch would have been more valuable to Pakistan in their semi-autonomous state than by their forced inclusion in a centralized administration [42].

The talks between the Khan and the government of Pakistan dragged out for fairly a long time. The Governor-General of Pakistan,

Muhammad Ali Jinnah, visited Balochistan in February 1948. He was welcomed by the Shahi-Jirga in Sibi. The sardars of the Kalat state were also present on the occasion. They were headed by Nawabzada Muhammad Aslam. As a pressure tactic, reports published in Pakistani newspapers gave the impression that Kalat would soon accede to Pakistan. An inspired item appeared regarding the meeting of Jinnah with the Baloch sardars. According to the report, the sardars expressed fears that the Khan might encroach upon their rights and privileges as independent feudal lords. Pakistani papers reported that sardars from Jahlawaan, Sarawaan, Kachhi, Lasbela, and Kharan claim independence while the Khan of Kalat claims sovereignty over them. The report authorized by the government of Pakistan, further maintained that these sardars had already applied for the accession of their states to Pakistan but their request had not been yet accepted by the government of Pakistan [43].

Negotiation between the Khan and the government of Pakistan appeared to have landed in trouble. In the meantime, the government of Pakistan pressurized the two states of the Kalat confederacy, Kharan and Lasbela and the province of Makkuraan, to join Pakistan. It was announced on 17h March 1948 that the Pakistan government had accepted the accession of Lasbela, Kharan, and Makkuraan. Their accession was illegal and without constitutional authority. These states were neither independent entities nor did their rulers have a mandate from the people to decide their political future.

The Khan of Kalat protested to the government of Pakistan over the report that it had accepted the request for accession from constituent units of Balochistan. The Government of Kalat demanded the denial of the report. In a telegram, the Kalat's Foreign Minister called the radio report mischievous and contrary to the Standstill Agreement concluded between the two countries. The telegram mentioned that Khan did not expect that the government of Pakistan as a Muslim neighbor will desire to take any high handed, unjust action against a Muslim neighbor. It recalled that the Khan had received a personal communication on behalf of Muhammad Ali Jinnah saying that relation between Pakistan and Kalat would be negotiated between the two countries. The foreign Minister further maintained that a formal approach to the government of Pakistan was under preparation, and protested strongly against any action in anticipation of receipt this [44]. The government of Pakistan, in a rejoinder, maintained that the Khan had not kept his word to Jinnah and that the Pakistan government had already accepted the merger request of Kharan, Lasbela, and Makkuraan [45]. The government of Kalat also issued a press statement declaring Kharan Lasbela and Makkuraan inalienable parts of Balochistan. A few days later the Khan, in a press interview, expressed his desire for an amicable settlement of the dispute with Pakistan over the accession of three constituent units of Kalat. The Khan also denied any talks which his government was allegedly having with Afghanistan or India [46].

The Khan had now become increasingly worried about Pakistan taking unilateral action against Balochistan. The talks between Jinnah and the Khan appeared to have broken down on the question of accession. This was apparent from a telegram sent by the Balochistan Foreign Minister, D.Y Fell, to Pakistan's Foreign Minister, Zafarullah, who was in the United Nations at that time, which said: 'on March 9th, His highness the Khan of Kalat received a communication on behalf of Quaid-e-Azam Muhammad Ali stating that his Excellency, the Governor-General of Pakistan had decided to cease to deal personally with the Kalat State and to leave the conduct of negotiation to decide the future relations between Pakistan and Kalat to the government of Pakistan. Please take steps so that no illegal or hostile action will be taken against Kalat by the Foreign office during your absence'. Asserting that Lasbela and Kharan were but two feudal states of Kalat and Makkuraan was one of its districts, the Foreign Minister maintained that 'Kalat desires to reach a satisfactory solution with Pakistan by negotiation and the government have taken no decision for or against accession and will take no such decision until you have yourself discussed the matter formally with Kalat's representative' [47].

The government of Pakistan considered the so-called merger of Kharan, Lasbela, and Makkuraan a great achievement in its hostile relation with Balochistan. An editorial in the daily Dawn on 22nd March 1948, fully reflects the attitude of Pakistani authorities regarding possible moves against Kalat. While welcoming the accession of these states, the paper rejects the protest by the government of Kalat saying that 'if his Highness the Khan now finds his position somewhat unenviable, he has been the architect. Thereof, his protest against Pakistan's acceptance of the accession of three members of the confederacy will ring unconvincingly to those who are familiar with the simulation. In their dignified and still friendly rejoinder to the statement issued on behalf of the Kalat state the Pakistan foreign office has revealed a number of illuminating facts and corrected several misstatements. The most important of them we think is that the Khan of Kalat had informed the Quaid-e-Azam during his recent visit to Balochistan that he had decided to accede to Pakistan. All that remained to be done, he had then said, was to make a formal communication to do so by the end of February'.

As pointed out by the Pakistan official organ, the Khan undoubtedly was the architect of this evil. He had given the impression to Pakistani ruler that he would join that country. His attitude was also encouraging to the member states of Kalat whose insensate rulers entered into a conspiracy against Balochistan. For instance, the ruler of Makkuraan, Baiyan Gichki, was his brother in law. It was generally believed then that the Khan himself had connived not only with Baiyan Gichki but with all other petty chiefs for their declaration of accessions. Since all the responsible tribal heads and prudent politicians were opposed to the suggestion of Kalat losing its independence, the Khan was instrumental in bringing an ignoble political catastrophe on the Baloch people and their state. In his paranoid approach, he was posing as a great Muslim nationalist contrary to Baloch sentiments. The Khan obviously did a great wrong to the entire Baloch people, or as put by the leader of the majority party in the Kalat Parliament, Mir Ghous Bakhsh Bizenjo signed the death warrant of fifteen million Baloch: a great crime which could not be remedied in a hundred year.

Pakistan continued to harass the Khan and his state machinery on various pretexts. The Government of Pakistan was preparing a showdown on the basis of a radio report from India that sometime back the Khan had contacted the Indian Union for a possible accession of Balochistan with India. The Khan may have tried to solicit Indian help against possible Pakistani aggression, which was afoot: in any case, he remained steadfast in his unpredictable stand to remain independent. This was confirmed by the Indian Secretary of the States Ministry, V.P Menon. He told a press conference in New Delhi on 27th March 1948 that Kalat had approached the government of India through an agent one or two months ago but we refused to have anything to do with that state. Menon described as utterly false, the report that there had been a negotiation between India and Balochistan, though the latter had made an approach. He repudiated the idea that India could think of giving any financial help or bribes to Kalat. The government of India, Menon maintained, would not have anything to do with any state within or contiguous to Pakistan [48]. Three days later, on 30th March 1948, the Indian Prime Minister, Jawaharlal Nehru, made a statement in parliament to clear up a 'misapprehension that had unfortunately arisen'. Replying to Balkrisha Sharma, he said, 'I greatly regret that owing to an error in reporting, the All India Radio announced on the night of March 27th that the Khan of Kalat had approached the government of India about two months ago through his agents to seek permission to accede to India, but the government of India did not agree. This statement is incorrect. No mention has been made at any time either by the representative of the ruler of Kalat or by the government of India of the accession of the Kalat state to India. In view of the geographical position of the Kalat state, the question did not arise. Certain reports which have appeared in the foreign press about political negotiation between the government of India and the Kalat State are also completely without foundation'. The Prime Minister further added that 'statement that any sum of money has been paid to the Kalat state on behalf of the government and that the government of India has sought air bases in Kalat is also wholly without foundation' [49].

The Khan was fairly scared over the reports of Kalat approaching India as Pakistan was making it clear through various channels that it is also considering appropriate actions against Balochistan if required in the face of new developments. The Pakistani prime minister summoned his military commanders on 26th March 1948 and ordered the Pakistan army to move into the Baloch coastal regions of Pasni and Jiwani. Troops were also sent to Turbat. This was the first act of Military aggression against Balochistan. Later, its garrison commander in Quetta was ordered to march on Kalat on 1st April 1948 and arrest the Khan unless he signed an agreement to accession [50].

The Khan's statement on 27th March declaring unconditional accession was prompted by the reports of the troop movements on the Makkuraan coast and the marching orders on Kalat. The Khan's capitulation ended 227 days of independence of the Kalat State after the British withdrawal. The Khanate had lasted nearly three hundred years. The Khan acceded to Pakistan without consulting the Parliament and ignoring the wishes of the people of Balochistan. In a statement to the press he said:

"On the night of March 27th, all India Radio announced that two months ago Kalat had approached the Indian Union to accept its accession to India and that the Indian union had rejected the request. This news is most surprising and disturbing to me as a Muslim neighbor of Pakistan. It has never been my intention to accede to India as my government or myself never moved the Indian Union either in writing or through an agent that it should accept the accession of Kalat state. A telegraphic request was at once made to the governor-general of India to contradict the announcement or as an alternative to release to the press for public information any correspondence that the Indian Union may have received on this subject. Prima facie, this is nothing but a piece of false propaganda carried on by a self-interested section in India with two motives behind it. First, to spoil the negotiation that is at present being conducted between Pakistan and Kalat and secondly, to give a false impression to the world that they are right in their policy in respect of Kashmir, Jamnagar, and Hyderabad. Let me make it clear in unequivocal terms that no earthly power separates Kalat and its ruler from Pakistan as we are all Muslims. Followers of the same prophet (Peace be upon him) believing in the Quran and worshipping a single god. We have to live and die together. We may have differences but not to the extent that may cause disunity and lead to separation. The efforts the ruler of Kalat has been able to make during the last ten years under the guidance of Quaid-e-Azam, for the achievement of Pakistan, are no secret.

Some time was and perhaps is still required for the clarification on differences of viewpoints existing between Kalat and Pakistan. But my very first reaction after hearing the news was that no time should be lost to put an end to the false propaganda and to avoid and forestall the possibility of friction between Muslim brethren in Kalat and Pakistan as a result of the mischievous news.

It is therefore declared that (a) from 9 pm on March 27th the time I heard the false news over the AIR, I forthwith decided to accede to Pakistan (b) whatever differences of viewpoint at the present exist between Kalat and Pakistan should be placed in writing before the Quaid-e- Azam whose decision I shall accept.

I trust that by the grace of God my sardars and people will welcome the decision taken by me.

Long live Islam; long live Quaid-e-Azam; long live the Muslim government of Pakistan; long live the Muslim Government of Kalat" [51].

Under the constitution of the Khanate, as the constitutional head, the Khan could not undertake a decision of such far-reaching consequences without the approval of the state Assembly, which had already refused to accede. No Khan was ever empowered to bring about any change which might affect the tradition and customs of the people. Accession to another country or surrendering the country's sovereignty was a grave issue which could not be decided by the Khan in any capacity whatsoever. Therefore, the Khan had transgressed in exceeding his mandate. His decision was illegal, immoral and unconstitutional. Many Baloch intellectuals still consider their continued inclusion in the country of Pakistan to be illegal and without any justification.

The accession was decided in haste after reports of Pakistan troops' movement. The ruler of Kalat was well aware that when Pakistan could not be deterred from organizing and sending a tribal Lashkar to achieve a forced merger of Kashmir, it obviously would do the same in the case of Balochistan. The government of Pakistan had already indicated its hostile attitude by inviting the nominal rulers of the Kalat constituent units to accede: now the way was clear for a military operation against Kalat under any pretext. The Khan was mindful that the report on all India Radio regarding the Khan's contacts with India would be taken very seriously by Pakistan. The Khan approach to the Indian Union was not denied by either the India spokesman, V.P Menon in his press conference on 27th March, or the Prime Minister in his 30th March statement in Parliament. What was, however, contradicted was the substance of the talks or the possible Indian moves in Balochistan. The decision to contact the government of India must have been taken by the Khan to determine the extent of support, military or financial he could have possibly obtained from that country in case of hostilities with Pakistan on the one hand, and on the other, to use the Indian interest in Balochistan affairs as a bargaining point in his negotiation for personal privileges with the government of Pakistan. But the Indian leaders were fully aware of the wavering personality and political virility, the Khan had shown throughout the period of the freedom movement and his close contacts with the Muslim League and its leader, Muhammad Ali Jinnah, who had also worked as Khan's legal advisor, had made the Indian leaders somewhat suspicious of the Khan motives. Moreover, with the Indian problem over Kashmir, where the Indian government was anxiously trying for a ceasefire, any action in support of Kalat could have put the Indian leadership in an awkward position on the world stage. The Indian analysis of the situation was completely correct. The Khan decided on the accession of Balochistan merely on the basis of a news story from a foreign broadcasting station and a threat of military action by the Pakistan government. This is without parallel in world history.

What prompted the Khan's action was the impending army operation by Pakistan. Orders for which had already been issued and deliberately leaked out scared the Khan. As an alternative, Pakistan could have organized a so-called tribal *Lashkar* from Kharan or Lasbela to attack Kalat, and then in an attempt to stop the fighting, the Pakistan army could have moved into the state. Pakistan was, however, taking the first option of direct aggression against Balochistan. In any eventuality, the Khan could fairly guess the pre-ordained fate of his state and rule. Declaring in haste his illegal decision to accede under the shadow of military intervention, he tried as a last resort to save the privileges the government of Pakistan had already offered in return for this disservice to the Baloch cause. With three of his member states already bribed away. Perhaps he saw very little room for maneuver for a more favorable agreement with Pakistan regarding his personal privileges and privy purse, which he discreetly referred to in his statement of accession as 'differences of viewpoint' which were not of an extent that might cause 'disunity and lead to separation'. Obviously, by that time, the Khan was little concerned with the gloomy destiny of his state and people but more with the facilities which he had been promised by his erstwhile trusted legal advisor, now the Governor-General of Pakistan, Muhammad Ali Jinnah. He was worried that under the shadow of rumors and reports from All India Radio which had been given credence because of his continued reluctance to announce an accession he might engender suspicion and end up in the wilderness.

The Baloch leaders, on the other hand never even entertained the idea of joining Pakistan. Lawrence Ziring, a well-known authority on Pakistani affairs, maintains that Baloch leaders did not enter into the arrangement to join Pakistan willingly. The government of Pakistan was threatening to use force to achieve the accession of the country.

The Baloch sardars and the Khan were ill-prepared to ignore this fact [52].

The Khan was a man of deep complexes. He was wholly responsible for the entire episode. In a misguided religious zeal, he started negotiation with Pakistan through his Prime Minister and Foreign Minister. Pakistani Foreign Secretary, Ikramullah Khan, spurned any discussions and demanded in September 1947 that Kalat should accede to Pakistan. The Khan also discussed the possibility of Balochistan joining even Iran or Afghanistan. Surprisingly, he was hesitant to entertain the idea of remaining independent as cherished by his subjects. He finally decided to merge his country with Pakistan and directed his Prime Minister, over the head of the Parliament and the people, to engage in talks with that country. It is ironic that a ruler should bargain away his county sovereignty without any genuine cause.

The accession to Pakistan was one of the epoch-making events in the entire history of the Baloch people and their country. The Baloch state came to an end after nearly three hundred years. The previous Khans fought gallantly in defense of the state while the present ruler bargained away the country's sovereignty and its people to a new state founded on a notion negating the right of any nationalities which may form part of it. Mir Naseer Khan resisted the most powerful Monarch of the region in the eighteenth century, Ahmad Shah Durrani, who not only dominated Afghanistan but most part of central Asia and the Indian sub-continent. He was successful in obtaining an agreement that guaranteed Kalat's sovereignty. The present Khan was in a most prestigious position in the twentieth century, with the entire Baloch people behind him and backed by world opinion and most probably the support from neighboring countries. He could have saved Balochistan from subjugation and strengthened the Baloch homeland, which would have been the center of nationalistic aspirations for the Baloch throughout the world. Mir Naseer Khan succeeded because he was determined and sagacious: Ahmad Yar Khan failed because he was myopic and lacked self-confidence. Mir Naseer Khan established Baloch confederacy on a firm footing: Ahmad Yar Khan destroyed it for no genuine cause whatsoever. Both will be remembered in history: the former for his bravery, political acumen and strong affection towards his people; the later for his cowardice to face the realities of political exigencies and for his betrayal of a cause which the Baloch cherished. Mir Naseer Khan gathered the Baloch into a well-knitted unit based on tribal affiliations and harmony; Ahmad Yar Khan created a wedge among his subjects and helped destroy the very fabric of Baloch society and its sovereign status. Mir Naseer Khan is revered while Ahmad Yar Khan is being scorned. Ahmad Yar Khan capitulated when the Pakistan army threatened to March on Kalat while Mir Mehraab Khan faced the invading British troops, giving his life in the battle so that the Baloch could live in honor and respect. He added a glorious chapter to Baloch history. Ahmad Yar Khan surrendered without a fight, disregarding the will of his people and in the process lost the country. If he had resisted, the geopolitical map of central Asia would have been quite different and the Baloch would have been ruling their country with honor and respect.

6- The Accession: Initial Reaction

The unconstitutional decision of Ahmad Yar Khan to accede sent a wave of alarm and deep resentment through the people. The reaction was one of shocked surprise among political workers and tribal heads. The Khan's younger brother and former governor of Makkuraan, Prince Abdul Kareem, reacted violently. Within two weeks of the accession, he crossed over to Afghanistan with a considerable number of followers. He wanted to solicit Afghan help in organizing and conducting a guerrilla war against Pakistan. His opposition to the merger put the Khan in a very bad light with his people and the government of Pakistan. While the people proudly referred to Abdul Kareem and lauded his courage and foresight. Khan himself was never accorded any respect after his announcement. The government of Pakistan was watching the situation in Balochistan with keen interest. Its leaders were suspicious of reports that the prince had taken a larger number of arms and ammunition from the state armory, sufficient ration to sustain his men for a long time and also jewelry which could not have been taken out without official knowledge or permission of the Khan himself. In a report filed by a special correspondent from Quetta, the official newspaper Dawn on 1st June 1948 dealt with this aspect of the issue and expressed doubts that all this could possibly have been done without official knowledge. The report noted that Jinnah, during his recent meeting with the Khan must have discussed the alarming situation, in Balochistan. The report also expressed concern over the activities of some elements disloyal to Pakistan, the allusion was clearly to the Kalat State National Party, which was opposing the accession. The paper suggested that a purge in the Kalat administration removing Prime Minister Fell would be advisable under the circumstances. Earlier the paper, in an editorial welcoming the accession of Kalat to Pakistan, had cautioned about the activities of the National Party and called for action against those opposed to Pakistan [53]. In another editorial on 2nd June 1948 captioned Kalat Affairs, Dawn again criticized the National Party as a coterie of discredited political workers known for close association with the Indian National Congress in the past and for its more recent opposition to accession. The paper charged the party with arousing sectional feelings in Balochistan. It urged a purge of disloyal elements from the state administration.

In the meantime, Prince Kareem's movement attracted favorable responses from various quarters among the Baloch. According to newspaper reports, two more officials of the Kalat administration crossed to Afghanistan on 3rd June 1948 to join the rebellious prince. The reports further add that they, along with some other persons crossed to Afghanistan at Shorawak carrying with them ration and ammunition. The report mentioned that the prince's original group who went to Afghanistan included several state employees. It maintained that surprise was expressed in political quarters that despite precautions supposed to have been taken by the state authorities, more officials, more food and more arms and ammunition should still be leaving Kalat on the traitorous mission [54]. In an editorial on 15th July 1948, the Dawn while expressing concern over the activities of Prince Abdul Kareem who, the paper said, could not have crossed the border with huge supplies without the knowledge and connivance of the Balochistan authorities also condemned the National Party for its anti-Pakistan role. The paper expressed concern that Kalat state employees were also playing a part in the anti-Pakistan activities of the Party and of Prince Abdul Kareem.

During his stay in Afghanistan, Prince Kareem tried to solicit help from that country and the Soviet Union. The Afghan government refused any support, because to them any movement for an independent Balochistan would negate their own stand on Pakhtunistan. The Afghan government, therefore, was not in favor of Prince Kareem staying in their territory and carrying out hostilities against the government of Pakistan. The Prince was also cold-shouldered by the Russians. The Russian officials in Kabul expressed their sympathy for the Baloch cause but promised no assistance [55]. Disillusioned, Prince Kareem decides to return to Balochistan after staying in Afghanistan for nearly three months. During this period, he was mostly encamped in Sarlat, an Afghan district adjacent to Balochistan. He returned to Balochistan on 8th July 1948. He was arrested along with scores of his followers after some minor clashes near Harboi with the Pakistan army. Earlier, on 24th May 1948, Prince Kareem was declared an anti-state person by the Khan of Kalat. He was tried by a special Jirga in Mach Jail and sentenced to ten years imprisonment on 4th December 1948. His colleague and advisor, Mir Muhammad Husain Unqa, a poet and intellectual also received the sentence of ten years imprisonment. His other followers received sentences ranging from one to seven-year confinement.

Prince Kareem's rebellion was the first in a series of insurrection against the government of Pakistan. Prince Kareem went to Afghanistan in the hope of acquiring support for a sustained war against Pakistan and finding the situation unfavorable in that country returned to Kalat. With the increasing pressure on the Khan by the government of Pakistan the Khan must have prevailed upon his younger brother, convinced him of the futility of armed resistance against the might of Pakistan and persuaded him to surrender. Obviously, the initial euphoria must have subsided and the prince decided not to pursue his hazardous course.

After their release from prison on 18th June 1955, Prince Abdul Kareem and Mir Unqa called a meeting of political workers, mostly belonging to the National Party, in Karachi on 14th July 1955 and formed a political organization, the Usthumaan Gal. Prince Kareem became the President and Qadir Bakhsh Nizamani it's General Secretary. The Party had identical objectives to those of the National Party. However, under the changed circumstances, Usthuman Gal mentioned its goal of creating a separate province for the Baloch people on the basis of ethnicity, geography, culture, and language. It demanded that all the Baloch areas of Balochistan were to be merged in a separate [56] Province where Balochi would be the official language. It also supported the establishment of a democratic federal political system in the country with equal rights and provincial autonomy for the constituent units. Earlier in 1950, the Baloch nationalists, headed by Abdul Kareem Showrish, a former General Secretary of the National Party had formed the Balochistan peace Committee with the aim of struggling for the right of self-determination for the Baloch people. This committee could not make any headway and was soon to be replaced by the Usthumaan Gal.

7- Balochistan in Pakistan: Initial Years

The government of Pakistan assumed absolute power in Balochistan on 15th April 1948 and the State was administered by officials from Karachi. In late 1950, the Pakistani government broached the idea of forming the Balochistan States Union by merging the states of Lasbela, Makkuraan, and Kharaan into Kalat. On 11th April 1952, a covenant was arrived at by leaders of these states, which was approved by the government of Pakistan. The covenant maintained that the leaders of the four states were convinced that the welfare of the people of the region can best be secured by the establishment of the United States comprising territories of the respective states with a common executive, legislature and judiciary, under the constitution of Pakistan. The document provided for a council of rulers. With one of the rulers elected as its president. The Prime Minister was to be a nominee of the government of Pakistan. An interim constitution provided for the legislative assembly of 28 elected and 12 nominated members. Elections to the first legislative Assembly were to be held by early 1952. As a consequence of this arrangement, the Pakistan government appointed Aagha Abdul Hamid, a civil servant, as the Prime Minister of the Balochistan States Union (BSU) in April 1952. On 16th June 1954, the Pakhtun areas of former British Balochistan were included in the BSU. However, nearly a year later, the whole phenomenon collapsed when the BSU was dissolved by the government, merging it in the One-Unit scheme in West Pakistan.

The Khan, Ahmad Yar Khan, felt betrayed. He never expected his exclusion from the government. He started maneuvering in order to influence political events in the country. He tried a workable relationship with the Pakistani President Iskandar Mirza. But he was unaware that Iskandar Mirza was using him to create an apparent uncertainty in the country to assume absolute powers.

The Khan, encouraged by the President, convened a meeting of the tribal chiefs of Balochistan on 17th September 1957. The chiefs submitted a memorandum to the Khan expressing their full faith and confidence in Pakistan and assured their continued cooperation and loyalty. The sardars claimed that they were keeping a strong vigil on the border against activities detrimental to the interests of Pakistan. However, they expressed their apprehension that the One-Unit type of government was dangerous to Baloch's socio-cultural traditions and their way of life. They demanded that the Baloch should be treated at par with the people of the Northwest Frontier Province (NWFP), where tribal customs and traditions were being respected [57].

The President of Pakistan agreed to meet the Khan along with his forty-four sardars to discuss their demands. The meeting was convened on 8th October 1957. The Baloch sardars demanded that there should not be any interference in their internal socio-cultural affairs by the government and that the ex-Khan of Kalat should be consulted when administrative or legal changes were to be introduced in Balochistan by the federal government of Pakistan [58].

With the active support and encouragement of President Iskandar Mirza, the Khan, for his part, was becoming instrumental in Pakistani power politics. He wanted to convey the impression that he had great influence among the Baloch and that he deserves to be accommodated in the government. The Khan was little interested in the welfare of the people or their political participation but wanted to have some position for him in power corridors of the state. In the beginning, he was instrumental in bringing in the One-Unit system which he later began to condemn. As the president of BSU, he had signed an agreement with the then Governor-General of Pakistan on 1st January 1955 for the accession of the territories of Balochistan States Union and the leased areas of Kalat into the proposed One-Unit of West Pakistan.

During the meeting with Baloch sardars, the President of Pakistan promised to consult his legal advisers on the question of the exemption of BSU and its leased areas from One-Unit and retaining its original position. He also hinted at the possibility of restoring the BSU after examining the constitutional and legal aspects of the issue. In the meantime, he promised that Baloch traditions and way of life would be preserved as far as possible. The Khan was also advised by Iskandar Mirza to avail himself of the services of a legal expert, preferably Lord

MacNair of London, and seek his advice on whether the withdrawal of the BSU from the One-Unit would weaken the position of the federal government. Iskandar Mirza also broached the idea of conducting a referendum in the BSU to back up such a decision [59].

The real intention, of Pakistani president in encouraging the Khan on this issue is not known [60]. However, later events showed that he wanted some pretext to abrogate the constitution and declare Martial Law in the country. He had groomed the Khan to provide that opportunity. Lawrence Ziring believed that the Khan was being ingenious and simple when the word was passed to him that the country's political system was about to crumble and that he would be restored to his crown, he quickly accepted the bait. It was his understanding that President Mirza had sanctioned the re-establishment of his kingdom and that it would be advisable to move with immediate speed to demonstrate his capacity to govern the state. The Khan had no idea that he was being duped, that his action would be publicized as a secessionist plot and that the whole affair would be used to justify not only military action against his person but throughout the entire country [61].

Meanwhile, the situation in Pakistan was getting worse and Iskandar Mirza was planning to assume dictatorial powers. The perceived threat of the disintegration of the country was the main excuse. It was propagated that the Baloch were preparing a *Lashkar* of eighty thousand men to fight for their liberation. The Khan, Ahmad Yar Khan, was arrested by the Pakistani army after a maximum show of force in Kalat on the morning of 6th October 1958, a day before Martial Law was formally proclaimed in the country. The Khan's wife and children were also taken into custody and exiled to Chowa Saidan Shah in Punjab. Many people were killed by the army during the operation in Kalat. The army occupied the Khan's residence, and possessions including ancient valuables, ancestral coins of the family, and numerous other antiques. The Kalat armory was taken away by the army. The palace was virtually looted. It was also thoroughly searched for possible anti-government literature and an alleged currency printing machine [62].

It was also reported by the government that some three hundred people were gathered at Kalat to obstruct the removal of the Khan from Kalat and that the Pakistan army had to open fire to disperse the crowd. The government of Pakistan put the casualties as three killed and two wounded of the Khan followers, while one was killed and two others received injuries from the army side [63]. The government announced that the Khan had been taken into preventive custody and divested of all the distinctions, privileges and annuities conferred upon him by the Pakistan government. The newspapers reported that Khan was involved in rebellious activities by pulling down the national flag of Pakistan from the Miri and hoisting his own ancestral flag a week before his arrest. He was also blamed for ignoring the President's invitation to meet him to discuss the situation. Instead, he was accused of asking the President to come to his ancestral Mirri Fort in Kalat for the meeting. The Pakistan Government alleged that Prince Kareem and an uncle of the Khan had been secretly negotiating with Afghanistan to get support for a full-scale Baloch rebellion. However, the only evidence brought to substantiate the allegations was the fact that Khan's Afghan wife had gone to Kabul for a holiday [64].

Although the Khan of Kalat neither had support nor enjoyed any respect among the people after his suicidal decision to accede to Pakistan, the latest events had given the people some hopes that Balochistan might at least gain some sort of autonomy. President Mirza's relationship with the Khan was an encouragement to nationalist political activists, who would welcome a semblance of autonomy for their country. Therefore, the Baloch elite was generally happy over the situation and expected some concession from the government of Pakistan. Khan's earlier journey to Britain seeking legal advice was taken as sufficient proof of the Pakistani government's sincerity.

The arrest of the Khan came as a big surprise for the Baloch. The killing of innocent people and the looting of Kalat was deeply resented by the people throughout Balochistan. A protest march took place in Quetta against the arrest of the Khan and the killings. Nearly fifty Baloch leaders and political workers were taken into custody. The happening reminded the Baloch of the extent of their political subjugation. They had also experienced a similar event a hundred and twenty years ago when the British forces had attacked Kalat and killed their Khan. But there was a qualitative difference between these events. Mir Mehraab Khan, true to his Baloch blood, resisted and was killed on the battlefield, while Ahmad Yar Khan simply surrendered before the advancing troops. On both occasions, the Baloch masses took the affront with courage and fortitude. The later happening revealed the mechanizations of Pakistan. In fact, all the encouragements to the Khan by the President of Pakistan were aimed at creating suspicion in the minds of the military men to pave the way for declaring Martial Law in the country. Ahmad Yar Khan in no way had the courage to unfurl the flag he had removed a decade earlier. He did not possess the capability and will to pose any threat to Pakistan.

The operations in Kalat sparked off a series of rebellious activities in Balochistan, especially in the mountainous regions of Jahlawaan. The people revolted not because of any respect for the Khan but out of deep fear of compromising their political sovereignty and a grave threat to their socio-cultural identity. The masses in consultation with the tribal elders now started mobilizing to face the advancing troops. On 8th October 1958, the Pakistani army moved into Jahlawaan and mounted a great search operation for arms and ammunition. The army movement was halted for the first time at Dancer, where only three youth stood in the way of advancing troops. They held them for three days till one was killed and the remaining two were critically wounded [65]. The army penetrated up to Wadh and ordered the villagers to surrender their weapons. Mir Norouz Khan, along with a sizable number of followers took to the hills of Mir Ghat. He demanded inter alia the unconditional release of the Khan. The army commander, Colonel Tikka Khan who afterward gained notoriety in the genocide in Bengal in 1971, ordered the bombardment of the house of Mir Norouz Khan, which was razed to the ground and all the property confiscated.

Mir Norouz Khan engaged the army for nearly a year. The government responded by bombarding the villages and imposing a reign of terror in the entire area. But the troops failed to counter the activities of the resistance fighters. In order to deceive the leader of the resistance, government envoys met his representatives and took an oath on the holy Quran, that if he stopped hostilities and surrendered to the government along with his comrades, he would be received honorably for peace negotiation and the Baloch demands would be considered sympathetically [66]. Mir Norouz, in his simplicity, could not imagine a mean deception after an oath taken on the Holy Book of Muslims by the government official. He agreed to meet the military officers, but when he came down from the mountains for discussion, he and his associates were arrested and removed to a concentration camp, Quli camp, in the Quetta cantonment area.

Mir Norouz Khan and seven of his colleagues, including his elder son, were tried in Hyderabad and sentenced to death on charges of treason. The death sentence on Mir Norouz was commuted to life imprisonment because of his old age. He was above ninety years at that time. He died in a Pakistani prison in 1964. Others, Mir Sabzal Khan Zehri, Mir Masti Khan, Mir Bahawal Khan, Mir Jamal Khan and the elder son of Mir Norouz, Mir Batay Khan were hanged on 15th July 1960 in Hyderabad and Sukkar jails. Their bodies were taken to Balochistan and buried in the graveyard of Kalat Nasiri as per their last wishes. There was a general mourning for the executed souls. Their bodies were received with all solemnity and greatest respect. Hundreds of people turned out to participate in the burial ceremonies in Kalat. Mir Jalal Khan Zarakzai, Mir Bahand Khan, Mir Muhammad Umar, and Mir Dilmuraad were given life imprisonment.

After the executions, the government ordered an intensification of the military operation. The leadership of the insurgency had now passed on the hands of political activists, who condemned the cruelties of the army against the people. On the eve of President General Ayub Khan's visit to Quetta in August 1962, a meeting of political workers was convened in which the Baloch leaders warned Ayub Khan against contemplating a military solution of the Baloch issue. The Pakistani military dictator was infuriated and publicly threatened the Baloch with total extinction if they continued with resistance activities [67].

By July 1963, the guerrilla activities had increased in Jahlawaan and Mari areas. The fighters had established a score of camps, where the people were given training in guerrilla warfare. It was estimated that there were nearly 400 hardcore militants in each camp, besides hundreds of loosely organized part-time reservists [68]. The guerrillas engaged the Pakistan army over an area of more than four thousand square miles, where a few hotly contested battles were fought between the militants and the government forces during 1964-65. In December 1964, some five hundred Mari attacked an army camp in the area, which resulted in heavy casualties on both sides. The battle was provoked by the army, which had bulldozed the agricultural fields of the relatives of one of the guerrilla commanders, Mir Sher Mahmad Mari. Another battle was fought in the Gharur area in December 1965, where the Pakistani army reportedly suffered heavy casualties. In another battle in Bambore that year, the army allegedly used napalm bombs in its air raids. Many more battles were fought in 1966.

Government troops advanced from Quetta into Mari's heartland. They met with stiff resistance. Reinforcements were rushed in to relieve the beleaguered soldiers. Large contingents of Pishin scouts from Zhob were ordered into the Mari area and troops from South Waziristan were also moved in. There was bitter fighting and both sides suffered heavy losses. General Ayub who wanted to show the world that he enjoyed universal support in the country tried to initiate a reconciliation process with the Baloch. During the insurrection, the government had replaced the chiefs of those tribes who were engaged in hostile activities with Sardar of its own choice in Jahlawaan, Mari and Bugti areas. Sardar Athaullah Mengal, Sardar Khair Bakhsh Mari and Nawab Akbar Bugti were replaced, but the new sardars were bitterly opposed by the people, all of them were murdered by their own tribesmen to register their opposition to the government move. This further aggravated the conflict. The government realized the futility of its actions, and after some maneuvering, a general amnesty was announced by the Pakistani Government in January 1967: the Baloch leaders were released apparently on the mercy appeal of the sardars of Kalat and Quetta divisions and their follies and misconduct, were pardoned [69]. The Government reinstated the tribal chiefs once again in their positions and promised to concede many of their political demands. The rebellion was called off by Baloch leaders in 1967 and Balochistan returned to an uneasy calm after nearly a decade of unrest and war.

References

1. Inayatullah Baloch: The Baloch Question in Pakistan and the right of self-determination. Wolf Gang-peter Single (ed) Pakistan in its Fourth Decade. Deutsches Orient Institute, Hamburg, 1983, p 11.

2. Ibid.

3. There is no proper evidence of any direct military support to Mir Gwahraam by the Sindhi Rulers. Cf, Anwar Roman: Ainae Baloch. Qasr e Adab, Multan, p 31. Mir Khuda Bakhsh Mari: Searchlight on the Balochistan Op.Cit. p 184.

4. It is generally believed that Rind-Lashaartribes had fought and defeated Mir OumarMirwadi of Kalat. But according to many folk accounts, the Mirwadis had already given way to Jadgaal over-lordship by the time of the Rind-Lashaarintrusion. Therefore, Kalat was captured from Jadgaal and not from Mirwadis.

5. In 1810 AD, a British Intelligence Officer, Major Pottinger, saw a register in Kalat showing Baloch armed strength as 250,000 men (A.W. Hughes: Country of Balochistan. Op. Cit, p 49). This may be the entire number of able-bodied tribesmen who could be mobilized in a national emergency. During the Khanate or Rind Lashaartribal union, even a portion of such a large number of troops had never been used in active hostilities.

6. Muhammad Sardar Khan Baloch: History of Baloch Race and Balochistan. Op. Cit, p 85.

7. Olaf Caroe: The Pathan, London, 1958, (Reprinted) Union Book Stall, Karachi,1973, pp 372-373.

8. Gul Khan Naseer: Balochistan: Qadeem o JadeedTharikhKi Roshni Mein. Nisa Traders, Quetta,1982. p 288.

9. Ibid. PP 191-192.

10. Ibid. PP 291-292

11. Ibid. P 293

12. Ibid. PP 297-298

13. Ibid. PP 294-295

14. Daily Zamindar, Lahore, 22nd October 1932.

15. Balochi Dunya, Multan, June-July 1970.

16. AL -Hanif, Jacobadad,1973, (Special number on Balochistan)

17. In the same convention, the Kalat State National Party elected Mir Abdul Aziz Kurd as its first President. Malik Faiz Muhammad and Mir Gul Khan Naseer were elected as the vice president and General Secretary of the party respectively.

18. Gul Khan Naseer: Balochistan: Qadeem oJadeedTharikhki Roshni mein. Op. Cit. pp 323-324.

19. Gul Khan Naseer: Tharikh-e-Balochistan, (VOl II) Qoumi Kitab Ghar, Quetta, 1956, p 476.

20. The president of the Kalat State National party, in one of his numerous communications to the government on 11th April 1941, criticized the

internment orders on the party workers and demanded that the orders should be withdrawn. The party also explained its stand on the question of political support to the Khan's government. In another letter addressed to Khan the Party again criticized his government's attitude towards the Party and its backing of elements and sardars responsible for breaking up the party convention in 1939. The Party asked the Khan to rescind the internment orders on its workers and leaders. The Prime Minister, on 3rd January 1942, in response to a communication from the Kalat State National Party refused its workers entry into the state without 'a formal written undertaking' individually that they would not carry out any subversive propaganda against either his Highness, the Khan, the officials or the Sardars of the state. The letter recalled that government orders were being modified allowing individual entry in the hope that the party workers would refrain from any such act which may impede the orderly progress of the state or the efficient prosecution of the war (Unpublished).

21. Gul Khan Naseer: Tharikh-e Balochistan (Vol II) Op.Cit.

22. Abdul Kareem Showrish, quoted in Inayatullah Baloch: The Baloch Question in Pakistan and the Right of self-determination, wolf Gang-peter Zingel(ed): Pakistan in its fourth Decade Deutsches Orient Institute, Hamburg, 1983, p 195.

23. Malik Abdur Raheem Khawajakhel, Mir Ghous Bakhsh Bizenjo, and Malik Faiz Muhammad attended many meetings of the Conference held in Jodhpur, Jaipur, and Delhi. They explained the Balochistan situation in the context of the Indian freedom movement. Balochi Dunya: Multan, June 1973. Nokien Dour: Quetta, 21st October 1966.

24. The Kalat State National Party Resolution: Balochistan Press, Quetta.

25. Partly reported in Ahmad Yar Khan: Tharikh-e- Khawanin-e- Baloch. Islamia Press, Quetta, pp 357-359.

26. Gul Khan Naseer: Tharikh-e- Balochistan (Vol II) Op. Cit. p 541.

27. Gul Khan Naseer: Thrik-e-Balochistan (Vol I and II) Kalat Publishers, Quetta,1979, p 503.

28. Jang (Quetta) 28th January 1985.

29. Ahmad Yar Khan: Inside Balochistan. Op. Cit. p 265.

30. Ibid. pp 262-266.

31. Inayatullah Baloch: Op. Cit. p.196.

32. Ahmad Yar Khan: Inside Balochistan, Op. Cit. pp 255-256.

33. Gul Khan Naseer: Balochistan: Qadeem o JadeenTharikhki Roshni Mien. Op. Cit. pp 328-329.

34. Announcement of the Government of Kalat (Pamphlet) Quetta, 1947, quoted in Inayatullah Baloch: Op. Cit. p 197.

35. Dawn, 17th October 1947. The Khan arrived in Karachi and stayed in the capital as the guest of the Pakistan government. He had discussions with the country's rulers concerning relations between Pakistan and Kalat. Surprisingly, the khan was not received by any political figure at the airport on his arrival and the visit got minimum coverage in Pakistani newspapers.

36. Dawn, 12th December 1947.
37. Ibid.
38. Ibid.14th November 1947.
39. Ibid. 29th January 1948.
40. Ibid. 4th March 1948.
41. D.Y. Fell, quoted in Lawrence Ziring: Op. Cit. p 160.
42. Dawn, 14th February 1948.
43. Ibid. 21st March 1948.
44. Ibid.
45. Ibid. 27th March 1948.
46. Ibid. 21st March 1948. ·
47. Ibid. 29th March 1948.
48. Ibid. 1st April 1948.
49. Selig S. Harrison: In Afghanistan's Shadow: Baloch Nationalism and Soviet Temptations. Carnegie Endowment for International Peace, New York, 1981, p,25. Muhammad Asghar Khan: Op. Cit. p 117.
50. Lawrence Ziring, Op, Cit. p 160.
51. Dawn, 30th March 1948.
52. Inayatullah Baloch Op. Cit. P 200.
53. Dawn,10th June 1948.
54. Inayatullah Baloch, Op.Cit.
55. Gul Khan Naseer: Balochistan Qadeem o Jadeed Tharikh Ki Roshni Mien. Op. Cit. pp 337-338.
56. Ouman (Karach) August 1955 p.3.
57. Ahmad Yar Khan: Inside Balochistan. Op Cit. pp 169-170.
58. Ibid. pp171-172.
59. Ibid.
60. The Khan maintained afterward that Iskandar Mirza had demanded five million rupees from him for the favors of withdrawing Balochistan from the One-Unit. (Ahmad Yar Khan: Inside Balochistan. Op. Cit. pp172-172).
61. Ziring: Op. Cit. pp 162-163.
62. Ahmad Yar Khan: Inside Balochistan, Op. Cit. pp 182-183
63. Dawn, 7th October 1958.
64. Selig Harrison: Op. Cit. pp 27-28.
65. Ahmad Yar Khan: Inside Balochistan. Op. Cit. p 185.
66. Ibid. p 186.
67. Ibid. p 189.
68. Selig Harrison: Op. Cit. p 30.
69. Ibid.p.95

CHAPTER VI

THE BALOCH STUDENTS ORGANIZATION: STRUGGLE AND ACHIEVEMENTS

After, the Anjuman, the Kalat State National Party, Usthaman Gal, and the National Awami Party, the most significant organization in the context of Baloch national struggle is the students' movement, the Baloch Students Organization, (henceforth referred to as) BSO. The BSO was primarily aimed at the promotion of educational and cultural activities among the Baloch youth.

Balochistan has been backward in education. During British rule, the country lacked a proper educational system. In 1891, there was only one high school and one middle school for boys and one middle school for girls. There were only 27 boys and nearly fifteen girls enrolled in these schools. This number was raised to 14 schools, mostly in Quetta municipality, in 1901. Two European schools in Quetta with only 31 students started functioning in 1902. The pupils were usually given some religious education and primary knowledge in Persian, the court language, through mosque schools. In 1903, it was estimated that some two thousand pupils were being given religious education in these mosques [1].

Until the early fifties, there were hardly any proper institutions of higher learning in Balochistan. Baloch youth began to join school and colleges, mostly in Mastung and Quetta, in the late fifties and early sixties. With the opening of a college in Khuzdar in 1963, there were

169

three centers of education: Quetta, Mastung, and Khuzdar. Kalat, the Khanate capital, where a high school functioned for a long time, attracted no students from outside Kalat proper.

Although, few in number, the influence of students and the educated class in the society were considerable. Socio-political and economic conditions cast their grim shadow on the thinking of educated people. The youth in schools and colleges began to realize the magnitude of their political subjugation and helplessness. These educated people belonged to a primitive society under a tribal system which was reshaped in its contemporary tyrannical form by alien rulers. To them, education was the only means of equipping themselves with the confidence and hope needed to shoulder the great responsibilities for the future of their nation.

In Quetta, students hailing from far-flung areas met nationalist leaders like Mir Ghous Bakhsh Bizenjo and Mir Gul Khan Naseer. The latter had considerable influence on them because of his revolutionary poetry. The National Party activists, like Abdul Kareem Showrish, who had started the newspaper Noukien Dour, had profound respect among the youth, who contributed articles to his paper on Balochi language and literature. Political commentaries, written by students, also began to appear in the paper. The Baloch leaders provided moral support to the youth and inculcated in them an intrepid spirit of nationalism. Mir Gull Khan Naseer's Poems and national songs were soon being sung and recited at youth gatherings. Although sometimes devoid of fine literary standards, the poems imbued the students with a sense of purpose and prepared them to withstand suffering for the national cause. Mir Ghous Bakhsh Bizenjo did the political teaching and made the students conscious of the need for a constant struggle for a better political and cultural environment where the people could achieve their national rights. The youth became aware of the glorious movement launched by the National Party for an independent and sovereign Balochistan and the role of the ruling Khan and his sardars in bringing a great catastrophe upon the Baloch people. The students organized themselves in literary societies and debating groups, mainly to discuss Balochi literature, politics, and history.

The events of 1958 and the subsequent military operations were an eye-opener for the younger generation. The Baloch leaders, including Mir Ghous Bakhsh Bizenjo, Mir Gul Khan Naseer and others were put in Quli Camp in Quetta, tortured and humiliated. The Khan's arrest and the killing of innocent people in Kalat had not only sparked off tribal unrest in Jahlawaan but also sent shock waves throughout the Baloch land. The most baffling event was the execution by the Pakistan government of seven colleagues of Mir Norouz Khan on the charges of treason on 15th July 1960.

In the background of intense political and social upheavals, the Warna Waaninda Gal, the educated youth forum, was formed in 1961 in Quetta. Siddique Azat became its first president. Its professed objective was of promoting Balochi language and literature. It initiated discussions and debates on the prevailing political condition in the country and their impact on the people.

By mid-sixties, the youth seriously considered forming an organization that would not only cater to their craze for Balochi but also struggle for better educational facilities and provides a forum for enlightened discussions regarding their political future. The students announced the formation of the Baloch Students Organization, the BSO, on 26th November 1967 after a three-day convention in Karachi. It replaced the WarnaWaaninda Gal. Youth from all over Balochistan and other parts of the country participated in the gathering. The convention issued a Dastural Amal, a manifesto, which called, inter-alia, for a campaign for free and secular education and the promotion of Balochi language, literature, and social traditions. The manifesto also demanded the break-up of One-Unit and complete provincial autonomy for Balochistan [2]. (A most striking amendment was introduced to the Dastural Amal in 1979, demanding the right of national-self-determination for the Baloch people [3]. The manifesto included the provision of Balochi as the language of education in Balochistan and its recognition as the official language. The BSO also expressed its opposition to imperialism, neo-colonialism and national oppression in Asia, Africa, and the Latin-American countries [4] A *Tharana*, a national anthem, was included in the manifesto, which was to be recited with all solemnity in national sessions and other important gatherings of the organization [5].

The predecessor of the BSO, the Warna Waaninda Gal was aligned with the National Awami Party (NAP), which was generally regarded as the successor of the National Party in Balochistan. The NAP and its predecessor groups were opposed to the Sardari system, which was considered instrumental in bringing political subjugation. Most of the sardars had favored Baloch accession to Pakistan. This anti-Sardari policy of the NAP was appealing to youth. But during the last years of the military regime of General Ayub, when the government, as a gesture of reconciliation towards the Baloch, announced the restoration of chieftaincy of the powerful Mari, Bugti and Mengal tribes, it was vehemently opposed by the BSO. Earlier, during the military operations, the government had deprived the chiefs of these tribes of their nominal titles and appointed government favorites as the heads of Mengal, Mari and Bugti tribes. The restoration of these sardars was symbolic and does not carry any privileges. Progressive elements considered this decision as a retrogressive step. Since these sardars were members of the NAP, the party came under severe criticism. The NAP itself condemned the government's decision. The party, however, believed that the system could be changed only through vigorous efforts in educating the people. The NAP was the only progressive party that opposed all forms of exploitation and was greatly feared by the government and its right-wing allies, who were trying to create differences in the party ranks on the one hand and among its most vigorous youth wing, the students, on the other. The differences among the students were first witnessed in early 1967. A few students, mostly from Makkuraan, started condemning the NAP and its Baloch leadership. Elements with clandestine support from the government penetrated among the students and began to exploit some isolated incidents of loot and murder by highway robbers that were identified with the Baloch militants fighting against the government in Jahlawaan. These elements who helped form the Anti-Sardar group of the BSO, published a handbill entitled *Bloodshed Must End* in Balochistan, which alleged that the sardars were responsible for highway robberies. The handbill, issued in Karachi in the name of BSO breakaway faction, rejected the argument that the militants were fighting for the Baloch cause. It appealed to the government to curb the activities of Baloch fighters which they are carryout in the name of nationalist politics.

During the 1960s, the armed opposition to the government in the mountains was mostly led in Jahlawaan by the Mengals. This group of tribal people used to ambush government convoys and their concentration points. However, occasionally some unscrupulous bandits used to loot truck owners or passengers on Karachi-Turbat-Panjgur routes. In order to discredit the resistance fighters, the government would promptly blame the hostile political elements for such crimes. The government agents among the students exploited such isolated occurrences to confuse the youth and achieve an estrangement of the students from the NAP.

The official propaganda charged the National Awami Party as 'the party of the sardars' opposing the government for selfish motives. The BSO rejected these allegations. One of its leaders, Manzoor Ahmad Baloch, wrote an article titled, Balochistan and the political parties, published in a booklet form, which refuted the charges that the sardars had manipulated the NAP in Balochistan. Manzoor Ahmad Baloch included a list of seventy important sardars recognized by the government who were heads of important tribal factions or entire tribes, including the chief of the chiefs, the ex-Khan of Kalat. Out of seventy, only five had leanings towards the policies of NAP or were regarded as its supporters, including Nawab Akbar Bugti, Nawab Khair Bakhsh Mari, and Sardar Atullah Mengal. All other sardars were opposed to the NAP due to its progressive stance and were aligned with various political ruling parties in the country, mostly the Muslim League [6].

The differences among the students led to the formation of rival organizations, the Baloch Students Organization Anti-Sardar which in the 1970s was renamed as BSO-Awami (henceforth referred to as Awami). The eponym Awami was added to denote its opposition towards the National Awami Party. It also indicated the organization's closeness to the Peoples Party of Zulfikar Ali Bhutto. Many of the group's activists supported the Peoples Party during the 1970s general elections and later on became members of the Peoples Party when it came to power in 1971.

The persons who masterminded the split among the youth did apparently achieve their goal. But the subsequent events were very distressing for the student who in their youthful enthusiasm had supported the breakaway faction. The military operations in Balochistan put the sincere members of the group in a very compromising situation. Desertion began in the ranks and file of the BSO Awami (anti-Sardar). The organization was reduced in popularity and strength. Quite a few of them tried to maintain the differences with the main organization, but the honest among them began to think of unity and even broached the idea of a merger with the BSO.

Since mutual recriminations and hostility during these years appeared unbridgeable, it took many years to agree to talk of merger openly.

The honeymoon of the Awami with the Peoples Party proved short-lived. After some of its senior members joined the party, the younger students bitterly criticized them and dissociated themselves from the group. Bhutto's military action made the situation worse for the organization whose earlier support for him was always referred to by the nationalists to prove their alleged anti-Baloch stance. When the BSO developed its own differences with the NAP, the two groups became closer and ultimately forged unity between them. The Awami had to its credit some pamphlets and a magazine, while the BSO could claim to have done its bit for the national cause by participating actively in the armed struggle. Its leaders, Khair Jan, Hakim Lehri, Aslam Kurd, Khalid Jamaladini and many others participated in the armed resistant movement of the 1970s. Khair Jan led a group of nearly forty men and carried out resistance activities against the army. Hundreds of BSO members were put behind bars and tortured by security authorities. One of its members, Abdul Majeed Lango, gave his life while trying to kill Prime Minister Zulfikar Ali Bhutto with a hand-grenade in Quetta on 12th August 1974. Yet another courageous youth, Hameed, was executed by the military regime in 1981. Several others were killed in actual combat. On the contrary, the Awami, during the period of its separate existence brought out only some hard-hitting pamphlets.

With the passage of time, it became clear that the two organizations had identical views on many issues, especially on the question of the Baloch political future. On the Sardari system, which was apparently the main cause of their differences, the BSO had a firm stand throughout its existence. When the government announced its decision to restore the sardars, the BSO strongly rejected the move. Its mouthpiece, Sangath, issued a pamphlet on 1st November 1969 opposing the restoration of the sardars. The BSO had gained immense prestige and strength due to its active participation in armed struggle and was in the mainstream of national politics, while the Awami, shy of its existence, adopted a negative approach to compensate for its inactivity. Moreover, the pressure was mounting on the Awami from sincere elements in the group and from the Baloch intellectuals, to merge with the main body. Hameed, in his last well before his execution, had appealed to the students to shun their differences and work unitedly for the Baloch cause. This appeal had an irresistible impact. Both the organizations formed negotiating teams for the merger of their groups. The leaders of both the factions, Habib Jalib of the BSO and Yasin Baloch of the Awami, signed a joint communiqué after prolonged discussions between the two-negotiating team on 18ᵗʰ October 1982, laying down certain procedures to be followed in connection with the merger. The joint communiqué discussing the geo-political and military situation in the region and expressed the determination of both the organizations to work in unison to face the growing challenge to their people. The communiqué alleged that Balochistan was being turned into a big military base to serve the interests of world imperialism. Ultimately on 25ᵗʰ September 1983; the two factions formally announced their merger with each other in the name of BSO. The announcement issued on the occasion was indicative of a sense of reconciliation and wisdom among the student leaders. The merger undoubtedly was a great event in student politics and was highly appreciated in all nationalist circles. The declaration, issued in the form of a leaflet entitled *Inzimaam*, merger, said that unity would enhance the cause of the Baloch people and all those who cherished a progressive set-up in the country.

Impact of BSO Politics

The Baloch Students Organization had played an appreciable role in Baloch politics. As early as 1968, it was in the mainstream of the national struggle. Presenting an address of welcome of Professor Muzaffar Ahmad President of the East Pakistan NAP, the BSO Chairman. Dr. Abdul Hai outlined the approach of BSO to national issues and its stand on matters concerning Balochistan. Speaking about the role of the students, he considered the students' movement an integral part of the democratic struggle in the country. The students of the smaller provinces of West Pakistan, he declared, have given a lead in the struggle for provincial autonomy and recognition of their languages as national languages. Taking into account the economic exploitation of Balochistan, the BSO chairman said that the income from natural resources in Balochistan was pocketed by foreign and internal monopolies. Even employment in Sui Gas installations is reserved for people from outside Balochistan, he added. While welcoming Mir Sheer Mahmad Mari on 27th May 1970 in a function in Dow Medical College Karachi, the BSO president Naseer Baloch expressed the determination of youth to follow the course chalked out by Baloch leaders to achieve a rightful place for their people. He demanded the inalienable right of sovereignty for the subject nationalities of Pakistan.

The BSO was in the vanguard of the nationalist movement launched by the NAP and its Baloch leaders. The NAP greatly valued the organization and its spirited youth in the struggle. In their speeches before BSO gatherings, they would ask them to work selflessly in the interest of their people. The BSO workers addressed Baloch leaders on 18th March 1969 in Karachi, were asked to be true to their great traditions. Sardar Athaullah Mengal and Nawab Akbar Bugti in their speeches opposed the Sardari system in Balochistan. Addressing the BSO workers at Mastung in 1970, Sardar Mengal praised the students for their historic role in achieving provincial status for Balochistan [7].

The Baloch student organization was given the highest consideration by the NAP. The BSO leaders were taken into confidence by the party leaders on major policy decisions. One of its leaders, Dr, Abdul Hai, was nominated to contest the National Assembly on the NAP ticket. He defeated Prince Yahya, the son of Ahmad Yar Khan, the last Khan of Kalat. The selection of Dr. Abdul Hai was the recognition of BSO sacrifices and their appreciable role in the Baloch national struggle.

Although, since its inception in 1967, the BSO worked closely with the National Awami Party, nevertheless, the student activists were by no means mere camp followers. They were a vocal faction in the party. In spite of its close association with the NAP, the BSO retained an independent posture and acted with more fervor than expected from a student's body. The NAP rapprochement with the Peoples Party in 1972 was severely opposed by a strong faction in the BSO because of inadequate guarantees of provincial autonomy in the PPP sponsored constitution.

The growing influence of BSO and its support for nationalist leaders was alarming to state establishment. The government and many other elements outside the government started manipulating the organization and courting its leaders in order not only to confuse the rank and file of the BSO but also to secure an estrangement with its main political ally, the National Awami Party, and its successors, the NDP and Pakistan National Party. The division in the BSO earlier in 1967 was also aimed at weakening the Baloch movement but since the breakaway faction did not come up to their expectations, efforts were made to penetrate the main organization. The BSO's influence in political circles made some of its leaders regarding themselves as indispensable. Some of the BSO top brass believed that the students could provide an alternative leadership to the people. Some Muhajir ideologues and pseudo-communists on the payroll of state establishment did play a despicable role in confusing the minds of some of the ambitious student leaders.

On a socio-political context, the students are a motley group of young activists with divergent social background, and their solidarity would last as long as they are in the educational institutions but after quitting those institutions, they would become part of their own class and pursue policies consistent with the requirements of that class. The students could never have provided leadership to a people, nevertheless, their role would be as a pressure group strong enough to influence many of the policies of the political parties. In East Bengal, now Bangladesh, the powerful Students Action Committee which at one time, during the absence of the Awami League leadership because of their imprisonments, posed as an alternative leadership, was severely rejected by the Awami League: and the idea of students as a parallel organization outside the mainstream of national politics was neither appreciated nor allowed. However, their 21-point program mainly for educational reforms was included in the charter of demands submitted to the government by the Awami League, and later the Awami League promised to implement them when it came to power. In all developing countries, the role of the students as agitators and as a pressure group is always recognized. Even in countries like France, the students played a significantly unexpected role in the downfall of General Charles de Gaulle in 1968. Such a role of the student's organization is always acknowledged in Third–world countries but nowhere have such organizations superseded the political parties.

A pattern was discernible in the BSO's relations with the NAP were on many issues, it influenced the party policies. Both organizations worked in unison to achieve the common goal of bringing greater support and strength to the nationalist movement. However, as mentioned earlier, many elements were at work within the organization including government groomed intelligentsia and non-Baloch ideologues often with dubious connections. Calling off the armed struggle in Balochistan was the culmination of relations between the BSO and the NAP. The BSO threw its weight into the armed resistance and its chairman, Khair Jan, and other important members were actively involved in the movement. Many more imprisoned for many years. When the Baloch leaders, released from imprisonment, called off the armed resistance, the BSO considered this a clear betrayal of the cause. Extremists and other elements in the BSO alleged that the NAP was never sincere in its commitment to the people and had gone back on its promises to liberate the country or at least gain significant concessions from the government in the form of political autonomy. In the annual report of the organization for the period ending July 1979, the General Secretary of the BSO severely criticized the NAP leadership. The 164-page report dealing with the BSO policies and programs, which was approved by the National Council Session of the organization and was later published in an exclusive issue of Sangath, alleged that the National Awami Party, contrary to its protestations, had never owned in letter and spirit the national struggle of the Baloch and Pakhtun Peoples [8].

While the NAP leaders, now realized the futility of continuing the armed resistance, wanted a respite, the youth were not happy on the overall conduct of the insurgency and believed that the armed resistance could have been further intensified in order to achieve desirable results. Even some important personalities in the NAP like Mir Mahmud Aziz Kurd believed that the leadership did not go far enough to compel the Pakistani authorities to come to terms with the Baloch. In a letter to a government advisor, Mir Mahmud Aziz Kurd said, that during all these years our leadership exercised extreme restraint in the face of brutal oppression of our people. We did not allow the situation to go beyond uncontrollable limits in spite of the fact that the entire might of the government of Pakistan was being used against us. You could imagine the situation if our leadership really wanted to dismember the country. There were many options. But we were not always guided by national interests. Influenced by such sentiments, the activists of BSO were apparently aggrieved by this self-imposed restraint of the Baloch leaders in the fight against Pakistan.

The Baloch politicians were by no means ready to accept the self-assumed role of the student in national politics as a parallel organization. They were very candid about this. Some of the BSO leaders, influenced by anti-Baloch elements and adamant in their newfound role, started an anti-NAP campaign to the distaste of many sincere youths and genuine nationalists. The BSO was so disgusted with the Baloch leadership that its Chairman, Mueem Khan who advocated continued support of the NAP and its successor party the NDP, was removed from the chairmanship and his basic membership of the organization was canceled through an overwhelming vote of no confidence in 1978. This was the first instance in the history of the BSO where a serving leader had been compelled to quit on the question of policy. When the PNP was formed, the BSO Chairman Habib Jalib, in a press conference on 22nd July 1979, categorized the party as a bourgeois group and declared that the BSO would continue its policies in pursuance of its objectives independently. In a written statement released to the newsmen on the occasion, Jalib said the BSO would not have relations with any bourgeois political party, particularly the PNP [9]. Thus, the BSO with a history of relentless struggle was getting out of the crosscurrents of Baloch national politics. It had become a recluse in extremism. By demanding the right of national self-determination, the BSO was now favoring an all-out struggle to achieve that right, which explicitly meant an independent Balochistan. The BSO had taken the Baloch politicians by surprise. That was the turning point in the history of the organization.

The self-assumed role of the BSO as an independent organization on the pattern of the political parties in the developing countries, working for drastic changes in the socio-economic and political structure of the society, is evident in an article written by its general secretary, Habib Jalib, and published in the BSO organ, Sangath in 1980. In the article, titled 'something about BSO' he declared that the ideological perfection of the BSO had encouraged people to withstand oppression. He said the BSO worked for inalienable socio-economic rights and the right of national self-determination for the Baloch. The article gave the impression that only the BSO could lead the people in the realization of the national rights [10]. Its chairman, Ayub Baloch, said in an interview that the BSO could not remain aloof from political crosscurrents, because the problems confronting the students were in fact political. He said the students believed that they could get national rights from the rulers only through a constant struggle. Therefore, the BSO had a dual role while it was striving to solve educational problems, it also wanted to solve the problems facing the people. The Baloch Students Organization, Ayub Baloch said, was proud of its dual status [11]. This had served as the main theme of the organization's political stance for the last several years. Its leaders consider all the political parties essentially anti-people.

The stand of the BSO in opposing the end of hostilities with the state was however vindicated by later events, which showed that the Baloch politicians were clearly mistaken about government intentions. The great sacrifices of the people achieved nothing. The struggle had not only added further miseries to the people but also brought a defeatist psychosis to the nation. At first, the BSO was hesitant in its opposition to leadership. They were selective in their campaign. The majority of student activists thought that Nawab Khair Bakhsh Mari, because of his Maoist leanings, was perhaps closer to them. During the Baloch conflict of the 1960s and 1970s, Khair Bakhsh's relation with certain Maoist elements from the Punjab and Sindh made him the only hope and gave the impression that he was opposed to the calling off of armed resistance. When the Baloch leaders arrived in Quetta after their release from Hyderabad Jail, the BSO received them and showed considerable enthusiasm towards Nawab Khair Bakhsh and Mir Sheer Muhammad Mari. The students, under the leadership of Aslam Kurd, took these leaders in a procession to the Jinnah Road office of the organization, where they talked to BSO workers [12]. But the students were soon disheartened when Khair Bakhsh Mari along with other leaders started negotiations with the government. The BSO now openly criticized the leadership. This suited not only the government whose agencies for many years have been cultivating many of the student activists in the organization but a lot of other student extremists and an influential faction in the bureaucracy.

The BSO did not call off the struggle officially though their members could not do anything more than to issue strong-worded statements against the Baloch politicians putting them in the same category of the exploitative class in the country. The BSO annual report referred to earlier put the NAP and its Baloch leadership at par with other right-wing political parties in the country. The report said that by aligning themselves with the reactionary and conservative political grouping, the PNA, the NAP had exposed itself as an anti-people organization [13]. Now the BSO and the government by implication were co-operating with each other in maligning the

National Awami Party and its successor, the National Party. The government-controlled media carried the BSO statements against the Baloch leadership prominently. The elements which masterminded the rift between the BSO and the Baloch politician also encouraged the BSO top brass to make frequent calls for student agitation on the slightest pretext in order to heighten the atmosphere and create an air of continued active hostility between the Baloch and the Pakistan government. When the Baloch students tried to agitate at the call of their leaders, they found themselves in jails and their leaders in hiding. Without political backing, the BSO, for the first time since its inception, was reduced to an insignificant faction in Balochistan politics. They found themselves without direction and without any support in the masses. While their leaders went into hiding, many of the members of the organization suffered immensely.

The most significant event was the execution of one of its active members, Hameed on the charge of the attempted murder of one Colonel Khalfan, a foreign delegate from the Sultanate of Omaan, in Turbat in 1979. The BSO opposed the recruitment of Baloch youth into the Omaani army, which had been fighting a war against the Dhofari dissidents in southern Omaan bordering Aden. The BSO believed that recruitment would earn notoriety for the Baloch in the eyes of progressive elements throughout the world and weaken the Baloch nationalist movement in Pakistan. Secondly, they saw it as aiming to pervert the younger elements in society by offering huge salaries for their services in a mercenary army [14]. Hameed was tried by a Special Military Court and condemned to death. The death sentence was carried out on 11th June 1981 in Mach prison. The event had a paralyzing effect. The BSO could not do anything to secure the release of one of its members. The execution was so demoralizing that for fear of government action none of its prominent members participated even in the burial ceremonies of their executed comrade [15]. Earlier, when the death sentence was challenged in the High Court by Hameed's relatives, the BSO members, fearing arrest, did not even come to attend the court proceedings except for a few personal and family friends [16].

In spite of its shortcoming and miscalculated political decisions and the penetration of agents provocateur in its ranks, the BSO nevertheless remained the strongest force among the Baloch youth. The organization cannot be dismissed easily nor its importance in the Balochi political struggle minimized. Although its members are united only for their short-term college or university life, the organization has produced devoted workers and political agitators during the last two decades of its existence.

The BSO has high ideals. Considering it the true representative of the people, the BSO aims at uniting the masses and working for their emancipation. The government efforts at creating differences between the two sections of the Baloch population, the Brahui and the Baloch, are severely rejected by the students. It has also vigorously opposed the government-sponsored moves in sectarian violence on the Numazi-Zigri issue. The BSO had undoubtedly created a deep awareness among youth. A brief analysis of the organization shows that it had played a significant role in the movement for the dissolution of the One-Unit. The organization helped the NAP not only in the electoral process but also in the armed struggle. It has always condemned the anti-people policies of the state and assumed the role of watch-dog over the Baloch politicians. After their split with the Baloch leadership, hard-hitting commentaries continued to appear in the BSO publications on various issues. Its organ *Pajjar* of November-December 1981, in a commentary titled 'Different Faces of usurper Government in Balochistan' strongly condemned the Pakistan government as an anti-Baloch one, looting their resources. The government functionaries, according to the article, are nothing but plunderers and killers. Condemning the execution of Hameed, it regretted that the world has become a pathetic witness to the barbarity of the military junta [17]. The *Pajjar*, in its issue of August-September, 1980, Which was exclusive for the members-only, severely criticized government policies in Balochistan. In a commentary titled 'the present situation and its requirements,' it expressed anger over what it termed intrigues and imperialistic manipulations and asked for joint efforts to secure the rights of the nationalities in the country. The commentary expressed the hope that the objective conditions were now very ripe for a struggle against the military regime. It also opposed the foreign policy of the government, which supports American imperialism. The article reiterated the stance of the BSO on the right of nationalities to self-determination and recognition of the peoples' languages as the official languages of the country [18].

Although the BSO publications and news bulletins sometimes express extreme opinions without any apparent flexibility, the organization has served as the most motivating factor among the students and molded public opinion towards nationalism to a considerable extent. Its publications from 1980 to 1984 progressively indicate political maturity and a softening attitude toward nationalist leadership. The BSO policies on various issues facing the Baloch also appear to be inching towards practical realities keeping in view the objective conditions prevailing in Balochistan.

The BSO stand on the question of provincial autonomy has now been replaced by the demand for national self-determination which clearly means the Baloch right to a sovereign existence. The BSO appears to have come to the conclusion that the Baloch can no longer live within Pakistan. It believes that the only way for the Baloch is to fight for their freedom. The demand for the right of national self-determination is being pursued with all ideological and theoretical forcefulness. The speeches and writings of the young activists show a marked deviation from the original policy of the organization. The *Pajjar* is now increasingly depicting an ideological pattern emphasizing the theory of national self-determination. The creation of Pakistan is generally seen by BSO as being a geo-strategic requirement of western imperialism rather than a religious imperative or political necessity. The BSO consequently disapproves of the often quoted, two-nation theory or the Pakistan ideology. The definition of nationalism in the subcontinent in terms of religion has scared the Baloch youth who consider such misinterpretation of history, a grave threat to their ethnocultural identity. The BSO is dissatisfied with the Baloch political position in Pakistan and elsewhere and considers a national struggle as the only logical option to settle the claim of Baloch sovereign status.

The BSO has drifted progressively from being a student body catering to the academic needs of the youth into a group of political activists with a secular outlook. On the ideological question, the organization sometimes vacillates from purely nationalistic motives to chauvinistic overtures and from a socialist stance to upholding the Marxist rhetoric of the supremacy of the working class. Such confusion explicitly persists in most of the writings in its publications.

The BSO stands for Balochi and the other languages to be recognized as national languages, and for the right of education in mother tongues. It wants drastic changes in the socio-economic set-up in the country to create a socialist economic system where exploitation of man by man would end and, peace, justice, and mutual harmony among the peoples of various socio-ethnic origins would prevail.

The Baloch Students Organization supports the April revolution in Afghanistan and strongly condemns the efforts by the Pakistan military regime to destabilize Afghanistan. The organization believes that the destabilizing efforts of Pakistan in Afghanistan will result in strong political fallout for the Baloch in the area. Every publication by the organization contains strong arguments in favor of the revolution and the need to support the people of Afghanistan in their fight against world imperialism.

The Pakistani government has been reacting with an iron-hand towards student politics spearheaded by BSO. The attitude of the government is fully reflected in a speech by the military Governor of Balochistan, Rahimuddin Khan in 1983. During the inaugural ceremony of the Grid Station at Khuzdar, he deviated from the written text and warned the Baloch students that he would not mind keeping all the Baloch as shepherds and laborers because of the students, whose attitude is far from accommodating. At no time since 1973 have the jails in Balochistan contained a larger number of students. Of those who happen to be at universities and colleges, at least 60% have been in goal on one charge or another for various terms of detention. This is evident from the fact that on the occasion of Pakistan Day on 23rd March 1985, the governor of Balochistan, General Khushdil Khan Afridi, declared a general amnesty for the students who were under detention in the province. Addressing the Pakistan Day parade, the Governor termed his action a gesture of goodwill towards the youth in the hope that they would not indulge in undesirable activities [19].

The students are not simply imprisoned but severely tortured and humiliated. Those interrogated by the Crime Branch of the police or army officers have been telling of inhuman treatment meted out to them during their confinement. Their interrogators, mostly Punjabis, always made it a point to express their deep dislike and hatred for the Baloch and their traditions. Not only the students of colleges and universities have undergone detention, but school children have not been spared. To quote only one instance, eight schoolchildren, mostly under fourteen, from the Government High School Turbat were sentenced to three months of rigorous imprisonment by a summary military court in May 1982 because they were demanding the restoration of electricity to their hostel during their examinations. The students are usually tried collectively without any specific charges being brought against any individual, and sentenced to undergo rigorous imprisonment. In October 1979, seven students were tried summarily by military tribunals and sentenced to rigorous imprisonment for one year. In December 1983, twenty-two students were tried collectively on charges of staging a demonstration in Turbat opposing recruitment of youth to the Omaan army. They were sentenced for one year with hard labor. One of them, Qazi Ghulam Rasool, was awarded ten lashes. The award of lashes to students invoked sharp protests because, for a Baloch, disgrace in public is worse than death. The BSO and the Pakistan National Party promptly condemned the sentences as insulting and unbearable [20].

Indiscriminate firing by the security forces on the slightest excuse is always resorted to without any regard to human life. Scores of students have been killed in police firing during the last two decades. Such occurrences have met with a news blackout. On 15th April 1978, Police opened fire on students in Khuzdar, including school children, killing and wounding at least fifteen of them. A press note issued by the government said the police opened fire in self-defense. A wave of resentment swept throughout the province at the police brutality. In a telegram to Pakistan's military ruler, General Zia ul Haq, Mir Mahmud Aziz Kurd, the then president of the National Democratic Party in the province, rejected the government press note as a classic example of a mischievous distortion of the facts.

Searches of student residences and hostels are a common phenomenon and resorted to frequently in all major educational centers in Balochistan. The government always puts the blame on students creating unrest on the campuses. The student forcefully rejects the allegations that they are responsible for creating lawlessness in the institutions and forcing their closure. *Pajjar*, in its May-June 1981 issue, charged the government with deliberately denying the Baloch the right to education by closing educational institutions and harassing the students [21].

Government policy in dealing with the students in Balochistan is aimed at achieving three distinct objectives: securing the estrangement of youth from the Baloch political parties, curbing student agitation, and curtailing the number of graduations of educated youth among the Baloch. The government's efforts have not been fruitless. The divisions among them and making them isolated from mainstream politics are the obvious dividends for the Government. The emotional approach of the youth and the dubious role of some of their top brass facilitated the government task.

References

1. MoulaiShaidai: Education during British Rule in Balochistan, Ouman, Karachi, August 1951, pp. 9-10

2. Dastural Amal of the Baloch Students Organization pp 5-6,

3. Ibid.

4. Ibid.

5. The English rendering of the BSO anthem is quoted in the chapter, Social Origins of the Baloch National Struggle. The following is the oath of membership of the BSO:
   "I do swear solemnly In the name of Balochistan, the Baloch masses and in the name of all oppressed and working-class peoples of the world; that I will abide myself to follow the manifesto of the BSO and its aims and objectives in letter and spirit; and that I will never hesitate to offer any sacrifices for the cause of the organization; and that I will not act in such a manner which may contravene the manifesto and aims and objectives of the organizations"(Dastur) Amal: (amended) Op, Cit.

6. Manzoor Ahmad Baloch: Balochistan and political parties. Kalat Press, Quetta, PP, 3-21.

7. Dawn, 20th October 1970.

8. Sangath (1979) Special PP 17-18.

9. The written statement of Habib Jalib released to newsmen on 22nd July 1979.

10. Habib Jalib: Something about BSO, Sangath, pp4-6.

11. Mujahid Brailvi: Balochistan what is the issue? Gosha e Adab, Quetta, 1984 p, 107.

12. Mashriq, Quetta, 6th January 1978.

13. Sangath, (1979) Special Issue p, 18.

14. Pajjar, May-June 1981, pp3-4.

15. Public sympathy was so immense that thousands of people from different parts of Balochistan and other provinces, including many from adjoining Iranian regions, and Arabian Gulf countries, visited the members of Hameed's family after the execution to express their grief. The family received innumerable messages of condolences from across the country and abroad.

16. Saleem Kurd, a medical student and personal friend of Hameed, who came to witness the court proceeding, was arrested in the court premises and was put behind bars for many years without trial.

17. Pajjar, Different faces of usurper government in Balochistan. November-December1981, p 3.

18. Pajjar, August- September 1980, pp,1-4.

19. Jang, Quetta, 24th March 1985.

20. Daily News and star, Karachi, 13th December 1983.

21. Pajjar, May June 1981, p 11.

CHAPTER VII

BALOCH RELATIONS WITH PAKISTAN: STYLE AND NATURE

Baloch relations with Pakistan have from the very beginning been marked by deep suspicion and open confrontation. The Baloch were not only against their country's accession to Pakistan but also actively thereafter continued to raise the question of their separate identity. Their fear of annihilation as a national entity and political subjugation appears to be intrinsic and can be discerned in their political and social thinking. Their literature has always depicted the proud existence of the people. Pakistan, born in hatred towards others, its religious narrow mindedness, and intolerance has never been appreciated by the Baloch. Reciprocally, Pakistani leaders adopted a policy of active hostility and deep mistrust toward the Baloch and their socio-cultural traditions and beliefs. The state policies adopted after the accession of Balochistan into Pakistan had given credence to the impression that Baloch political rights and economic wellbeing are a lost cause in a society where the cultural rights of the peoples are being denied and where efforts are made to impose alien cultural influences as part of the state policy. The Pakistani rulers' determination to subjugate the Baloch and completely absorb them into a Pakistani national identity that is being designed and controlled by an alliance of Urdu speaking immigrants, religious elite and the Panjabi army, has been a compelling reason for the Baloch to give serious consideration to their political allegiances.

British domination in Balochistan had created a feeling of exhaustion and deprivation. The tribal chiefs, who had earlier resisted the British authority in various ways, including sporadic armed confrontations, had come to the conclusion that imperial Britain could not be defeated by any tribal force. World War I gave further credence to the invincibility of British might. This psychological strain was fully depicted in the political attitude of many tribal elders and opinion leaders in their subsequent relations with Pakistan. Initially, the British were not in favor of including Balochistan into the Partition scheme, nor were the Pakistani leaders enthusiastic about the region; but when the birth of the new country was in sight and the question of its viability came under continuous scrutiny, Balochistan assumed immense importance. Its vast resources and the geographical area would give the country a strategic depth and guarantee its economic workability. The long coastline could open an immeasurable opportunity to the new state to become an important country at the mouth of the Gulf in the Indian Ocean.

Many political and psychological compulsions worked in favor of Pakistan in convincing the Baloch to eventually accept Pakistan as a political reality. Most of the leaders who had opposed their country's amalgamation into Pakistan, after absorbing the initial shock of losing their sovereignty, were willing to co-operate with the new rulers, but they were soon to be disillusioned by their attitude. Prince Kareem's rebellion was short-lived, but when he came back from Afghanistan, instead of reconciliation, the Prince and his followers were awarded severe punishments. They remained behind bars for several years. This was perhaps the first sign of political intolerance by the rulers towards the people of a former independent country, whose accession they had secured through coercion.

The Baloch struggle within Pakistan started soon after the country's inclusion into Pakistan in 1948. They demanded provincial status by merging all the Balochi speaking areas into Balochistan with reasonable internal autonomy. Instead of any direct confrontation, the Baloch started a peaceful political movement to realize their rights in a federal structure where Balochistan as a unit could enjoy sufficient autonomy and where the Baloch could pursue a way of life commensurate with their deep-rooted traditions. They were soon disappointed. The Panjabi politicians, after their failure to provide an agreed constitution for the new state, dissolved the existing provinces in the western wing of the country to form the province of West Pakistan. This was also to counter the Bengali in East Bengal that was also renamed as East Pakistan. This was an ill-advised attempt on the part of Punjabi and Muhajir elite. East Bengal constituted more than 54% of the country's population but was compelled to accept the parity formula in the name of the national solidarity. After the forming of One-Unit in October 1955, the country was given a constitution in 1956 which was aimed at perpetuating the domination of the Panjabi-Muhajir clique to rule the country.

The case for One-Unit was put forward on the one hand within the overall ideological framework of Islamic solidarity and separate Muslim nationhood, and on the other hand, as a practical means of achieving that unity through regional co-ordination, by ensuring the domination of the most loyal of the country subjects: the Panjabi-Muhajir ruling clique. When confronted with the common notion that Pakistan would achieve stability by pursuing the same approach as India, which is accomplishing the task of mutual harmony under the same strenuous conditions and is enjoying unity through cultural and political diversification, the rulers rejected the arguments in the name of Islam and Muslim patriotism. To the Pakistani mind, the grave condition of grinding poverty and social contradictions demanded stricter control on its peoples and that unity could be achieved only through coercion. At the time it was suggested that the dissolution of the provinces was a prerequisite for the greater unity of the peoples. Geographical distance and socio-cultural and national distinctions should not come in the way of closer comradeship between East and West Pakistan on the one hand and among the peoples of West Pakistan on the other. Differences in language and culture and the inherent administrative problems resulting from the merger of these provinces were considered insignificant in the light of their larger national interests. It was argued that diversification and distinctions between the peoples if any, were of design rather than fabric. It was felt that cultural personality was less pronounced among the people of the various provinces in Pakistan than in most of the advanced states of Europe. The language factor was easily discarded as inconsequential. Economically, all of West Pakistan was regarded as one single unit. Moreover, it was maintained that undeveloped regions like Balochistan would benefit from the One-Unit system. It was said that the system of administration in which units, the machinery of government, assemblies and public offices duplicated in various regional capitals was wasteful, and the solution lay in the formation of a one-unit administration. It was argued that the quantum of provincial autonomy demanded by Bengal could not be managed by the smaller provinces of the Western wing unless the provinces of West Pakistan were merged to form a greater province. It was implied that it was not because of the One-Unit that the country was lagging behind in development, and that it was because of the provinces that the question of the political system had not been resolved.

The One-Unit scheme, instead of bettering the lives of the peoples or creating a stable government plunged the country into chaos. The majority province of East Bengal realized that the parity system of the One-Unit scheme was in fact aimed at denying the rights of the Bengalis and perpetuating Punjabi-Muhajir rule in the country. In West Pakistan, the Baloch, Pakhtuns, and Sindhis expressed their bitterness on the curtailment of political and economic rights and opportunities. The 1956 constitution, based on the 'Parity Formula' -meaning equal representation in parliament for East and West Pakistan, was soon manipulated by the ruling circles in tune with the requirements of the time and political exigency. Within two years of the promulgation of the constitution, the military brass overthrew the shaky government, imposed Martial Law, abrogated the constitution and banned political activities. The country's armed forces chief, General Ayub Khan emerged as the strongman. He ruled through Martial Law regulations and orders for several years but ultimately gave the country his own brand of a constitution, which provided a workable setting for the changeover from military dictatorship to authoritarian rule with a façade of parliamentary institutions. The constitution lacked the provision of sufficient autonomy to the provinces. The One-Unit and parity systems were made the basis of the relation between the two wings of the country. The rule of General Ayub Khan can be regarded as a true model of military-civilian dictatorships in developing countries. It precipitated enormous political issues and created a wedge among the various classes of the peoples in the country.

The One-Unit and parity system invoked a sharp reaction among the constituent national entities of Pakistan. While the demand for the dissolution of the One-Unit took a less violent turn in West Pakistan, in East Bengal the demand for greater autonomy gained ground across the cross-section of the population. The Awami League, a political party dominated by Bangali nationalists, became the champion of the rights of Bengali masses. The presidential elections under Ayub's basic democracy system caused further bitterness between East and West Pakistan on the one hand and the smaller provinces under the One-Unit on the other. The Bengalis now demanded complete provincial autonomy, allowing minimum powers to the central government in Islamabad to the point of ineffectiveness. Only the defense, foreign affairs, and communication were proposed as the domain of the federal government, while all remaining powers were to be vested with the provinces. The party leader, Sheikh Mujeeb ur Rehman, issued his six-point formula on 23rd March 1966, and this remained the main thorn in the political polemics in the country for another five years until the separation of East Bengal in 1971.

The Indo-Pakistan war of 1965, which was provoked by the Pakistan military ruler in a miscalculated attempt to boost his authority, proved a complete disaster. The war, however, remained inconclusive and did not cripple the military machine of Pakistan only because the Indian leaders were ill-prepared for such a conflict and could not bring it to its logical conclusion in the context of the long-term security of India, but it proved to be a strong factor in the overthrow of the military regime of General Ayub Khan. The agitation in East Pakistan was led by the Awami League while in West Pakistan, there was another scenario. A section of the army became against the protracted rule of General Ayub. With the help of intelligence agencies, they launched a former foreign Minister and general secretary of ruling Muslim League, Zulfikar Ali Bhutto as "a leader of masses" and supported him to led the agitation against Ayub Khan in the Panjab and Sindh. With the sponsored projection of Bhutto as a progressive leader, the main nationalist opposition party, National Awami Party (NAP) was left in the wilderness in these provinces. However, in NWFP and Balochistan NAP was spearheading the movement for the restoration of democracy and provincial autonomy.

The Government's efforts to save the situation through negotiations, by convening a round-table conference of all significant political parties proved even more disastrous. Sheikh Mujeeb ur Rehman, who was under detection in the famous Agartala Conspiracy Case, had to be released unconditionally to participate in the conference. Sheikh Mujeeb had been charged by the Pakistani government with conspiring with India to disintegrate Pakistan and secure the independence of East Bengal. His release on the eve of the round table conference enhanced his position in East Pakistan and his party gained the overwhelming support of Bengali masses. The buildup of mass pressure unnerved General Ayub Khan and he succumbed and a new general, Yahya Khan took over as the ruler of the country. General Yahya Khan proclaimed Martial Law, banned political activities and abrogated the constitution.

The military regime headed by General Yahya was not unaware of the political frustration in the country. He trod carefully in the initial period to bring the country out of chaos. General Yahya restored the former provinces in West Pakistan by dissolving the One-Unit, and also rejected the parity formula. However, he did one of the great disfavors to the country by not demarcating the provinces on the basis of language and geography but restored the provinces without substantial adjustments which were necessary. Balochistan was declared a separate province but a large number of Pakhtun in three districts of Loralai, Zhob, and Pishin were included in the province against the wishes of the Baloch. Many Pakhtun leaders who had publically supported the inclusion of Pakhtun areas of former British Balochistan in the Frontier Province were also disillusioned.

Elections were held in 1970 but the army brass was not ready to accept the result of the elections and refused to hand over power to Sheikh Mujeeb-ur-Rehman's Awami League that had secured the majority of seats in the National Assembly. It was not because any threat was really seen as coming from the nationalist Sheikh Mujeeb but because power was slipping from Punjab to Bengal. The election results also nullified many notions regarding the political approaches of the people. The Punjabi-Muhajir vested interests, represented by the religious parties, raised slogans deriving from "the ideology of Pakistan" and "Nizam-e-Mustafa" in the election campaign, which by implication meant a religious orientated system of government with a partisan approach to country's socio-economic and cultural problems and a denial of rights to the subject nationalities. These parties were utterly defeated in the elections. The Awami League emerged as the sole representative of the people in East Bengal. The only consolation for the army came in Punjab and Sindh where its sponsored Peoples Party secured the majority of seats. The National Awami Party claimed considerable legislative support from the NWFP and Balochistan. The net result was that the parties with a secular approach toward politics were returned to parliament while the religious and right-wing groups were completely routed.

Peoples Party leader Bhutto as the ally of the military establishment began a campaign to work against the transfer of power to the Awami League and demanded in a most undemocratic way a share of power. Encouraged by the unwillingness of the military junta to hand over power to the elected representatives, Bhutto as the trusted politician close to the junta, became instrumental in bringing the political crisis to a climax by boycotting the National Assembly session scheduled to be held in Dacca on 25th March 1971. The boycott threat gave the regime an opportunity to postpone the opening session of parliament and precipitated political agitation by Bengalis. The army and the Peoples Party miscalculated the hazards involved in such a situation. The people of Bengal were furious and took to the streets for a solution to the intricate constitutional and governmental problems.

The military regime of General Yahya Khan put a ban on the NAP on 26th November 1971 accusing the party of acting against the state interests.

The genocide in Bengal culminated in the military intervention of India, freeing the Bengalis from the clutches of the Pakistan army after a costly but mostly uncontested war in East Bengal. The army, claiming to be one of the best fighting machines in the world, spirited by the Muslim faith, armed with the fervor of Jihad in the way of Allah, surrendered ignobly before a few battalions of advancing Indian paratroopers in Dacca, on 17th December 1971, thus ending one bloody chapter in the saga of creation of Pakistan. East Pakistan became Bangladesh.

The separation of East Bengal settled the ideological contradictions of the "two-nation theory" and the Muslim-nationhood in the sub-continent and in effect nullified the very basis of the creation of the country. Muslim nationalism, the only basis of the new state, was certainly weakened on the theoretical plane by this sudden but not unexpected jolt to the shaky foundation of the state. However, instead of any re-appraisal of the ideological and theoretical basis of Pakistan, the rulers engaged themselves with more vigor in finding flimsy justification for spurious notions and self-contradictory concepts, to advocate a continued denial of the rights of the smaller nationalities. The military rulers, disgraced and completely nervous, summoned their ally Zulfikar Ali Bhutto from the United Nations, where he had been sent to represent Pakistan in the UN debate on East Bengal crisis, to be sworn in as President and Chief Martial Law Administrator of a truncated Pakistan.

Zulfikar Ali Bhutto lifted the ban on the NAP and started negotiations with the Party to achieve a political consensus to evolve a constitution for the country. The provincial government of NWFP and Balochistan were given to the NAP-JUI coalition, only to be dismissed after nine months in a glaring act of unconstitutionality. An interim constitution was proclaimed, to be followed by a permanent one in 1973. Although Bhutto enjoyed enormous powers by virtue of his majority in the National Assembly, and by enjoying the confidence of the military officers, who were still too unnerved to resist any civilian rule, the new leader lacked the political wisdom to give the country a constitution and a democratic system which could have ensured the non-interference of too eager an army in the country's political life. Zulfikar Ali Bhutto, could not foresee the gloomy future for him and the country's minority nationalities including the Sindhis. He caused irreparable damage to the body politic with his denial of provincial autonomy and his military adventure in Balochistan.

The country's armed forces by now had licked the wounds of their ignoble defeat and were once again ready to take over the authority of the state. On their part, the politicians were so disgusted with the autocratic behavior of Bhutto that they were ready to welcome the military coup d'état. Wali Khan, the chief of the National Awami Party, who was also the leader of the combined opposition in the National Assembly gave an interview to Peoples' Front, London which was reproduced in the Pakistan Times, Lahore, On 28th December 1974. In his interview, he said that if I can get rid of Bhutto and somebody is prepared to come and help me then, be it the devil himself, I would shake hands with him. Ultimately Bhutto like his mentor General Ayub Khan stepped down as the result of mass agitation. The peoples of Pakistan got rid of him and his Party by shaking hands with General Zia ul Haq.

The Threat to Baloch Socio-cultural Identity

i. Assault on Balochi language

Language is an inseparable part of a culture representing the true historical and cultural personality of the people. It is also an important factor in the cultural and religious relationships among various peoples. It becomes an integral part of Nationalism. Peoples with linguistic distinction have been able to preserve their national identity. The Basque, the Quebecois, the Kurds, the Baloch, the Pakhtuns and many others in Asia and Africa have clung to their languages, thus claiming a separate identity and distinction.

The system of education and communication in Pakistan is a carbon copy of the nineteenth-century British scheme in India when the alien rulers systematically eliminated the indigenous languages in favor of English. The education policy, masterminded by Thomas Babington Macaulay in 1835, aimed to affect a broad range of traditional institutions and behavioral tendencies. The aim was creating a group of natives brought up in elite education, Indian in blood and color, but English in taste, in opinion, in morals and in intellect [1]. The system of education in Pakistan derives its strength and logic from the spirit of Lord Macaulay. The languages of Sindhis, Panjabis, Pakhtuns and the Baloch are being replaced by Urdu—as alien as English was in India during the colonial era. Many people especially the Punjabis, have rediscovered in Urdu a stake in exploiting the peoples of Pakistan. The class of ruling elite created by the system has a similar attitude towards the people as the colonized intellectuals of the English educated elite had during 150 years of foreign rule in the Indian sub-continent.

The Pakistani rulers, in an attempt at forced cultural assimilation, imposed Urdu as the medium of education. The syllabi in various stages of education are indicative of a strange mentality. The Baloch are taught about alien personalities but never told about their national heroes, who made their names in war and peace. Every society or people remember and glorify the heroic acts of an individual. These acts of heroism are remembered and preserved in folk literature for centuries and people invariably feel proud of past glories. If such heroes or acts of heroism did not find proper recognition, the people feel extremely bitter. The Baloch child, apart from being taught in an alien language, is also required to read exaggerated accounts of the deeds of various personalities who are regarded as heroes by the immigrants (Muhajirs) from India. The Baloch child is always in a fix. The heroes and folk-personalities about whom he is told by the elders at an early age are never mentioned in their school books. A certain Syed Ahmad Khan, a Jamaluddin Afghani, a Liaqat Ali Khan, a Muhammad Ali Johar and many many others from united India and of recent history are there for a Baloch child to memorize in school, but never Mir Shahwash, Mir Shahsawaar, Mir Jalalaan, Mir Chaakar, Mir Gwahraam, Mir Mehraab Khan, Mir Baloch Khan, Balaach Gorgeij, Mulla Fazal, Mulla Izzath or Jam Durruk. The people and personalities who have been traditional enemies of the Baloch are usually depicted as the national heroes of a non-existent nation of Muslims, for example, Mahmud of Ghazna, a predatory ruler, and his son fought many hotly contested battles with the Baloch, in whose folk tales and history Mahmud is a contemptible foe that deceived the Baloch to death. But in Pakistani school and college textbooks, he is taught as a distinguished character who paved the way for Muslim rule in India. Similarly, Muhammad bin Qasim, who massacred thousands of Baloch before invading Sindh, is always painted as another illustrious personality for the students, including the Sindhis in whose annals Muhammad bin Qasim is no more than a cruel freak who perpetrated a reign of terror in Sindh. To a Sindhi, history speaks of Raja Daher as one of their greatest rulers who resisted the invaders. Such contradictions are visible in every field. Many textbooks in schools and colleges have references to the Baloch and their country which are grossly incorrect and without any substance [2].

A mother tongue of a child may not be rich in knowledge but the fact that he can learn and acquire basic education in his own tongue more quickly than in another form of speech is absolutely indisputable. Moreover, many languages in Pakistan are more archaic and richer than Urdu, which can by no criteria be regarded as a language of knowledge. Professor Le Page, an eminent educationalist, believes that education in a foreign speech will have an undesirable impact on the child. There can be no doubt that to educate a child in a language which is not that of either of his parents tends to alienate him from his parents and to educate him in a language which is not one of the indigenous languages of the country, tends to alienate him from the culture of his country. Professor Le Page also opposes the very morality of education in an alien speech by saying that education through the medium of a foreign language may encourage a kind of opportunism that is not prepared to give unselfish service back to the community. He further argues that whenever the language of the government and law differs from that of the mass of the people, plans for economic, agricultural and industrial development are more difficult to make and more difficult to put into effect [3].

The aim of education is to help the child develop roots in society. It is to prepare him for a lifelong learning process involving mental, moral and spiritual growth by fostering a spirit of inquiry and critical thought, and to equip him with the intellectual means to find his way through the experience. The system of education being imparted to the Baloch child is superfluous and absolutely worthless in objective substance. Instead of offering an opportunity to the child in structuring him physically emotionally, intellectually and spiritually, this education is having a negative influence on him. The child grows in culture. He is part of the Baloch collective personality. But when he goes to school, he is taught from the very beginning something alien to him. The pertinent question to every Baloch is whether the education which is being given to his child is worthy of the nuisance of all these years of the formative phase of his child's life.

Pakistan is not ready to recognize the languages of the peoples of the country. It has adopted the language of the Muhajirs from India as the national language. The official wisdom is that Urdu or English should be taught to the child from the beginning but not his mother tongue. The culture of Indian immigrants depicted by Urdu is as alien as any other language and culture for the peoples of Pakistan. The Baloch child is doubly disadvantaged. He is required to express ideas and gain comprehension of subjects in a language with which he is totally unfamiliar. Therefore, the process of learning is slowed down and gravely impaired, because he cannot understand the language which is being taught to him. He is put under unnecessary stress and strain at an early age. Not only this, the ruling circles want to introduce Arabic in the educational system. Steps are underway. Radio and Television Corporation is organizing programmers in this language. Even a demand to introduce Persian had been voiced by individuals who claim official backing [4].

Pakistan undoubtedly is a unique country. The philosophy behind adopting Urdu, Arabic, Persian or any other alien tongue as the national language or the medium of education and communication, cannot be comprehended by an ordinary intellect except those whose thinking has embraced a host of obnoxious idea since the formation of this State. The Baloch and other nations in Pakistan have been opposing Urdu's national status. One of the Baloch leaders, Nawab Akbar Bugti, who served as Governor of Balochistan in 1973, even refused to talk in Urdu as a mark of protest against the socio-political set up dominated by a particular class in the country [5]. Akbar Bugti, in fact, represented the sentiment of a vast majority of the people who desire a proper status for their languages in the country.

Balochi still lacks a standard script that is needed to cater to the requirements of the language. The present script borrowed from Arabic cannot fulfill the demands of the language. The speakers of various areas use different sounds-different allophones and even different phonemes in pronouncing the same word. Balochi has various dialects. People living in Irani Balochistan and the western part of Makkuraan have their dialectical variation, generally referred to as the western dialect. The Balochi dialect that is being spoken in the Mari-Bugti region, upper Sindh and Punjab are known as the Eastern dialect, while the people in central Balochistan, including parts of Afghani Balochistan, speak the Rakhshani dialect. It is generally agreed by all shades of Baloch intellectuals that a Roman script with necessary modification can be adopted in Balochi but Baloch efforts to standardize their language are always strongly opposed by the Government. The short-lived NAP Government in Balochistan tried for the first time to adopt a script. A conference of all known Baloch writers, poets and scholars were convened to formulate suggestions to give an agreed scrip to the language. The convention was presided over by the renowned poet and historian, Mir Gul Khan Naseer, who was also the Minister of Education and Information in the NAP cabinet. The convention recommended the adoption of the Roman script for Balochi.

The convening of such a gathering was considered an undesirable act by the Pakistani government. A campaign was soon started in the mass media against the decision of the conference. The federal government obtained the co-operation of many Baloch writers who challenged the move on frivolous grounds. Although the efforts by

Baloch intellectuals and scholars to give a script to their language crumbled after the dismissal of the NAP government, the Pakistani authorities and their various agencies are still making constant efforts to secure the opposition of a large number of government-hired Baloch writers to the adoption of the Roman script. It is argued that Islam is linked with Arabic and that adopting Roman would mean that Baloch youth could not read and write Arabic and would thus become further estranged from the Islamic faith. Numerous articles have been printed in newspapers, including government-controlled papers voicing their strong disapproval of such an "anti–Islamic" step by the Baloch nationalists [6]. Baloch intellectuals and scholars, however, are unanimous in their view that the Roman script is best suited for Balochi. The youth are particularly enthusiastic. The Baloch Students Organization, before the language convention in 1972 led a march demanding the adoption of the Roman script for their tongue [7].

The subsequent political struggle and military operations after the dismissal of the NAP government in 1973, threw the language issue into the background but the question has been agitating the minds of the Baloch social, political and literary elite. About a decade after the language convention, the script for Balochi once again became the subject of discussion in an informal gathering in Kunchiti, a village sixty kilometers west of Turbat where many intellectuals were assembled on the first anniversary of the execution of Hameed Shaheed. About a dozen writers and poets participated in the discussions. Majority of them favoring a Roman script. They agreed that the Roman script would be helpful in the speedy advancement of the language. It was also agreed that the new script would make it easy to incorporate the internationally recognized signs and symbols into Balochi, helping the students to acquire scientific knowledge within a shorter span of time in comparison with any other script including Arabic. Manuscripts of two books in Roman script for children written by Mir Lal Bakhsh Rind also came under discussion [8].

Such a gathering even in a remote village could not go unnoticed by Pakistani official press. An editorial comment on the decision of the Baloch intellectuals in Dawn conceded that language plays a decisive role in peoples' search for identity and advancement and that the Baloch concern with the problem of the script in the context of the evolution of the Balochi literary genius deserved understanding and sympathy, but the paper took a generally hostile attitude in maintaining that a changeover to Roman would create the compulsion for the child to learn two scripts, Roman and Arabic in which the Holy Book is written [9].

Pakistan Radio and Television Corporation are engaged in a malicious distortion of the Balochi language. Balochi is being corrupted. It is estimated that more than seventy percent of the words and phrases used in the Balochi programs of the state-run Radio and Television are alien words used inappropriately and very purposefully as being Balochi [10]. Baloch intellectuals and writers have often objected to programs by both the corporations. Significant was a statement signed by fifteen intellectuals including poets and writers, expressing their disapproval of the programs sponsored by Pakistan Television. They called the programs ridiculous and an insult to Baloch culture and language. They maintained that what they are presenting in the name of Balochi is completely new literature based on animosity and an insult to the Balochi linguistic and literary traditions [11].

The hostility of the state against Balochi is evident from the fact that a foreign scholar of the Balochi language, Professor Joseph Elfenbeine who was appointed to Balochistan University and was engaged in research with the help of some Baloch writers was harassed and compelled to leave the country. His research activities were reported by the Pakistani press as mysterious. It was also alleged that he was engaged in anti-Pakistan activities [12]. In reality, the only fault of Professor Elfenbeine was that he had undertaken the tremendous task of compiling a Balochi-English dictionary and was perfecting a Roman script for Balochi.

ii. Cultural Aggression

Cultural aggression is attempted in subjugated societies mostly through falsification and misrepresentation of their national history. National tradition and socio-political values and institutions are undermined and ridiculed to achieve a gradual value re-orientation of the nation. Everything connected with the nation's past is dubbed outdated and reactionary. The Pakistani rulers have shown a deep contempt for the Baloch and their socio-cultural traditions from the very beginning. In order to combat the rising trend in Baloch nationalism, they started a cultural offensive to motivate and convince the younger generations of the Baloch of the futility of their own traditions and lure them into adopting alien customs. Baloch traditions have been subjected to a systematic vicious campaign. Services of some of the Baloch have been hired for the purpose. They were tasked to make slanderous attacks on the Baloch and their traditions. In their works, they regarded Baloch customs as barbaric, based on class differentiation, and its social structure as outdated and full of evils. The individual Baloch is portrayed invariably as a robber or swindler. It was also mentioned by these hired writers that to be considered a true Baloch, a person must first commit some heinous crime: and he must withstand some barbaric tests of chivalry before he is recognized as an enterprising individual [13]. The Baloch is considered the quintessence of evil. He is provoked on the slightest pretext. The people are said to be insensible to ethics denoting a negation of values. The Baloch state, the Kalat Confederacy, has been portrayed to be devoid of any civilized conduct.

In multi-national states, cultural non-interference is regarded as the essential ingredient to achieve mutual harmony and trust. The Pakistan rulers have never been reconciled to the idea of the integrity of the peoples through diversity. They believe that the peoples of Pakistan should be forcefully assimilated into the culture of Indian immigrants, which is not only alien to the peoples of Pakistan but is in open conflict with the traditional values of the masses.

A very interesting insight into the culture of immigrants which has been adopted as the national culture of the religious state of Pakistan has given by Muhammad Hasan of Jawaharlal University, Delhi, in an article published in a compilation by Qalam Qabila, Quetta. He deals in considerable detail with the educational system and socio-cultural tradition of Muslims in northern India. On the role of institutions and individuals, he has maintained that two elements can fairly be distinguished. One is the institution of prostitution and the other is homosexuality. He says that prostitutes were regarded as a symbol of honesty, civilized behavior, and deep possessive love and affection. The common people were always inspired by the prostitutes whose manners and lifestyle were copied not only by the youth but by the ruling elite, the landed aristocracy and even the clergy. The prostitution centers were regarded as places of civilized behavior, where many nobles and aristocrats would send their sons and daughters to be trained and educated. Another factor was homosexuality, a cultural innovation derived mostly from the Muslim invaders of the sub-continent, beginning in the 8th century of the Christian era. The long sojourn of the troops and their absence from their homes for a long time found an outlet in homosexuality, which later found its way in the Indian society of the settled immigrants and their dependents. The Muslim rulers and nobility not only encouraged but by and large practiced homosexuality. Such a cultural pattern is fairly evident in the literature, particularly the poetry, of the time. The conclusion he has drawn is that the culture of the Urdu speaking Muslims of northern and central India was to a large extent visibly shaped and determined by the prostitution centers of Delhi and the adjoining areas and the homosexuality of the nobility and upper classes [14]. Urdu itself is the product of these prostitution centers, where it became the vulgar tongue of communication with strangers, especially the soldiers of Central Asian origin.

No one can very well imagine the cultural conflict between two drastically different sets of peoples in a varying cultural setup. Among many of the Pakistani national entities, especially the Baloch and the Sindhis, prostitution is deeply abhorred and despised as the greatest evil of all. It is absolutely impermissible; everything connected with it is highly disliked. Hundreds of murders are still committed every year on slight doubts of infidelity. During the formative phases, the Urdu speaking rulers were, therefore, quite an alien community, in the cultural terms, for the peoples in the country.

The Punjabi-Muhajir rule has been commensurate with the introduction of a set of laws and administrative edicts that are very much alien to the people, who by and large consider such regulation repugnant to the spirit of the Baloch traditions. The de facto rulers of Balochistan are not only alien to the people but they neither understand the language nor the deep-rooted cultural traditions of the masses. Therefore, a mere realistic comprehension of the native cultural values, their behavioral tendencies are never achieved by them. Consequently, the government officers are little bothered by the sentiments of the people and always act like masters of a captured people of inferior stock. Like the colonialists, the government of Pakistan regards the people and the area as a zone that requires different sets of laws to ensure continuity of rule in order to organize, administer and develop the backward nation and the region.

Balochistan is being run on the misconceived assumption that the Baloch people are unaware of the art of rule and civilized behavior. They have to be raised from backwardness to full maturity, and until then the people of Punjab or their ruling partners should manage the affairs of the province to the good of all concerned. This unquestionably reflects the colonial mentality. The colonial masters believed that the peoples under their rule were devoid of civilized behavior, so they should be organized trained, guided and groomed to the position of responsibility to administer their area. The Pakistani attitude in relation to the Baloch and other peoples appears to be the same as that of the colonial masters. They never hide their belief that the Baloch are unqualified to be given a position of political responsibility. The emphasis is always on the development of the province. When the government opens a school, which is its primary duty, or gives some drinking water facility to the people of a village, it is publicized so much that it appears to be regarded as a great favor which the people do not deserve.

Systematic pressure on the Baloch has taken many forms and has been directed mainly against their socio-political system. The Baloch, like many other peoples, had tribalism as the main system to regulate society. The Sardar or the head of the tribe was the executive branch of the system. Any people in the modern world must have passed through this primitive stage of development. Therefore, to single out the Baloch for condemnation on the basis of tribalism betray the intention of the rulers. The insurgency in Balochistan provided the Pakistani government the question of justifying its military operations. A two-pronged attack was made, one was directed at maligning the Baloch leadership and the other was a cultural war against the people. The Baloch leaders were painted as cruel Sardars fighting for their own selfish ends. In fact, the Baloch nationalist leaders were always opposed to the sardary system and as early as 1972, the NAP dominated provincial Assembly recommended the abolition of the sardari system in the province. The decision to declare its abolition was delayed by the federal government for many years and NAP leaders who had advocated the end of the system were made the target of a vicious campaign that had no truth in it.

The systematic campaign against Baloch traditions never ends with a particular regime. It appears to be a permanent phenomenon of the state's Baloch phobia. The military regime under Zia ul Haq tried to institutionalize this trend by founding an organization named Qalam Qabela, headed by the wife of Balochistan military governor, Rahimuddin Khan. The Qalam Qabila was aimed at grouping together all the local talents who would work to defame Baloch culture and traditions. During the first year of its formation, no Baloch intellectual joined the Qabala. All its members were non-Baloch. Efforts were made at all levels including putting pressure on Baloch literary men in the Government services to join the organization, and as a result, its membership eventually included quite a few local writers. A huge complex was planned for the organization, which was inaugurated by General Zia ul Haq in September 1980. It was completed at a huge cost. This amount is estimated to be equal to at least thirty years grant in aid to three language academies of Balochi, Brahui, and Pakhtu in the Province.

iii. The Humiliation of the Elite

Pakistan's rulers always adopted an attitude of disrespect towards the Baloch and their leaders. When arrested, they were subjected to torture and ill-treatment. Leaders like Mir Ghous Bakhsh Bizenjo, Mir Gul Khan Naseer and Sardar Athaullah Mengal served prison terms in Quli (concentration) camps and were subjected to objectionable and harsh condition during General Ayub's regime. During the period when Zulfkar Ali Bhutto was ruling the country, the Baloch political prisoners were treated in an inhuman manner. Students took the brunt of brutalities. Even leaders such as Mir Mahmud Aziz Kurd, a senator, were treated improperly and the Senate of Pakistan had to intervene and asked the government to give proper facilities to the detained leader, to which he was entitled as a legislator. As a result of this maltreatment, he was taken seriously ill with liver malfunction. The government did not respond to requests from members of his family to arrange speedy transport to carry the ailing leader to Karachi for emergency treatment. He died on 14th August 1981.

The attitude of the rulers towards the Baloch appears to be one of deep contempt and intolerance. There are numerous instances that reflect this trend. Nasir, a Baloch employee of the official Pakistan International Airline (PIA), was one of the four accused and sentenced to death by a military tribunal in a hijacking case. The death sentences of his three co-accused were commuted to life imprisonment, but the sentence on Nasir was carried out on 5th March 1985 in spite of appeals from many people, including newly elected members of the national assembly and provincial assembly from Sindh. Many believed at the time that he would not have been hanged if he were not a Baloch. In the case of Hameed, all shades of public opinion in Balochistan were against his execution. More than three hundred notables had made representations to the president of Pakistan to commute the controversial death sentence. A former governor of Balochistan, Mir Ghous Bakhsh Bizenjo, asked for a meeting with the military governor to request clemency for the young student. The Governor refused to meet him. During military operations in Balochistan, the savagery of the law-enforcing agencies can be understood in the general context of the conflict, but in peacetime, such an attitude betrays a particular frame of mind.

There are numerous examples where the Baloch were subjected to extreme insults and maltreatment. On 22nd February 1979, the Pakistan Coast Guards conducted a search of a village, Bullu, near the Pak-Iran border in Kech district, and subjected the people to grave insults. Valuable possession of the people was taken away. Earlier a shepherd in Buleda was abducted in mysterious circumstances, allegedly by the army. But when the people voiced their protests to visiting high ranking officials on 25th March 1979, they were verbally abused by the officer and fired upon, which resulted in many casualties [15]. On 13th Mach 1982, the police and the army allegedly entered into many villages in the Pat Feeder area and killed many innocent people, while more than a hundred and fifty were arrested. A BSO bulletin alleged that some seventy people were killed or wounded in the operations [16]. Official sources confirmed eleven dead and twenty wounded. On 21st February 1984, the army raided a village, Dalesar, near the Iranian border, to apprehend outlaws. There was resistance to the army entering the village and there were casualties on the army side, four dead and three injured, including the troop's commander, Captain Muhammad Asghar. The army reacted with excessive ferocity. Reinforced heavily, the troops destroyed the entire settlement. The destruction was ordered by a high-ranking officer, DIG frontier Corps, who flew in from Quetta in a helicopter to supervise the punitive operation. The village was destroyed and all belonging including domesticated animals and cattle were gutted with fire. The army arrested the entire population of the settlement, 118 persons, including women and children.

Apart from general harassment, various government agencies have set up numerous check posts and search squads throughout Balochistan, to harass and humiliate not only the common villagers but also passengers on the highways. A report published in the BSO organ Girouk mentioned the inhuman treatment of the people at the hands of various law-enforcement agencies. The report said the treatment meted out is so extraordinary as to give the impression that the Baloch are a colonized people [17].

iv. Divisive tactics

To drive a wedge between various sections of the Baloch society appears to be a permanent endeavor of the state. When Kalat was truncated by illegally securing the accession of Kharan, Lasbela, and Makkuraan into Pakistan, one of the arguments at that time was that it was to secure the autonomy of these regions from the Khanate of Kalat which is dominated by the Brahuis. Therefore, Lasbela, Makkuraan, and Kharan, where the majority are Baloch, should secede from the Confederacy of Kalat. Apart from such a factional approach, the government of Pakistan has always encouraged and patronized tribal rivalries, such as between the Maris and Bugtis, or between Zehri and Mengal or among the various factions of a single tribe. Sardar Doda Khan Zarakzai was patronized and used against the Mengal chief, who was a leader of the NAP. Zahri chief was used in eliminating a faction within the Zehris. The killing of Safar Khan Zarakzai, a guerrilla commander of the 1977 insurgency was more a machination of the Zehri chief than an act of the Pakistani army.

Most important are the government efforts to fuel the imaginary differences between the Baloch and Brahuis. The latter has been portrayed as being Dravidians. The minor differences in their speech are taken as proof of their non-Baloch origin. Many writers were discreetly commissioned to prove the Brahui's non-Baloch origin on the one hand and their gruesome crimes, against the Baloch during the Brahui rule in Kalat on the other. According to these hired writers, the Khanate of Kalat was always a Brahui rule over the Baloch. The Baloch system of governance was portrayed as a permanent curse decimating the vigor and vitality of the entire race [18]. The history of the Baloch Confederacy of Kalat was said to be a history of intrigues, feuds and tribal jealousies, the entire reign as anarchic and Machiavellian in the competitive ingenuity of its misdeeds [19]. In their plan of creating divisions, various dialects of Balochi language have also been put forward to counter the Baloch demand for recognition of Balochi as the medium of education.

On the political front, the theme of Baloch-Brahui's separate identity was propagated as a possible means of checking Baloch nationalism in the early sixties, when the *Warna Waaninda Gal* and the Baloch Educational Society demanded an official status for Balochi. The government immediately devised a plan to have certain individuals assert the bilingual character of the Baloch region and ask that Brahui should be treated equally with Balochi on the eve of the regional languages conference at Lahore in April 1961.

What was sinister is not the demand for the promotion of Brahui which is a language of the Baloch, but the way it was used to counter the demand for Baloch socio-cultural and political rights. The Baloch never opposed the Brahui language or those who insist on its promotion, but certainly disliked attempts to divide the Baloch and create factionalism, with disastrous consequences for the entire people. The students, in their publications always include a Brahui section alongside the Balochi. In all the meetings of the NAP and its successor the PNP, and in BSO gatherings, both the languages are freely used. As regards Balochi, it was declared the official language of Balochistan during the Kalat States Union. The parliament of Balochistan, elected after its independence, in its meeting on 14th December 1947, recommended that Balochi should be declared the national and official language of Balochistan [20].

Vigorous resistance by political leaders against attempts to divide the people into linguistic or racial premises did not deter the government in adopting more subtle ways such as the non-existent Zegri-Numazi issue. After the apparent failure of the attempts at division on the basis of ethnicity or language, the government agencies encouraged religious clergy or the mullahs, belonging to various religious parties and based outside Balochistan, to raise the bogy of sectarian intolerance. The move is directed mainly against the Zigris. Zigri, a religious sect of Indian origin, has been practiced in Balochistan since the early fifteenth century. From the evidence available so far it appears that the sect was founded by one

Muhammad (C.1442-1505 AD) of Jaunpur, in India who was expelled from there because of his religious beliefs. He visited Mecca and some other Muslim holy places and made his way to Persia. He or one of his descendants came to Makkuraan and took up abode at Koh e Muraad, a hill in the suburb of Turbat and preached his faith to the people of the area, who became his followers. He also had disciples in Sistaan and Kirmaan.

A systematic campaign against the Zigris was started by the orthodox clergy with official encouragement. The mullahs not only incite the people to violence but openly condemn the Balochi traditions and their cultural heritage.

The Baloch belonging to any sect, whether Zigri, Sunni, Shia or Ismaili are secular in their approach; however, the clergy has started a campaign of vilification against the Baloch in general. Many books and pamphlets have been brought out by the mullahs and widely distributed in the area in which highly objectionable language has been used against the Baloch. The tirade against the Zigris is a movement against the Baloch and their traditions. It is inconceivable that the Baloch will ever change their beliefs no matter how much of coercion is used. Obviously, the clergy is not unaware of this cultural trend. The aim is not to convert the Zigris to any other Islamic sect Sunni or Shia, but to continue the diatribe against the Baloch and reduce the entire region to a zone of religious intolerance.

Distribution of material preaching communal hatred, which should have been brought to the attention of the law is never objected to by the government while any other reasonable book is promptly confiscated under the relevant clauses of the omnipotent Press and Publication Ordinance. In a brief period of five weeks in early 1985, the government proscribed 22 books and magazines. These were said to have contained objectionable material [21]. But anything against the Baloch unity is not only allowed free circulation but its authors are encouraged. Not only this, the clergy in their regular sermons, are openly preaching violence and have been instrumental in many acts of killing and looting of the Baloch settlements transgressed every limit. They preached that intermarriages with people believing in Zigrism are prohibited and existing marriages stand revoked.

The first-ever example of violence organized by the clergy against the Zigris was in 1958 in Pasni, where eleven persons were killed, including a notable, Kahoda Noor Mahmad. This resulted in a sharp reaction against the mullahs who remained silent for a long time. More recently under active patronage and with Saudi petrodollars, they are becoming more organized and delivering invective harangues against the people. Hundred of religious educational centers are operating in far-flung areas throughout Balochistan producing religious fanatics. The main target is the Jahlawaan and Makkuraan regions. Madrassas (Islamic schools) are operating under foreign guidance with enormous funds. Preachers, *thablighi*s, from the Punjab, NWFP, and Sindh are visiting the area more frequently. Their annual gathering, *ijthimah*, in even remote places are attended by the Mullahsto preach hatred amongst the Baloch. These gatherings are very well organized and well-financed.

v. The Import of the Workforce

Despite loud claims by the Pakistan authorities, the Baloch are being denied job opportunities. The former Chief Minister of Balochistan, Sardar Athaullah Mengal, talking to writer Tariq Ali in 1981, had this much to say of the Baloch representation in the services: when I was in Mach Jail in Balochistan, the situation was brought home to me very vividly. A prison warder is the lowest-paid government employee. There were 120 warders in the goal but only eleven of them were Baloch. He estimated that out of twelve thousand government employees only three thousand were Baloch, the remainder Pathan, Hazarawals and Punjabi. The situation in other services, including the army and the police, was no better. Sardar Mengal said in the same interview that there are only a few hundred Baloch in the entire Pakistan army. The famous Baloch Regiment has no Baloch in it. The Kalat Scouts was a para-Military force raised during the reign of General Ayub Khan. There were only two people from Kalat recruited to its ranks. The same is the case with the Sibi Scouts, created to police the Mari area. Not a single Baloch is in its ranks. The officers were from Punjab and the soldiers from the Frontier province. He observed that if you land at Quetta airport today and visit the city, you will soon realize that 95% of the police constables have been brought from outside [22]. Robert G. Wirsing estimated that out of forty thousand civil employees of all categories in the early seventies, only two thousand (5%) were Baloch: most of them held inferior jobs [23]. The Baloch demands for a share in the services

209

have been met with allegations of their being traitors and anti-state. When the Mengal ministry wanted to recruit the Baloch and into the police service, which was overwhelmingly a force derived from Punjab, the federal government looked at it with considerable suspicion and planned to defeat the move by any means. Sardar Mengal, recalling the event in 1981 to Tariq Ali, said: when we tried to correct the Balance (in the Police force) Bhutto and his Punjabi aide Mustafa Khar organized a police strike against our government, creating a law and order situation in the province [24].

The Baloch share in the civil service is negligible. Of all the administrative officers in the province, only a few are Baloch. During the period from 1973 to 1984, out of the officials appointed in seventeen districts as district magistrates or Deputy Commissioners, the number of the Baloch never exceeded one or at the most two at a time. Out of twenty administrative secretaries to the government, three were Baloch in 1984 and this number is the maximum known. Out of thirty-two directors of various departments in the province, with the rank of grade eighteen and above, there have not been more than three at a given time. Similarly, all high officers in the police and other law enforcement agencies are reserved for officers from outside, mostly from Punjab or from their junior partners, the Pakhtuns of NWFP. Of all the officers of grade eighteen and above in the province, only 4.3% are filled with the Baloch. Of grade sixteen and seventeen officers, the Baloch share is however slightly higher, which is 9.5%. The Education Department appears to be an exception where the Baloch fills nearly 12% of the officer posts in grades sixteen and seventeen. In the Higher grades, the share is progressively lower. Baloch representation in lower grade jobs, however, constitutes some eleven to thirteen percent. Out of nearly seventy-five thousand provincial government employees of all grades, the Baloch constitute ten thousand mostly in lower grades. According to a survey carried out in June 1980, out of 830 higher grade officers in Balochistan, there were only 181 Baloch and out of 499 officers attached to the federal services in the province only 16 were Baloch. The survey showed that 95 percent of Baloch graduates were unemployed in the year 1980.

The Baloch has no representation in the federal services. A different trick is being played to fill the vacancies reserved for Balochistan in the federal departments. They are given to candidates who produce documents of domicile in the province. Since the majority of issuing authorities of such certificates are non-Baloch, candidates from other provinces especially from Punjab quickly obtain the necessary papers and get the jobs on the reserved list. Moreover, such papers can be secured easily on payment of a small amount. Every year thousands of such documents are issued. The district magistrate of Quetta alone, an army colonel from the frontier, who is now the commissioner of Quetta, issued the amazing number of three thousand domiciles certificates in fifteen months from 1979-1980 to people belonging to other provinces, most of them not registered in the books. No Baloch officer is working as secretary to the federal government; no Baloch is serving as an ambassador or on any other assignment in any of the embassies of Pakistan abroad, nor any officer in higher grades serving in any government-controlled corporation or semi-government agency. In the National Shipping Corporation, out of 816 employees in 1979, there were seven persons working in clerical jobs claiming domicile from Balochistan, five of them were non-Baloch. Mir Ghous Bakhsh Bizenjo a former governor of Balochistan, in an interview in 1983, said that most officials in the province have come from outside. We have never had a chief secretary or I.G. police or additional chief secretary from our own people... these discrepancies must be removed if we are to be equal. If Pakistan is to be strong, there must be equal representation in the armed forces. What is the Baloch Regiment doing in Abbottabad? How many are Baloch in the regiment? We have qualified and experienced people amongst us; so why are we never consulted about our own affairs? [25].

The Baloch youth who pass the examinations conducted by the Federal Public Service Commission found it difficult to get a job. A report, published in Dawn on 30th August 1984, says that out of twenty-one candidates who qualified for the federal services in 1983 less than one-third of them were offered jobs. Even a presidential assurance to the candidates was not kept and according to the Daily Star (24th January 1985), they were not provided with the jobs reserved for Balochistan.

The rate of unemployment among Baloch youth is the highest in the country if judged on population ratio. A large percentage of jobs provided by the unemployment cell; which has functioned for many years under the ministry of Communication have been captured by non-Baloch. A permanent unemployed Graduate Action Committee has been formed, whose job is to approach various government ministeries and ask for job opportunities for those registered as unemployed with the action committee. It is estimated that several thousand Baloch graduates and postgraduates are jobless in the province and this includes doctors and engineers. Given the low rate of literacy among the Baloch these figures mean that the highest percentage of educated among the Baloch are unemployed as compared to other ethnic groups.

The Baloch cannot even sell their labor to industries operating in the province or mines being extracted from Balochistan. Ninety-nine percent of the labor engaged in mining is from outside the province. The Baloch cannot get jobs in industrial units set up in Hub in the Lasbela District. Sardar Athaullah Mengal, addressing a gathering soon after his release from prison, regretted that the Baloch were not getting employment in the Lasbela industries. He said: our people merely want to sell their labor. They neither demand any share in the profit nor do they aspire for managerial or executive posts. He alleged that out of ten thousand workers in the Gaddani Ship Breaking Yard, none of them were Baloch [26]. Not only this but the Baloch workers have never received proper wages. Jabal (November 1977), the mouthpiece of the Baloch Peoples' Liberation Front (BPLF), alleged that out of forty employees at the Goonga Baryte Mines near Khuzdar in 1975, non-Baloch workers received wages three times higher than the Baloch laborers there.

Sui Gas provides fuel to houses in the Punjab and other provinces and saves a huge amount in foreign exchange. But the Baloch are not only deprived of its benefits but even refused entry to its installations. A monthly magazine, Siyasiyat-e-Pakistan, published from London, quoted an interesting notice on the perimeter of the Sui Gas installation, reading: Bugtis are not allowed to enter [27]. This notice tells the full truth about the Baloch and their future in their own land.

Baloch officers should be entitled to the same facilities which the officers from the Panjab and other provinces may be receiving, but non- Baloch officers always get the priority. Residential accommodation in the provincial capital usually goes to non-Baloch officers. Not only this: the officers who serve in the province are allowed subsidies for their travel expenses from the other provinces to Balochistan. PIA issued a directive to its ticketing staff on 30th January 1980 which says: All civil servants who are not domiciled in Balochistan will be allowed to make payment at 50% of the actual fare. This pertains to travel between points in Balochistan on the one hand and points outside Balochistan on the other. This is applicable to travels for personal reasons or for those on vacation. Their immediate family members and dependents are also eligible for this discount [28]. Such a bonus is not only available to civil servants, but also to a variety of officials including the nurses in government hospitals and teachers in the education department who hail from other provinces [29]. Similarly, teachers are allowed additional money to defray their traveling expenses during vacations [30].

In matters of promotions, officers belonging to the provincial services, who include many Baloch and indigenous tribes, cannot get promotions in years while officers belonging to the federal services, mostly Punjabis, are catapulted within a fixed time span. Discrimination between federal and provincial services is more pronounced in the case of Balochistan. Officers belonging to the federal services are given grade twenty within fifteen years of service, while officers of provincial cadres require that period to be promoted from grade seventeen to grade eighteen.

Bureaucracy has an overwhelming role in the province. Nothing moves until the powerful civil-military bureaucracy wishes it. When the Baloch leaders wanted the government to replace certain individuals known for their anti-Baloch stance, including the then Chief Secretary, Raja Ahmad Khan, a Punjabi, the demand was rejected outright. The Baloch leaders raised this demand with General Zia ul Haq in a meeting in Quetta on 28th July 1978. In a statement after the meeting, Sardar Athaullah Mengal said bureaucracy was given preference over the Balochistan issue [31].

vi. The Perception of Exploitation

'We can survive without Pakistan. We can remain without Pakistan. we can prosper without Pakistan. But the question is what Pakistan would be without Us?' This question, posed on 14th December 1947 by Mir Ghous Bakhsh Bizenjo, a young parliamentarian in the sovereign assembly of Balochistan, is still pertinent. What is Balochistan, to Pakistan? Geographically, it has provided strategic depth, a long coastline and an area of immense importance in the heart of central and southwest Asia. Economically it is sustaining the entire state by providing billions of rupees annually from its natural wealth. Without its immeasurable riches, Pakistan could never be an economically viable state. Apart from minerals and gas, there are huge oil reserves that are still to be tapped, Balochistan produces more than 70,000 metric tons of marine fish annually earning foreign exchange to the tune of 500 million dollars [32]. Balochistan produces important minerals such as chromate, fluorite magnesite, copper, marble, limestone, and barytes. Mineral production during 1982-1983, according to government statistics, was 930,850 tons of coal, 4,257 tons of chromites; 20,953 tons of marble; 16,309 tons of barytes and 1,687 tons of magnesite. The latest figures for limestone were not revealed, but during the year 1972-1973, some 52,105 tons of limestone was extracted. Similarly, the production of fluorite for 1981-1982 was 2696 tons. As for natural gas, the Pakistan government has not revealed the figures for nearly a decade. However, some 4,77,436 units were produced in 1976-1977 when the new gas field at Pirkoh had not been commissioned [33]. The federal government had an income of more than 10,426 million rupees from gas in 1976-77. The latest estimates indicate that the government has an income from the gas of nearly 22,000 million rupees [34]. Another 10,000 million is saved from minerals, Gaddani Ship Breaking Yard saved 400 million rupees in foreign exchange in 1975 [35]. The saving has gone up to 820 million rupees in 1985 [36].

Balochistan is the richest land in Central Asia. The per capita income, if it were to have at its disposal its entire resources and income, would be one of the highest in the world. But the people of Balochistan are not the beneficiaries of the huge resources and income the province provides to the federal exchequer. It is getting only a nominal royalty from the Sui Gas production. During 1979-1980, Balochistan received only 1.23 million dollars. The royalty rate in 1981 was 12.5 Percent of the well-head price, as against the 45 percent rate enjoyed by the petroleum-producing provinces of Canada, and the wellhead price was 0.06 dollars per 1,000 cubic feet, as against 1.90 dollars in Canada [37]. If only fifty percent of the more than three thousand million dollars Balochistan contributes were spent in the development of the province, it would become a prosperous and developed land within five years. It is poor not because it lacks resources, but because the Pakistani rulers neither desire its development nor are ready to allow some of its income towards the uplift of its people. The Baloch are well-aware of the wealth of their land. There is saying in Balochi that: "A Baloch child may be born without socks on his feet, but when he grows up every step he takes is on gold".

Gas was discovered in 1952. It was brought into use in other provinces of Pakistan from October 1955 but it was not provided to Balochistan for decades. The Sui Gas was provided to the Quetta army garrison and other non-Baloch areas but had never reached the Baloch homes of the provincial capital. While every town and village of Punjab, Sindh and the Frontier Province is lit up with gas from Balochistan, the Baloch cannot imagine this for many decades to come. Natural gas is the backbone of Pakistan economy. It is running more than thirty percent of the industrial units in the country and providing energy to forty-five percent of the households in the Punjab and other provinces. Without it, Pakistan would have to spend more than two thousand million dollars in foreign exchange to import energy. A Punjabi Minister, Saifullah Paracha, has admitted that Balochistan resources are being utilized in a wasteful manner and that within fifteen years the present gas reservoir will be exhausted [38].

All the industries producing and refining minerals extracted from Balochistan are located in other provinces. Therefore, the Baloch are not given the opportunity to sell their labor to the factories in which their resources take their final shape. Coal is produced in great quantity, but its prices are higher in Balochistan than in Punjab. People cannot get coal easily in the winter. All the small industrial units in Balochistan, including those recently set up in Hub in the Lasbela District, are owned by big businesses from Karachi. In fact, industries functioning in Lasbela, a few miles from Karachi, have been set up for the benefit of Karachi as observed by Sardar Athaullah Mengal [39].

The development is a big hoax. According to former provincial Chief Minister Sardar Athaullah Mengal, in 1973-1974, the development projects in the province included the construction of big military camps throughout the province. Fortified buildings were built for the army, each at a huge cost [40]. A great misinformation campaign has been launched by the government regarding its development initiatives. A former finance minister in the NAP cabinet, Mir Ahmad Nawaz Bugti, rejected government claims as meaningless because no infrastructure for development has been created. He said a major portion of the fund allocated for development were manipulated by government officials. The entire development work in the province circles round official propaganda. The amount which is incurred on the propaganda of development works, if spent in the province, would have made a lot of difference in the peoples' lives, he added [41]. Nawab Khair Bakhsh Mari has been skeptical of government intentions. Mari told an American author, Harrison, that the Baloch wanted to modernize their country in their own way while Pakistan authorities want to modernize us in their own way without listening to us. On the overall strategy of development planned by the Pakistan government, Mari alleged that most of the roads built in Balochistan were not for our benefit but to make it easier for the military to control us and for the Punjabis to rob us. The issue is not whether to develop, but whether to develop without autonomy. Exploitation has now adopted the name of development, Nawab Mari alleged [42]. In 1977 the BPLF alleged that Pakistan considered the Baloch country a vast estate for plunder, an arid desert floating in oil and minerals. A large part of their political strategies is dictated by the desire to extract this treasure for the benefit of the Pakistan bureaucratic bourgeoisie and foreign imperialist interests. The Pakistani oligarchy needs Balochistan's oil and minerals to overcome the severe economic crisis gripping the whole country [43].

No developmental work which can benefit the people of Balochistan has ever been started by the government for the last thirty-eight years. The RCD Highway connecting the port city of Karachi to the Balochistan capital of Quetta is a glaring example. It was proposed in 1953. A survey was conducted by a UN team n 1954-55. The work started in 1956. The 440-mile highway is still to be completed and cannot be called a highway in the real sense. Many governors and other government dignitaries have inaugurated this road several times for the benefit of propaganda. The last time the Balochistan's military governor inaugurated it on 25th July 1982. Another highway that connects the Punjab and Sindh with the province via eastern Balochistan is also in a dilapidated condition. Yet another 358-kilometer road connecting Balochistan to Multan through the Mari-Bugti mountainous country is under construction [44]. This is a strategic link between Balochistan and Punjab mostly for the movement of the armed forces in a future eventuality. Except for these strategically important roads, there is hardly any road throughout Balochistan worth traveling. The government is only interested in keeping Balochistan open to carry its mineral wealth to other provinces for refining and marketing. Another road that was given FrontPage coverage in the newspapers is the Coastal Highway connecting coastal townships with Karachi. This is also perceived to be of strategic importance for the military.

The publicity campaign on the development is aimed at hoodwinking the people and misguiding public opinion abroad. All development projects are on paper, with nothing visible on the spot. This was also felt by General S.F.S Lodhi, who remained governor of the province for a brief period in 1984. Speaking before government official at Dhadar, he expressed his dissatisfaction with the state of development works. He said instead of paperwork, the efforts should be made to uplift the province in a real sense [45]. Presiding over a high-level meeting in Quetta on 15th may 1984, to review the Annual Development Plan, Governor Lodhi again expressed dissatisfaction over the quality of work carried out on roads and buildings [46].

Development is an integrated process in which all aspects of the life of a society, social, cultural, political, moral and economic usually advance on parallel lines to achieve certain given objectives. Real development can be achieved only if the peoples' co-operation is obtained and institutions are created. No institution can flourish unless it caters to the moral, socio-cultural, economic and political realities of the society. However, the advancement of subjugated people is perhaps the favorite theme of all third world military or civilian dictatorships to justify their ruthless domination of minority nationalities. In the case of Balochistan, the development has other dimensions. Even if developments claimed by the rulers are taken for granted, it is merely the construction of building for government officers or constructing some military-strategic roads connecting Balochistan to important centers in the Punjab and other provinces. As regards the Baloch, they are alienated because they are out of any decision-making process. The rulers of the state would not allow a Baloch government in their land to function smoothly even for nine months out of 38 years of the county's existence. The province is being run through emergency laws and regulation since the establishment of the military regime in 1977. The representatives of people in other provinces have been associated in a limited way in administering their province but no ministers or advisors to the government were appointed in Balochistan, which is being ruled directly from Islamabad.

References

1. Thomas Babington Macaulay: Speeches of Lord Macaulay. Oxford University Press, London, 1935, (Re-Printed in 1979) p 359.

2. To give only an instance, the Sindh Text Book Board approved a book of history for ninth class students contains a much-distorted version of Balochistan and its people. The write up in the book is a crude attempt to show the Baloch, Brahui, and Makkuraani belonging to distinct racial groups. A non-existent dialect of Makkuraani has been added to the Balochi Language. The customs and tradition of the Baloch are depicted in a very objectionable manner. (Badal Khan Baloch: Rajekebebeit Gung Namaniet. Sanj, Op. Cit. pp 269-272).

3. R.B. Le Page: The National Language Question, The Institute of Race Relations, London, 1964, pp,18-25.

4. Jang (Quetta),10ᵗʰ May 1985.

5. Ibid. 11ᵗʰ October 1983 and 6ᵗʰ January 1984.

6. Qazi, Abbur Rahim Saabir: (Sougaath, March 1982) Faqeer Muhammad Ambar: Sougaath, May 1962) InayatullahQoumi: (Sougaath, August 1982) Ghulam Akbar Baloch: (Sougaath, August 1982).

7. Sun, Karachi,19ᵗʰ May 1972.

8. Siddique Baloch: Heat Waves: Script for Balochi language, Dawn 27ᵗʰ June 1982.

9. Dawn, 29ᵗʰ June 1982.

10. Jan Muhammad Dashti: The Baloch Cultural Heritage. Royal Book Company, Karachi,1982, p.42.

11. Jang (Quetta) 29ᵗʰ January 1979.

12. Daily News (Karachi), 5ᵗʰ September 1982 and Jang (Karachi) 28ᵗʰ August 1982.

13. Muhammad Sardar Khan Baloch: History of the Baloch Race and Balochistan Op. Cit. pp 120, 178. The Great Baloch. Op Cit p 77.

14. Muhammad Hasan: Atharaween Sadi Mien Dehli Ke Afrad o Mushaira Ka Thaaruf (A compilation of articles) Qalam Qabela, Quetta, 1983, pp, 69,108.

15. Balochi (Quetta) March-April p 15.

16. Pajjar,1982, p 6.

17. Girouk, February- March 1983, p 17.

18. Muhammad Sardar Khan: The Great Baloch, Op.Cit. p

19. Muhammad Sardar Khan: History of Baloch Race and Balochistan. Op. Cit, p 120.

20. Gul Khan Naseer: Tharikh-e-Balochistan. Vol I and II. Kalat publishers, Quetta, 1979, p 499.

21. Dawn, 10ᵗʰ February 1985.

22. Tariq Ali: Op. Cit. p 177.

23. Robert G. Wirsing: The Balochis and Pathans (The Minority Rights Group Ltd) London, 1981, p 9.

24. Tariq Ali: Op. Cit p177.
25. Mir Ghous Bakhsh Bizengo: (Interview) Balochistan Byways: A Star Report Op. Cit. 32.
26. Peoples Front (London) Vol 3 No. 2. June 1978.
27. Siyasathe-e-Pakistan (London)July August 1978, p 8.
28. PIA Directive (No TF Pak D 129). Dated 30th January 1980.
29. Mashriq (Quetta), 26th October 1983.
30. Jang (Quetta), 30th January 1985.
31. Mashriq (Quetta), 29th July 1978.
32. Source: The Directorate of Fisheries, Government of Balochistan.
33. Source: Planning and Development Department, Government of Balochistan.
34. Balochistan Assembly Debates, 2nd June 1985. quoted in (Jang, Quetta, 3rd June 1985).
35. Dawn, 25th April 1975.
36. Source: Department of Industries, Government of Balochistan.
37. Selig Harrison: In Afghanistan's shadow: Baloch Nationalism and Soviet Temptations. Op. Cit. p162.
38. Source: Directorate of Mineral Development, Government of Balochistan.
39. Mujahid Brailvi: Op. Cit. p 29.
40. Sardar Athaullah Mengal, Quoted in Parcham, (Karachi) Vol I No 6-7 p 12.
41. Ahmad Nawaz Bugti, quoted in Mujahid Brailvi Op. Cit. p 71.
42. Khair Bakhsh Mari: Interview with Sleg S. Harrison: Op. Cit. p 47.
43. Imperialism, Oil and the Balochistan Revolution. Jabal July 1877 p 6.
44. Dawn,18th February 1985.
45. Jang (Quetta), 13th May 1984.
46. Dawn, 16th May 1984.

CHAPTER VIII

THE BALOCH RELATIONS WITH PAKHTUNS

After the ban on the NAP, the party workers, on the advice of the detained leaders, formed its successor, the National Democratic Party (NDP) on 6th November 1975, nine months after the ban on the NAP and merely a week after the Supreme Court upheld the government decision banning the party. Five basic principles of the NDP were announced by Sardar Sher Baz Mazari on 15th November 1975 in the Karachi meeting of the Party workers and these were subsequently included in the party manifesto. The new Party apparently did not deviate from the NAP manifesto on the question of provincial autonomy. It stood for a federal set-up, where only Defense, Foreign Affairs, Currency and Communications were to be given to the Federation and all residual powers would remain with the provinces. The Party asked for re-demarcation of the provincial boundaries on the basis of racial, cultural and geographical affinity and for distinct cultural and racial units to be allowed to progress within the Federation. It advocated non-alignment in external relations. It also demanded that basics education should be given in the mother tongue. The only slight deviation from NAP objectives was noted in its vague stand on the secular polity.

The National Democratic Party was regarded as the sole spiritual and political heir of the defunct National Awami Party. The NDP, within a few months of its existence, entered into an alliance with other groups, forming the Pakistan National Alliance (PNA), to fight the ruling Peoples Party. PNA, which was comprised of nine major opposition groups, accepted the NDP stand on Balochistan and boycotted the polls in the province in protest against the military operations in the province and the detention of prominent Baloch leaders.

After their release from prison, the Baloch politicians found a very distressing situation in the country, especially in Balochistan, where the party workers were not happy over the performance of the NDP and the role of its President, Sardar Sher Baz Mazari. Begum Naseem, the wife of the Pakhtun leader, Abdul Wali Khan, had been exercising considerable influence on the Party chief on his decisions and activities. Abdul Wali Khan also had developed differences with Baloch leaders regarding the question of political reconciliation with Prime Minister Bhutto and later with General Zia ul Haq. When the Pakistan government offered to release the detainees in the Hyderabad conspiracy case, Wali, Khan and five other Pakhtun leaders accepted the offer against the wishes of the Baloch leaders. They submitted petitions and were bailed out while the Baloch politician demanded the withdrawal of the case and the unconditional release of all political prisoners. This was the parting of ways and the end of the political alliance of the Baloch and Pakhtun for many years to come.

The Baloch were deeply aggrieved at the Pakhtun indifference to their struggle. During the period when the NAP was engaged in negotiations and afterward when it was enjoying power in NWFP and Balochistan, the party president, Abdul Wali Khan played a dubious role in spoiling the working relations of the provinces with Bhutto's central government. Moreover, he had promised not only the wholehearted support of the Pakhtuns in the Baloch armed struggle, but moral and material help from the government of Afghanistan, where he had considerable influence. Nothing came out and he also left behind the Baloch leaders in the wilderness by getting out of prison on bail. Not only was no help offered by the Pakhtuns during the conflict but they remained absolutely unconcerned throughout. The role of many of the Pakhtun leaders and government employees, especially those hailing from NWFP and serving in Balochistan was regrettable. On many occasions, the Pakhtun army officers and men showed greater enthusiasm in crushing the Baloch resistance than their Panjabi counterparts. Various troops of scouts fighting against the Baloch were from the NWFP.

The revolution in Afghanistan and the overthrow of the Sardar Daud regime also served as a cause for political estrangement between the two peoples. While the Baloch leaders wholeheartedly welcomed the new socialist government of President Noor Muhammad Tarakai, Wali Khan and many Pashthuns, because of their personal relationship with Daud Khan, resented the overthrow of his regime. The Baloch politicians also wanted the question of the four nationalities and their rights to be included in the manifesto of the National Democratic Party. On foreign relations, Mir Ghous Bakhsh Bizenjo, considered the entire zone of South Asia to fall within the Russian sphere of influence while Wali Khan and the Party chief, Sher Baz Mazari, opposed such open talk in view of the political exigencies within the country. After the Baloch politician left the NDP, its president told a press conference on 29th June 1979 that the Baloch leaders had left the party on the question of the four nationalities and foreign policy preferences. Their stand, he maintained was not acceptable to the party [1].

The differences of the Baloch leaders with the Pakhtun leadership became unmanageable. After their release from prison. The Baloch leadership decided to leave the National Democratic Party and form a separate organization. The decision was announced by Sardar Ataullah Mengal in a press conference in Karachi on 19th April 1979. He criticized the attitude of Wali Khan and Sardar Sher Baz Mazari and said the Baloch faction in the NDP had decided to leave the Party[2].

Sardar Sher Baz Mazari, the founder president of the Party, could not work with Pathans himself for very long. He resigned from the basic membership of the party in August 1985. Mazari experienced the chauvinistic attitude of the Pathan leaders towards other peoples. In his letter of resignation, issued to the press on 19th August 1985, he pointed out that issues pertaining to the Frontier Province and the Pakhtuns are raised without taking into consideration the feelings and aspirations of other nationalities[3].

The Baloch leaders convened a meeting of the party workers belonging to the defunct NAP and NDP and formed the Pakistan National Party (PNP) on 1st June 1979. The convention held on 1st and 2nd June approved a manifesto along with six guiding principles to be incorporated in the manifesto. The PNP advocated equal rights for the provinces with maximum autonomy within a federal parliamentary form of government. All powers except Defense, Foreign Affairs,

Currency and Communications would be exercised by the provinces. The PNP demanded a secular administration and non-alignment in external relations. The Pakistan National Party put forward the concept of national democracy in order to safeguard the rights and privileges of nationalities. It also advocated the creation of provinces on the basis of socio-cultural, geographical and historical unity and affiliation of the people and recognition of the languages of the federating units as official languages. The party stood for a socialist economy with the public sector taking precedence over the private sector.

As far as the government of Pakistan was concerned, it had welcomed any differences between the Baloch and Pakhtuns on the national level. Lawrence Ziring writing on Baloch-Pakhtun relations says: clearly Pathan and Baloch claim some of the same territories, and this makes them suspicious of one another and often brings them into conflict. Transcending of this narrower nationalism, however, had been attempted more by them than by the Pakistan government, which has over the year gained some advantage from these rivalries[4].

The Pakhtun areas in Balochistan were never claimed by the Baloch. Their insistence on the demarcation of the provincial boundaries on the basis of language and culture means the exclusion of these areas from Balochistan and the inclusion of the Balochi-speaking districts of Harand and Dajal (now Dera Ghazi Khan) and Jacababad(Now Sindh), into their country. The Pakhtun demand for provinces on a linguistic and cultural basis was supported by the Baloch. In fact, the Baloch have always opposed the inclusion of the Pakhtun speaking areas into Balochistan. When the Pakistan government wanted to merge the Kalat States Union and formerly leased areas with the Pakhtun districts, it was opposed by the Baloch. The move of inclusion of Pakhtun areas into Balochistan was backed by Pakhtoon leaders but severely criticized by the Baloch elders in a memorandum of 16th February 1954 addressed to the members of the Constituent Assembly of Pakistan. The memorandum opposed the inclusion of the Pathan areas into Balochistan and proposed that in view of the racial affinities they might be merged in the North West Frontier Province (NWFP) or retained as tribal areas under the direct administration of the Centre through a political resident. Later, 18 Baloch sardars and leaders of opinion sent telegrams to the Pakistani authorities voicing their opposition to the proposed inclusion of Pathan districts of British Balochistan into the Balochistan States Union. They termed such an action by the Pakistan government illegal and unconstitutional[5]. Notwithstanding the expressed wishes of the Baloch and their tribal elders, the Pakistan government decided on 16th June 1954 to merge the Pathan districts with the Balochistan States Union.

The Pakhtun speaking areas never formed part of Balochistan or the Baloch Confederacy. The Pakhtun districts included Hernai, Dukhi, Pishin and Chaman tehsils, a portion of Sibi Tehsil, Loralai and Zhob tribal territories. These were under the administrative control of Afghanistan and had formed part of the provinces of Kandahar and Hirat from time immemorial. After the creation of Pakistan, these areas were inherited by Pakistan as parts of British Balochistan.

The Question of the linguistic basis for the provinces and the formation of a province comprising the Pakhtun speaking areas of Balochistan were first raised by Abdul Samad Achakzai after the Partition of India. His organization, Wrore Pakhtun (the Pakhtoon Brotherhood), formed in 1954, was clearly aimed at creating a Pakhtun province incorporating all the Pakhtun areas. Earlier, the People Party, founded by Abdul Ghaffar Khan with Samad Khan as its General Secretary, also demanded a Pakhtun province. The Wrore Pakhtun aimed to achieve that goal. In a statement submitted before justice Shabir Ahmad of Lahore High Court on 26th October 1956, Abdus Samad Khan Achakzai said Wrore Pakhtun wished to create an autonomous unit within Pakistan comprising all Pakhtu-speaking areas. He told the court: Let me mention that the creation of Pakhtunistan, comprising contiguous Pakhtun areas separated by the British under various nomenclatures, is my life mission. I cannot give up that struggle, nor can I give it up to avoid punishment or torture on my body[6]. Samad Khan merged his party into the NAP in 1956 and worked for a separate Pakhtunistan on the NAP Platform. However, the NWFP leaders did not press the demand for the creation of provinces on linguistic bases when they were restored after the dissolution of the One Unit in July 1970. Samad Khan was disillusioned and formed a separate group. Pakhtunkhawa NAP, and worked to establish a Pakhtun province on the basis of language.

The Baloch leaders always supported the demarcation of the provinces on a linguistic and cultural basis. Addressing a BSO meeting on 18th March 1969 in Karachi, Nawab Akbar Bugti demanded the demarcation of the province on a linguistic and cultural basis. Mir Ghous Bakhsh Bizenjo unequivocally supported provinces on a linguistic and cultural basis[7]. When the government made known its plan to dissolve the One Unit, the Khan of Kalat wrote to the military leader General Yahya Khan on 27th January opposing any move to include the Pakhtun areas in the province of Balochistan. Balochistan, the Khan said, was not only a state but also an institution of Baloch culture and ideology. He suggested that the Balochistan States Union including the leased areas should form part of a separate province of Balochistan[8]. Sardar Ataullah Mengal supported the demarcation of the provinces on a linguistic basis and a separate province comprising the Pakhtun areas of Balochistan. He maintained that the Baloch by no means desire to rule the Pakhtun although they (Baloch) wanted to have their separate status[9]. Another Baloch politician, Sardar Sher Baz Mazari, the leader of the National Democratic Party, also strongly favored the demarcation of the provinces on the basis of geography, culture, and ethnicity. He maintained that since the provinces demarcated during British rule did not conform to the geopolitical realities, these should be reshaped in the interest of the country[10].

Baloch-Pakhtun political relations in Balochistan have never been cordial. Samad Khan, the only member of the Pakhtunkhawa NAP returned to Balochistan Assembly in 1970, never cooperated with the NAP Government in the province but continued to oppose it as anti-Pakhtun. He demanded an equal share in the services for the Pakhtuns, although, they never constituted more than one-fourth of the total population of the province. He also demanded that one of the two top posts in the province, the Governor or the Chief Minister, should go to a Pakhtoon. After his assassination in 1973, his son and political successor, Mahmud Khan Achakzai, followed the same line. In his various speeches, he demanded a Lebanon Model in Balochistan, where the Government high offices would be divided among various ethnic and religious groups[11]. The Pakhtun Students Federation has also demanded an equal share in the services for the Pakhtoons[12].

The Baloch Student Organization believes that the Pathans, who are in a minority are dominating the province politically as well as economically. In a statement issued by Aziz Baloch, Unit Secretary of the BSO in the NED University Karachi, in July 1985, alleged that all the top officers serving in Balochistan were Pakhtuns. Of the government secretaries and other higher assignments, seventy percent were held by Pakhtuns. Aziz Baloch alleged that all the aid-to-Balochistan funds granted by the United States and its allies were being manipulated by Pathan officials and were being spent in the three Pakhtun dominated districts of Pishin, Loralai, and Zhob, ignoring the remaining fourteen Baloch districts of the Province[13].

During the brief period of NAP-JUI rule in the province, differences between the Baloch and Pakhtuns came to the surface. The government of Pakistan had no trouble using the Pakhtuns against the predominantly Baloch provincial government. Abdul Samad Achakzai spearheaded this opposition and kept stressing the bi-lingual and bi-national character of the province, demanding a share in cabinet posts on the basis of ethnic numerical strength. The political divide between the Baloch and Pakhtun was the reason, the NAP government declared Urdu as the official language of the province. They did this reluctantly and not because they had any love for the language or because Urdu had any place in the social and political life of the province, but because adopting Balochi as the official language would have been severely opposed by the Pakhtuns who would have demanded that their tongue should also be given official status. The Baloch leaders could not reconcile themselves with the idea of declaring Pakhtu the official language of Balochistan. This would have created more complications in the long run than adopting Urdu, a totally alien language in the province. Deviating from their earlier political stand on languages, the Baloch leaders declared Urdu the official language of Balochistan, much to the dismay of the Baloch people and the alienation of many intellectuals and political activists from the party. The decision in a way encouraged the Muhajirs to start an anti-Sindhi campaign in Sindh, where Sindhi was to be adopted as the only official language. Today, many Sindhi nationalists recall the Baloch decision as very intriguing but they ignore the compelling reasons for their action.

As early as in 1976, Ahmad Yar Khan, the governor of Balochistan and ex-Khan of Kalat, openly opposed a continued political alliance of the Baloch with the Pakhoons. Talking to newsmen in Quetta on 20th March 1976, he said that the Baloch leaders, Mir Ghous Bakhsh Bizenjo, Nawab Khair Bakhsh Marri and Sardar Ataullah Mengal, should break their political relation with Wali Khan and come to a settlement with Prime Minister Bhutto. Such a decision, he said would be in the interests of the Baloch and the Country[14]. This remark can be seen from the perspective of Baloch-Pakhtun differences.

The Baloch form a majority in the province of Balochistan. They believe that the incorporation of Pakhtun dominated districts into Balochistan is a ploy and as a strong check on Baloch national aspirations. The Baloch politicians are not unmindful of this Pathan factor in their land. From the very beginning, the Baloch supported the demand that the provinces after the disintegration of the One-Unit should be demarcated on a linguistic and cultural basis. If this demand had been accepted, the Pakhtun speaking districts would have been incorporated into NWFP and a permanent source of dissent and pressure would have been removed from the body-politic of the province.

The ethnic distribution in the province was not so menacing in the beginning but continued migration from the Afghan parts of the adjoining Pakhtun-speaking areas brought about a change. Moreover, the arrival of a large number of Pakhtun refugees, after the Afghan revolution, could change the population balance because these refugees, due to the unwise policies of the military regime, may very well remain in the province. The refugees in Balochistan are roughly one million in number; most of them have acquired Pakistani nationality and have bought the property and engaged in trade and commerce. This situation has changed the population balance and the Baloch, after a decade would have been reduced to a minority in their own province.

The armed resistance in Balochistan and the government ban on the National Awami Party accelerated the process of alienation between the two peoples, which came to a climax when the Baloch leadership formed a separate party of their own, the Pakistan National Party, on 1st June 1979.

References

1. jang,(Quetta) 20th June, 1979.
2. Ibid. 20th April 1979.
3. Dawn,20th August 1985.
4. Lawrence Ziring op cit,p 161.
5. Nawa-e-Wathan, Quetta,1st June 1954.
6. The written statement of Abdus Samad Achakzai before Justice Shabir Ahmad of Lahore high court on 26th October 1956. Reproduced by Pakhtunkhwa NAP, Mizan Printing Complex, Quetta, p. 31.
7. Pakistan Time, Lahore, 20th June 1969.
8. Ahmad Yar Khan: Inside Balochistan, op, cit, pp,197-198.
9. Sangath, Quetta 15th 1972, Sun, Karachi,30th August 1972.
10. Jang,(Quetta), 5th January 1979.
11. Ibid.11th, October 1975.
12. Ibid. 20th, November 1984.
13. A signed statement issued by BSO Unit Secretary in the NED University Karachi, in July 1985, op, cit.
14. Jang,(Quetta)21st March 1976.

CHAPTER IX

PERSO-BALOCH RELATIONS: AN OVERVIEW

Despite the fact that the Baloch and Persians share common linguistic roots and geographical boundaries, their relations have never been cordial. They have been fighting the Persians intermittently for the last 2000 years. It is also a fact that the Baloch have been part of armies of various Persian empires and at the same time, the Persian emperors had given the orders for the total annihilation of the Baloch. This pattern of events in the relationship between the Baloch and the Persians continued in medieval times where the Baloch faced massacre, genocide and forced migration and at the same time siding one ruler or the other in the perpetual rivalry of many dynasties in the Iranian plateau. It can be said that the hallmark of Perso-Baloch relations had been a fierce and sustained struggle by the Baloch to maintain their national identity and the ruthless and brutal retaliation from the Persians to suppress the Baloch national aspirations.

1- The Persian Empires and the Baloch

One can observe a "love-hate" relationship between the Baloch and ancient Iranian empires. Intermittent hostilities between the Baloch and Persians, which led to massacres and forced deportations of the

Baloch on many occasions might have been the cause of wholesale migration of them from their original abode of Balashagan[1].

The Persian empires of Achaemenians (550–330 BC) and Sassanid (AD 226–651) came into confrontation with the Baloch. In the bloody conflict of Sassanid with the Baloch, which culminated in the slaughter of the Baloch, religious or sectarian aspects cannot be ruled out. The Baloch might have been caught in the conflict of orthodox Zoroastrian priests with that of Mazdakis. Emperor Shahpur and Khusrow I was known religious fanatics and for them, the annihilation of so-called heretic Masdakis (The Baloch are believed to be the followers of Mazdaki sect of Zoroastrian religion) might have become a divine obligation. The conflict initiated a process of distrust between the Baloch and the Persians that might have been one of the reasons for the defection of some of the Baloch tribes to invading Arabs during the last years of the Sassanid Empire.

2- Perso-Baloch Relations after the Arab Occupation

First to emerge as powerful Persian dynasties after the collapse of Arab rule in Iran, were the Tahirids, Saffarids and the Buyids. It was the period when the Baloch were mainly concentrated in Kermaan. Saffarid ruler Yaqub bin Laith in AD 863, attacked and captured Baam and advanced toward Kermaan. The Baloch and their ally Ali ibn Husain (also called Kursh) were defeated and a number of Baloch families were deported into various regions in Persia. Some of the Baloch tribes fled the area and settled in Makkuraan and Turan during this period.

The Buyids ruled major parts of north and west of Iran between AD 928 and AD 1055 and the Baloch came into conflict with them. During this period, the Baloch tribes (Koch o Baloch) were effectively dominating Kerman and southwestern Makkuraan. Buyids General Abid ibn Ali marched towards the Baloch dominated areas, captured Tiz and the surrounding territory and forcefully converted

---

[1] For a detailed study on Balochi origin and migrations see Dr Dashti's books: Dashti Naseer, The Baloch and Balochistan; a Historical Account from the beginning to the fall of the Baloch state, 2012. Trafford Publishing
Dashti Naseer, The Baloch Conflict with Iran and Pakistan; Aspects of a National Liberation Struggle, 2017. Trafford Publishing

the   Baloch to Islam. The Baloch resisted fiercely. In AD 933, Ali Buya, recruited an army of 1,600 Deylamites and 500 Turks to subjugate the Baloch. His younger brother Ahmad Buya was the commander of the force. Ahmad Buya took Baam while the Baloch vacated Jiruft and Ali Kulwaihi (Ali Guluya), chief of the Baloch tribes agreed to a ceasefire. The Buyids violated the agreement and set out to attack the Baloch off guard. A bloody conflict ensued at the mountainous pass of Dar-e-Farid or Dilfiirid in which the Baloch had the upper hand and only a few of the Buyids forces could escape. Ahmad Buya launched a reprisal attack from Sirjan in which the Baloch were defeated massively. The Buyids launched many punitive expeditions against the Koch and Baloch. The court poet of Buyid ruler Adud ad-Daula, Mutanabbi, in AD 965, mentioned in a verse that his patron was the one who offered cups of death to his foes on the one hand and cups of wine to his intimates on the other hand. In AD 970 and AD 972, two campaigns were launched against the Baloch, and, as a result, the Buyids authority was extended to the whole of Makkuraan. The Buyids generals Kurkir ibn Jastin and Abid ibn Ali marched southward from Jiruft, defeating an army of the Baloch and the Manujaniyans in the south of Jiruft in December AD 970. In the battle, five thousand of the Baloch were killed, including two sons of their chief, Abu Saeed. The Buyid army penetrated into Barez Mountains, defeating the Baloch under the leadership of Ali Barezui, slaughtering their males, and enslaving the women and children in AD 972. The remnants of the Baloch were deported from the Barez Mountains. Maqaddesi (1906) observed that after repeated aggressive and extensive campaigns, the Buyids ruler had scattered the Baloch and laid waste to their lands, taking some into slavery and settling others elsewhere.

3- Perso-Baloch Relations During Safavid Rule

After the collapse of the Seljuq Empire, Iran was engulfed in a state of anarchy and chaos and witnessed the onslaught of Mongols and Timurid hordes. The Safavid established a Persian empire in the 16th century. The Baloch were in constant resistance against the Safavids, and Shah Esmail Safavi, in 1515, was forced to seek Portuguese assistance in suppressing the revolt in Makkuraan. During the reign of Shah Abbas, under the command of Ganj Ali Khan, a strong Persian force attacked Bampur and the Baloch forces under the command of Malik Shamsuddin were defeated. However, in the later Safavid era, various Baloch chiefs ruled different regions of Balochistan in a semi-autonomous relationship with Safavids. Around 1620, Kech was taken over by the Buledai tribe, who dominated the whole of Makkuraan up to Jaashk until 1740. Malik Dinar was the ruler of Bampur, Purdil Khan was the ruler of Jaalk, and Khusrow Bozorgzada was the ruler of Shustun while Shah Salim Nosherwani ruled the Kharan region. During 1691, a huge Baloch army under the joint command of Shah Salim Nosherwani and Khusrow Bozorgzada invaded Kermaan. In 1700, Shah Salim Nosherwani and Sardar Purdil Khan renewed their attacks on Kermaan, and this time, they occupied Baam and retained it for many months. Shah Salim Nosherwani attacked the Rudbar region in 1701. The Persian Army, under the command of Alexander, the nephew of Gurgin Khan, the governor of Kandahar attacked Sarhad, devastating the area, killing hundreds of the Baloch and burning their settlements. Shah Salim Nosherwani was captured in an ambush set by Persian forces along with several of his chiefs and fighters. The captured Baloch were executed, and Alexander sent the heads of sixty-six Baloch chiefs to Isfahan, including the head of Shah Salim Nosherwani.

Nader Shah Afshar tried to consolidate Persian power in Balochistan by sending many expeditionary forces in Sarhad and western Makkuraan. The Persian Army captured Bampur, Pahraj, Laashaar, and Tiz after bloody conflicts. Another force was sent to the Sarhad region, and the Baloch tribes of Sanjarani and Narohi were heavily defeated in the region of Kharan. Kech and other places in Makuraan were also occupied by an expeditionary force sent from Fars. In 1739, a Persian expeditionary force under the command of Admiral Thaqi Khan invaded Gwadar on his way to Sindh.

4- The Perso-Baloch Relations During the Qajar Dynasty

After the British occupation of Kalat, Qajar rulers of Persia made sustained efforts to strengthen their grip on Western Balochistan. The Baloch for a while became involved in the rivalry of the Ismaili spiritual leader Aagha Khan and his brother with the Qajar for the throne of Iran. Under the leadership of Mir Muhammad Ali (the ruler of Sib), the Baloch decided to support Aagha Khan and his brother in their endeavors to overthrow Qajar from power. To confront the Ismaili challenge, a formidable contingent of the Qajar army was permanently stationed at Kermaan. This army in 1843 moved eastward and occupied Bampur. From their base in Bampur, military expeditions were periodically mounted into the surrounding regions in order to chase or disperse the Baloch tribes allied with the Aagha Khan. Several thousand Baloch were captured from the surrounding regions of Bampur and sold them into slavery.

The Baloch could not resist the might of the Persian state for a long time and one by one, Baloch chiefs of Dezzak, Sarbaaz, Geh, and Kasarkand agreed to pay taxes to the Persian governor. The resistance from the ruler of Sib, Mir Muhammad Ali, was overcome by a strong Persian contingent sent from Kermaan in 1856 and the Fort at Sib was occupied after a fierce battle. The Persians successfully exploited differences between Mir Abdullah Khan Buladai of Geh who controlled the coast from Jaashk to Chahbaar, and Mir Din Muhammad Sardarzai in Bahau who, besides Dashthyaari, controlled the coast from Chahbaar to Gwadar. In southern Sistaan, the Persians occupied the Sarhad region by defeating Sardar Said Khan Kurd, who was the chief of Baloch tribes in Sarhad. During 1888, a Persian force crushed the resistance of the Yarmamadzai tribe in Sarhad.

The general uprising in Western Balochistan during the last years of the 19th century ended with the agreement that recognized Sardar Husain Khan as the ruler of southern Balochistan under the Persian sovereignty. In return, the Baloch leader acknowledged the sovereign claim made by Persians on Baloch territories. This was the beginning of a semi-sovereign Baloch chiefdom in Western Balochistan. On the death of Sardar Husain Khan in 1907, his son Sardar Sayyad Khan and the Barakzai chief Mir Bahraam Khan tried to consolidate their power in Western Balochistan by asserting control on Geh, Benth, Kasarkand, Sarbaz, Bampur, and Fahraj. However, under increased military pressure from Persians, Sardar Sayyad Khan later submitted to Persian authorities by accepting the title of Sardar-e-Nizam. The Persians recognized him as the nominal ruler of the region. While Mir Bahraam Khan refused to submit, he rallied Baloch tribal chiefs and became the actual authority in Western Balochistan. An army was sent from Kermaan against Mir Bahraam Khan in 1910. The

Persians, however, failed to overcome the Baloch resistance and retreated without achieving this objective. This event improved the credentials of Mir Bahraam Khan among the Baloch and paved the way for the establishment of a short-lived Barakzai chiefdom in Western Balochistan.

The history of the Baloch and Qajar is one of the bloodiest in the Baloch memory. The Baloch resistance against the advances of Qajar was not successful despite the sacrifices of thousands of the Baloch and their tribal chiefs and Hakoms from different regions in Western Balochistan. In the absence of any united and organized resistance, tribal chiefs, Hakoms, and regions fought against the Qajar on their own. The mighty power of the British Empire which was allied with Qajar rulers was another cause of Baloch miseries. The Khanate of Kalat was facing a period of degeneration under British domination.

The division of Balochistan during the final decades of the 19th century brought far-reaching consequences. The British policy of appeasement toward Persia against Russian advances, their obsession for establishing Afghanistan and Persia as viable buffer states, together with the protection of Indo-European Telegraph Line were immediate causative factors in the division of Balochistan. This division caused tremendous geographical, political, cultural, social and psychological consequences for the Baloch. The permanent division of their land is one of the causes of the Baloch national resistance being so ineffective in Iran and Pakistan in recent decades.

5- Perso-Baloch Relations During the Pahlavi Regime

During the years preceding the fall of the Qajar dynasty, while Iran was in chaos; the Baloch chiefdom in Bampur consolidated its foundations. After the death of Mir Bahraam Khan in 1921, his nephew Mir Dost Muhammad Barakzai became the ruler of the state. He tried to establish relations with the Khan of the Baloch at Kalat, Sultan of Muscat and Omaan, and the king of Afghanistan. Attempts were also made to establish contact with the newly established revolutionary government in Russia.

Reza Khan after assuming power in 1921, embarked upon an ambitious program of nation-building and territorial unification. The situation changed for the newly independent Baloch chiefdom as Reza Khan began exploring strategies to bring the Baloch areas west of Goldsmid Line under Persian control. In 1927, the Persian Government gave an ultimatum to the ruler of the Baloch chiefdom Mir Dost Muhammad Barakzai to accept the sovereignty of Persia. After the rejection of the ultimatum, the Persian army, under the command of General Amir Amanullah Jahanbani, began the advance on Balochistan in 1928 which lasted for a year, resulting in the murder of thousands of the Baloch and the permanent occupation of their newly emergent chiefdom. Fierce battles were fought between Persians and the Baloch in different regions. Persians had to fight for every fort in Western Balochistan. The Baloch resistance, however, weakened considerably with the use of airpower by the Persians.

The Baloch chiefdom collapsed because it was no match for the power of the Persian state. The Baloch lacked the structural and organizational capacity to withstand a modern army with limitless resources, artillery, and air power. Mir Dost Muhammad Khan Barakzai did not have enough time to consolidate his authority over an inherently divided tribal society where local Hakoms were liable to defect to powerful forces. His failure to make any connection with powerful tribes of the Sarhad region was exploited by Persians to their advantage. Lack of any external support, the desertion of some Baloch Hakoms to the Persian side, lack of supply provisions for the besieged contingents in different forts, and lack of modern weaponry were factors which forced Mir Dost Muhammad Khan Barakzai to surrender after many months of struggle to preserve the independence of the Baloch chiefdom. He was detained in Thehraan and after a year's detention, was tried and hanged by the Persian authorities in 1931.

The Baloch resistance against the Persians did not end with the collapse of Barakzai's chiefdom. In Sarhad, there was an ongoing resistance by Ghamshadzai, Yarahmadzai, and Esmailzai tribes against the Persians. In order to forestall any German political or military advance in the region during the First World War, the British sent an expeditionary force under the command of General Dyer to deal with the Baloch resistance in Sarhad. At this time, Sardar Khalil Khan Ghamshadzai held the area around Jaalk and Safed Koh, while Sardar Jiand Khan Yarahmadzai who was also the nominal head of the confederacy of the Baloch tribes of Sarhad, controlled areas west of Safed Koh. Areas west of Khwash were under the control of Sardar Juma Khan Esmailzai. In a prolonged campaign, General Dyer and the Persian forces succeeded in defeating Baloch forces and crushing the Baloch resistance in 1920. The Baloch in Sarhad again rose in rebellion in 1925 but was overcome by Persian authorities in 1926. From then onwards, the resistance against the Persians was only manifested by intermittent outbreaks of disorder in this part of Balochistan until the late 1930s. A rebellion of Sardar Juma Khan Esmailzai was crushed in 1931, and another uprising in Kuhak was defeated in 1938 with much bloodshed by the Persian Army under the command of General Alborz.

Valiant chiefs such as Sardar Jiand Khan Yarahmadzai and Sardar Khalil Khan Ghamshadzai were eliminated from the scene. General Dyer and his successor General Tanner together with the Persian forces were successful in getting rid of the trouble created by the Baloch tribes for the Persians and they claim that it was imperative in order to deter any German activity in the region.

It took many years for the Baloch to overcome material losses and psychological traumas that they suffered during the confrontations in the early period of the Pahlavi dynasty. During the 1960s, a new phase of organized Baloch resistance began under the banner of a clandestine organization, the Balochistan Liberation Front (BLF). This resistance was different from previous ones in many ways and attracted the attention of a large segment of the Baloch society. During the 1960s and early years of the 1970s, the Baloch resistance against Iran by BLF got some kind of support from the revolutionary regime of the Baath Party in Iraq. That was in response to Iran's interference in affairs of Iraqi Kurdistan, where Iranians were believed to support Kurdish rebels in their activities against Iraq. This backing included the supply of arms and ammunition, provision of military training to Baloch volunteers, and extension of financial and publicity assistance to the Baloch resistance. Baghdad Radio began to broadcast Balochi programs, highlighting the plight of the Baloch in Iran. Several Baloch tribal chiefs and political activists affiliated with BLF were based in Baghdad directing the resistance from exile. Prominent among these included Mir Abdi Khan, Mir Moosa Khan, Akber Barakzai, Mir Jumma Khan, and Abdul samad Amiri. Baloch youths received basic guerrilla tactics and training for armed insurgency from Iraqi army instructors. The armed resistance under the banner of the

Balochistan Liberation Front (BLF) engaged a vast number of Iranian forces mainly in southern Balochistan.

Believing that BLF volunteers might get sanctuary and assistance from their Baloch brothers in Eastern Balochistan, increased cooperation between Iran and Pakistan occurred. Both countries were convinced that the resistance in Western Balochistan was part of the struggle for a greater Balochistan. A map was widely publicized by security establishments in Iran and Pakistan showing a liberated Balochistan reaching from the Soviet border to the Indian Ocean, showing Western Balochistan and Eastern Balochistan as part of a greater and united Balochistan. This propaganda was perhaps a tactical maneuver in order to warn the US and its allies and to invoke the long-held fears of Western powers that an independent Balochistan might provide the Soviet Union with access to the warm waters of the Indian Ocean. This increased cooperation between Iran and Pakistan which began to counter the resistance in Western Balochistan also played an important role in crushing the Baloch uprising in Pakistani Balochistan during the 1970s in which the Iranian air force became significantly involved in the Chamalang operation against the Mari tribe.

The Baloch political and armed mobilization in Western Balochistan during later decades of the Pahlavi dynasty was undoubtedly influenced by increased political activities and armed resistance by the Baloch in Eastern Balochistan. Many political activists which became part of the resistance in Western Balochistan during the 1960s and 1970s were initially refugees from Western Balochistan who settled in Eastern Balochistan and Sindh where they became active in nationalist movements of the Baloch and Sindhis. In the 1970s, the Baloch resistance against Iran received a much-needed boost with the establishment of a Baloch nationalist government in Eastern Balochistan in 1972 under the leadership of Sardar Ataullah Mengal, Mir Gous Bakhsh Bizenjo and Nawab Khair Bakhsh Mari. The nationalist uprising, which began after the dismissal of the government in 1973, the Baloch in Western Balochistan took great inspiration for their political and armed resistance. The BLF continued its struggle for more than a decade but in the face of a massive crackdown on its fighters and supporters inside and outside Balochistan together with the end of external support from Iraq in 1975, it reduced its potential to be a potent organization. There developed serious ideological and personal differences between its exiled leadership. The ideological and strategic differences between tribal chiefs and the middle-class political cadre caused much damage to the prospects of BLF surviving as a leading resistance organization.

The Pahlavi regime's policy was to keep the Baloch politically weak by denying any access to even local power centers. The regime also cleverly manipulated personal and tribal differences of the various Baloch Hakoms and tribal chiefs, forestalling any united Baloch resistance. Their culture, language, and national identity were mortally threatened by the increased cultural and religious invasion from the Persian state. The use of the Balochi language was ruthlessly depressed, and the Baloch were forced to adopt Persian dresses. The Persians also created some new Baloch tribes, giving them names of their choice. The Balochi personal names were forcibly replaced in official documents and Shia Mullahs were encouraged to convert the Baloch to their sect. Although attempts to persuade the Baloch to adopt the Shia doctrine of Islam failed, in reaction, however, it prompted some of the Baloch to become strict Sunni followers. In the coming years, this action and reaction phenomenon nearly changed the character of a secular Baloch society, and religion increasingly began its intrusion into the Baloch society in Western Balochistan.

6- The Perso-Baloch Relations during the Rule of Ayathullahs

The Persian state came under the firm rule of religious fundamentalists, Ayatullahs in 1979. In the absence of freedom of expression, freedom of the press, freedom of assembly and organization, together with the ban on political activities during the Pahlavi regime, the Baloch national struggle in Iran remained under the leadership of tribal chiefs and Hakoms. Only during the last decades of the Pahlavi dynasty and during the early years of Ayathullahs, the Baloch middle class and educated youth became prominent in the national movement. The political activists started their activities by joining the democratic forces who were openly advocating the cause of the minority national entities in their manifestoes. They joined left-wing political organizations such as Toudeh Party, Fidaheen e Khalq, Mujaheddin e Khalq and Paikaar.

They began organizing demonstrations throughout Balochistan highlighting the Baloch demand for socio-political rights. The publications of some periodical in Balochi began to appear containing pro-autonomy, pro-independence and pro-revolutionary materials.

The democratic political groups to which the Baloch nationalists affiliated themselves became the prime target of the Ayathullahs and were brutally crushed. The Baloch were beginning to acquaint themselves with the formation of political organizations after decades of brutal political repression under the Pahlavi dynasty. The numbers of educated Baloch were limited. Nevertheless, even with their limited resources, various resistance organizations were established with different political or social orientations by nationalist elements. Some of them began to form networks for future militant activities against the state. Many tribal chiefs who were earlier pacified or neutralized by the Pahlavi regime also sympathetic and Supported resistance groups.

Later, Nationalist elements organized themselves in a broad-based organization of Sazman e Democratic Murdom e Balochistan. It participated in democratic politics which was allowed at the beginning of the revolution and took part in the first parliamentary elections for the drafting of a new constitution for Iran. Prominent personalities in the Sazman included Dr. Rehmatullah Husseinbhor, Durra Raisi, Rahim Zard Kohi, Shafi Zaindini, Rahim Bandoi, Aziz Daadyar, Jamshed Amiri, Khusro Mubaraki, Muhammad Ali Dehwaari, Abdul Malik Dehwaari, Reza Shah Bux, Rustom, Laashaari, Mohandas Ashkani, Rehamath Khuda Banda, Ahirdad Hossienbhor, Ahmad Hasan Raisi, Abdul Ghani Raisi, Ibrahim Lashkarzai, Karan Shahnawazi, Wali Muhammad Zaindini, Dr. Dedwar, Muraad Amiri, Chirag Narohi, Gazabek Raisi, Chaaker Chaakerzai, Peer Bux Amiri, Ayub Hoshang, Rehamat Sayad Zada, Thaj Muhammad Sayad Zada, Chiraq Muhammadi, Faqeer Muhammad Raisi, Ghulam Hussein, Nazar Muhammad Hashimzai and Abdullah Zarpanah. The Sazman did not openly advocate an independent Balochistan but stressed the demand for an autonomous Balochistan within the Iranian federation. They openly dissociated themselves from the political activities of tribal chiefs and former Hakoms and administrators who were affiliated with the Pahlavi regime but had now joined the national resistance. Sazman's demand for autonomy was to get administrative autonomy for Balochistan, recognition of Balochi as a medium of instruction in educational institutions, and ownership of Baloch natural resources. This organization was soon dissolved and became ineffective because of the crackdown on its leaders by the Islamic regime. Its leader, Rahmath Hosseinbor was attacked and critically wounded by the Iranian secret services. Another short-lived organization in the name of Sazman e Inqilab e Rahkargir was founded by Ali Chaakarzai, Fateh Muhammad Abadian and Ahirdad Sepahi failed to be effective. The religious elements formed Hezb e Ithihad al- Musleminwhich led by Moulvi Abdul Aziz. Moulvi Abdul Aziz advocated an autonomous status for Balochistan with the guarantees of securing the cultural, religious and economic rights. Saazman e Democratic Murdom e Balochistan and Hezb e Ithihad al- Muslemin jointly began a political agitation in Balochistan after the approval of the new constitution in a referendum boycotted by the Baloch. The constitution of Iran denied any right to the Baloch as a national entity. In the ensuing agitation against the constitution, dozens of people were killed before the Iranian forces were able to establish a semblance of peace in Western Balochistan. After the death of Moulvi Abdul Aziz, his son, Abdul Malik, made an alliance with the Sunni religious elements of Kurds in Shura e Mili e Ahle Sunna. This too was disbanded after the murder of Abdul Malik in Pakistan, by Iranian secret services in the early 1980s. Tribal chiefs and former Hakoms in Balochistan, who have been involved in personal and tribal feuds, in an unprecedented move, agreed to work in coordination under the banner of an alliance called Wahdath e Baloch soon after the Islamic revolution in Iran. This union included Sardarzai, Maliky, Laashaari, Shiraani, Naarui, Ghamshaadzai, and Esmailzai chiefs. The Mubaraki chief Amanullah formed its own movement Fidaeen Baloch.

The militant wings of various Baloch organizations and united fronts' carried out armed activities mainly in the south of Western Balochistan. The regime reacted using brutal tactics and the full power of the state to crush the resistance. A large number of political activists and combatants were killed by Iranian forces and agents of the secret services. Thousands of the Baloch were imprisoned and the leadership of organizations was forced to flee into neighboring Pakistan, Afghanistan, and the Gulf countries.

The Baloch political activists in exile formed Jumbish e Azaadi Khuahan e Balochistan in 1981 which was mainly comprised of left-wing elements previously affiliated and later became disgruntled with the policies of the left-wing parties in Iran. Baloch Raaj e Zrombesh which was dormant after the murder of its founder, Rahim Zardkohi, was reorganized in 1983. During 1985, Laashaar chief Mir Mohammad Khan in alliance with the Narohi, Ghamshaadzai and Esmailzai chiefs formed Jumbish e Mujahideen e Baloch (renamed as Sazman e Mubarizin e Baloch in 1992); while Baaranzai chief formed his own organization. While in Afghanistan, the Naarui chief Sardar Sher Ali created his own united front, Ithihade Milli in 1986.

Things were not rosy for the Baloch exiles. Some prominent tribal chiefs including Laashaari Chief Mir Mohammad Khan and his nephew Mir Amin Laashaari narrowly escaped death but sustained serious bullet injuries in assassination attempts on their lives in Pakistan. Some of the activists and tribal elite were killed in infighting between the leadership of Wahdat e Baloch while they were living in exile in Pakistan. The unfortunate murders of Mir Mouladad Sadarzai and Mir Amanullah Mubariki in the 1980s were caused by the dispute over the running of the finances and the armed activities of the Wahdath e Baloch.

During the early years of the Islamic regime, the Baloch resistance groups obtained significant moral and material support from the revolutionary government in Afghanistan. The increased cooperation between Pakistan and Iran to counter the Baloch activities, the collapse of the revolutionary government in Afghanistan, and the end of Iran-Iraq war caused serious blows to Baloch resistance organizations operating in exile. After exerting their importance during the early phase of the Islamic regime, the Baloch political and armed resistance could not manage to sustain their activities in Iran and became ineffective. Politically, the Baloch were organized in small disparate groups and could not form a united front. This was probably the reason why their armed resistance despite foreign assistance could not find roots and was unable to make an impression either on the Baloch masses or on the regime of the Ayathullahs. The leadership in exile became vulnerable. Fearing for their life, the exiled Baloch nationalists in Afghanistan and Pakistan migrated in large numbers to various European and North American countries. Thus, the Baloch resistance against the Ayathullahs was a short-lived phenomenon.

CHAPTER X

EPILOGUE: THE BALOCH AT THE CROSSROADS

Since the publications of these essays in1988, a lot of water has flown under the bridge. Baloch politics has undergone various transformations and been facing new kinds of challenges from within and from outside.

The defeat of the resistant movement in the 1970s caused much political upheaval in the ranks of the Baloch nationalists. A process of division and disunity was initiated which is still haunting the Baloch national struggle. Disenchantment developed between the leadership and political activists, which caused political anarchy in nationalist circles for many years. After the banning of NAP in the 70s, in 1980 Sardar Ataullah Mengal and Mir Ghous Bakhsh Bizenjo tried to unite the scattered elements of the Baloch national struggle into a new party, the PNP. However, soon Sardar Mengal parted ways with Mir Bizenjo and went to London. A period of intense and heated political debates was witnessed in the 1980s among the nationalist circles regarding future strategies of the Baloch national movement in Pakistan. Sardar Ataullah Mengal and Nawab Khair Bakhsh Mari went into exile and Nawab Akbar Bugti successfully managed to re-enter the folds of the Baloch nationalists. Once regarded as the father of the Baloch nationalist politics, Mir Bizenjo was severely criticized and accused of abandoning the Baloch national cause. The student wing of NAP, BSO, with the banning of the party and imprisonment of its leadership and divisions among the leadership after their release from the prison, performed as a political party, with far-reaching negative consequences on the future Baloch politics.

Many events caused the renewal of armed resistance in Balochistan and for the last many years, Balochistan has been engulfed in an unprecedented violent confrontation between the Baloch and the security forces. The decision to end armed activities after the release of leaders in 1978 was believed by a section of the BSO activists as a great betrayal of the Baloch cause. For many years, the BSO got out of crosscurrents of the Baloch national policies and they adopted a hostile attitude towards the Baloch national leaders especially with Mir Ghous Bakhsh Bizenjo who talked to adopt a realistic view of the prevailing situation facing the Baloch national movement. From the beginning of the 1980s, the BSO was transformed from an educational organization, affiliated to the nationalist politics of Balochistan as the student wing of the NAP into a political organization on its own. This caused much damage to Baloch politics and caused an unending process of division and fragmentation of the organization which continued into the 21st century. Although, heavily infiltrated by the state security agencies; nevertheless, the BSO during the 1980s remained the strongest student force and attracted the sympathies of a large number of people.

The unity of BSO was not long-lasting. Soon, a process of disintegration began. It again split into two factions led by Dr. Yaseen Baloch and Dr. Kahur Khan Baloch. In later years, from two newly emerged groups (Yaseen group and Kahur group), emerged two youth movements and both groups of the BSO remained affiliated with these youth movements. They abandoned their previous stance of considering the BSO as a political organization capable of leading the national struggle on its own. Nevertheless, the division of the BSO resulted in many violent infightings among students. A prominent activist of the BSO (Yaseen group), Fida Ahmad was murdered in Turbat on May 2, 1988, by the rival faction of the BSO (Kahur group) to revenge an attack on one of their activists, Mullah Sathar. The division of the BSO did not end and with the formation of new alliances and parties by the Baloch nationalists; the BSO also underwent similar divisions and bifurcations. By the end of the last century, the BSO was mainly divided into two groups; one supported the BNM headed by Dr. Abdul Hayee, the other supported the Balochistan National Party headed by Sardar Ataullah Mengal.

Mir Bizenjo's Party, PNP, adopted a manifesto calling for greater autonomy for the provinces of Pakistan as enshrined in the Lahore Resolution of 1940. The resolution, which became the founding document for Pakistan, called for the creation of a group of 'independent states' for Muslims in north-western and eastern zones within British India. In the resolution, it was demanded that the constituent units or states were to be autonomous and sovereign. Although, the party failed to gain the support of the majority of former political activists of the NAP and the Baloch Students Organization; nevertheless, Mir Bizenjo still commanded respect and a significant following of educated and a rising middle class, during the 1980s. Although, the majority of the conscious elements did agree with Mir Ghous Bakhsh Bizenjo; nevertheless, a significant section of students and former activists of the NAP became alienated with him and his party.

After their release from prison with the disbandment of Hyderabad Tribunal in 1978, Nawab Khair Bakhsh Mari and Sardar Ataullah Mengal left Pakistan and went into exile in Afghanistan, and the UK. Under the instructions of Nawab Khair Bakhsh Mari, thousands of Mari tribesmen also migrated to Afghanistan. While in Europe, Sardar Mengal and Nawab Mari apart from having medical treatments began to analyze new developments regarding the Baloch national resistance and to explore the prospects of gaining international support for the Baloch cause. They also explored the possibilities of strengthening the organizational framework of the Baloch resistance in preparation for a possible renewal of a political and armed struggle.

Sardar Ataullah Mengal became active highlighting the Baloch national question in Europe and North America. He repeatedly expressed his lack of confidence in a solution of the Baloch national question within Pakistan. He played a prominent role in the formation of the World Baloch Organization in 1981 which was to consolidate the political activities of the Baloch Diaspora in Europe and North America. In 1985, he joined hands with Sindhi and Pashthun leaders in the formation of the Sindhi-Baloch-Pashthun Front (SBPF). The alliance is popularly known as the 'confederation front' was a political platform of oppressed nations in Pakistan demanding a confederation of nations comprising Pakistan. He was also instrumental in the formation of a discussion group 'Sindhi-Baloch Forum' in order to initiate political debates on the national struggles of these nations.

The socialist revolution in Afghanistan led by the Peoples' Democratic Party in 1978 was seen by the West as the end of Afghanistan as a buffer between Russia and the West in Asia. This was unacceptable to them as they saw in it the Soviet temptation to reach the Indian Ocean thus threatening their monopoly in the oil-rich Gulf region and giving an unprecedented strategic advantage to Russia in the Middle East and South Asia. The Western powers began to counter this apparent Soviet move to change the balance of power in the region. They organized a massive insurgency in Afghanistan in order to destabilize the pro-soviet government in Kabul. Islam was again found to be useful in this new confrontation with Russia. Thousands of Jihadists from all over the world were encouraged and paid to participate in the "holy struggle" to oust the "atheist and infidels" from Afghanistan. At the behest of the Western alliance and with money from Arab countries, Pakistan began training Islamic Jihadists on its territory and funneling arms to insurgents inside Afghanistan. A protracted Jihad was fought by the West in Afghanistan until the collapse of the Soviet-backed revolutionary government in 1992.

The Afghan revolutionary government extended the hand of friendship to the Baloch and Pashthun who were struggling for their national rights in Pakistan. Many Baloch activists from Pakistan and Iran took refuge in Afghanistan. Thousands of Mari tribesmen were given shelter. Several of the BSO leaders also crossed into Afghanistan. The Baloch exiles were not only given refuge but were also given access to the educational institutions of the Soviet Bloc countries and hundreds of the Baloch youth were educated in Russia and other socialist countries in Eastern Europe. However, no military or diplomatic support was given to the Baloch.

Nawab Khair Bakhsh Mari and his tribesmen remained in Afghanistan until the collapse of the revolutionary government. One of the unfortunate happenings during Nawab Mari's sojourn in Afghanistan was the parting ways of his close associates, Mir Sher Muhammad Mari and Mir Hazaar Khan Rahmakani. These two personalities played significant roles in the Baloch struggles of the 1960s and 1970s. Their dissociation with Nawab Mari proved to be the beginning of an unending dissent within the exiled Mari tribesmen which only came into open after the return of Mari tribesmen in Balochistan during the 1990s.

In the 1980s, the leaders of the Baloch Student Organization tried to fill the gap created by the absence of the Baloch leadership by forming their own political group. Their manifesto was no participation in the political process of the state. They believed that participation in the state political process dilutes the Baloch national struggle. They believed that the struggle should only result in an independent and united Balochistan and not for provincial autonomy within Pakistan. As the slogan was very attractive for the Baloch youth after the debacle of the 1970s, for a while it appeared that a new popular political leadership had arisen on the Baloch political scene with a significant following. The new youth leadership vehemently opposed the line adopted by Mir Ghous Bakhsh Bizenjo and his party, the Pakistan National Party which demanded the resolution of the Baloch national question within Pakistan according to 1940 Lahore Resolution.

Two separate youth movements were created in 1987. The group under the leadership of Dr. Abdul Hayee and Sardar Akhthar Mengal was named as Balochistan National Youth Movement (BNYM) while two former chairmen of the BSO, Raziq Bugti, and Habib Jalib, founded their own group named as Progressive Youth Movement (PYM). These two youth movements commanded the support of divided sections of the BSO. Soon these factions began to hurl various accusations at each other and activists of their student wings became involved in violent clashes.

The phenomenon of youth movements did not last long. Not only the political philosophy of their leaders changed diametrically but the two youth movements effectively became dissolved within a few years. The BNYM which was against any participation in the political process within Pakistan became a component of a nationalist alliance called the Balochistan National Alliance (BNA). This was formed to jointly contest the general elections in 1988 held after the death of military ruler General Zia ul Haque. In 1989, BNYM was transformed from a youth movement into a formal political party and renamed as Baloch National Movement (BNM). In 1990, BNM split into BNM-Mengal headed by Sardar Akhthar Mengal and BNM-Hayee headed by Dr. Abdul Hayee. The PYM which was supposed to be a radical and progressive nationalist organization with the objective of a revolutionary armed struggle for the liberation of Balochistan merged itself with the PNP following the death of Mir Bizenjo in 1990. These short-lived youth movements did not play any significant role in Baloch politics. During their brief life span, much damage was inflicted on the degree of respect the BSO commanded among the Baloch masses as a trustworthy organization devoted to the Baloch cause.

In 1988, the Baloch nationalist groups and individuals formed an alliance in the name of the Balochistan National Alliance (BNA). The main political organization in the BNA was Baloch National Youth Movement (BNYM). It was supported openly by Sardar Ataullah Mengal and covertly by Nawab Khair Bakhsh Mari and led by Nawab Akbar Bugti as both Sardar Mengal and Nawab Mari were living in the United Kingdom and Afghanistan respectively. In the context of the broadened political rift which developed during the second half of the 1970 decade, Mir Ghous Bakhsh Bizenjo's Pakistan National Party (PNP) was not included in the alliance. Nawab Akbar Bugti as the leader of the Balochistan National Alliance again emerged as one of the main leaders of the Baloch national struggle after his split with the Baloch leaders in 1972.

The election in Balochistan was mainly fought between BNA and PNP. The PNP was heavily defeated with the BNA winning a large number of seats in the Balochistan Assembly. The towering figure of the Baloch national struggle, Mir Ghous Bakhsh Bizenjo himself was defeated in two parliamentary seats. The alliance formed the government in Balochistan with Nawab Akbar Bugti as Chief Minister in November 1988. The BNA government was dissolved on August 6, 1990, when Prime Minister Benazir Bhutto's federal government and all democratically elected federal and provincial assemblies were dismissed by President Ghulam Ishaque Khan. This move was orchestrated by the army establishment. With the formation of an alliance of nationalists and the inception of a second nationalist government in Balochistan after 17 years, new hopes were raised among the Baloch masses. However, neither the alliance nor the government was long-lasting. BNM, the party that emerged from the dissolution of BNYM, soon dissociated itself from the government of the national alliance. With the withdrawal of the party in the alliance, the BNA ceased to exist as a political entity. The government of the alliance was for a brief period and its functioning created no impact on the masses.

Death of Mir Ghous Bakhsh Bizenjo in 1990 was one of the important happenings in the context of the Baloch national struggle in Pakistan. He was diagnosed as suffering from cancer of the pancreas in 1989 and died on August 11, 1990. His eldest son, Mir Bizen Bizenjo, was made the president of PNP after his death, but he was unable to keep the party together and many followers of Mir Bezanjo became dissatisfied with his leadership capabilities. A significant section of the party along with family members of Mir Ghous Bakhsh joined Sardar Mengal's Balochistan National Party in 1996. Mir However his sons and family members left BNP in 1998 and ultimately, they joined the National Party (NP) in 2003.

Baloch National Movement (BNM) attracted the attention of a vast section of the Baloch society, especially the educated elite. Having the blessing of exiled leader, Sardar Ataullah Mengal and with a very active BSO as its student wing, it became the major political party of Baloch nationalists following the banning of the NAP. It soon became the target of the state establishment. Many of the Baloch analysts believed that it was because of the active manipulation of powerful state agencies, which caused the immediate division of the movement, soon after its creation. Within two years it was divided and in 1990, it split into two groups; BNM-Mengal led by Sardar Akhthar Mengal and BNM-Hayee led by Dr. Abdul Hayee. At the time, activists belonging to BNM-Mengal accused the group headed by Dr. Abdul Hayee of hobnobbing with the establishment and of betrayal of the nationalist cause. BNM-Mengal was merged into BNP in 1996 while BNM-Hayee suffered further divisions in 2003.

In 1990, Nawab Akbar Bugti, after the dismissal of his government and the dissolution of the Balochistan National Alliance, formally launched his own political party and named it Jamhoori Wathan Party (JWP). The party pledged to struggle for the rights of the Baloch people. For various reasons, the party could not be organized in other parts of Balochistan, and it remained limited to Dera Bugti and its adjacent districts. Nevertheless, in the early days of the 21st century, it played a pivotal role in the political mobilization of the Baloch against the state aggression on Baloch natural resources and coastline. JWP under the leadership of Nawab Akbar Bugti raised the slogan of securing the Baloch coast and resources in order to mobilize masses in opposing the leasing out of Gwadar port to Chinese and exploitation of natural resources of the Baloch. In 2003, with the announcement of the ruling military to build new military cantonments in Balochistan and extensive land grabbing by the establishment in Gwadar and other parts of Balochistan, JWP became part of a loose four-party 'Baloch Alliance' to oppose these moves. With the martyrdom of Nawab Bugti in 2006, JWP split into various factions and ceased to be a potent player in the nationalist politics of Balochistan. The political heir of Nawab Bugti, Mir Brahamdag Bugti decided to form Baloch Republican Party (BRP).

While in exile, severe differences of opinion developed between Nawab Mari and some of his staunch political, tribal and armed supporters. Famous guerrilla commanders of the 1960s and 1970s and prominent leaders in the Baloch Peoples Liberation Front (BPLF), Mir Sher Muhammad Mari and Mir Hazaar Khan Rehmakani parted ways with their long-time tribal chief and political leader, Nawab Khair Bakhsh Mari. Sardar Athaullah Mengal ended his exile in 1996 and returned to Balochistan to play an active part in the political process. He was successful in the creation of a united nationalist party with the merger of PNP and BNM-Mengal. The party became the largest and most popular. It won the 1997 general elections and formed the third nationalist government in Balochistan in alliance with Nawab Bugti's Jamhoori Wathan Party. Nawab Khair Bakhsh Mari after his return became active in politics and formed a discussion group of its followers. This was named as Haq Thawar (the voice of truth). His sons-Mir Jangeez Mari, Mir Gazzain Mari, and Mir Hairbyaar Mari participated in provincial elections as independent candidates and became members of various nationalists and non-nationalist governments in Balochistan as ministers.

After a prolonged period of near political anarchy among nationalist forces, the BNP became a beacon of hope for a united struggle. The right of self-determination for the Baloch was included in the party manifesto. The Party participated in the general elections held in 1997 and became the single largest party in the provincial assembly of Balochistan. An alliance of BNP, JWP of Nawab Bugti with the support of Nawab Mari, the third nationalist government in Balochistan was formed in 1997 and Sardar Akhthar Mengal became the Chief Minister of the province. For many Baloch nationalist activists, it was the reincarnation of the NAP government of 1972 as the whole Baloch national leadership was together for the first time in a political alliance since the traumatic events of the 1970s. It was not only the true representative of the Baloch nationalists but joining of Nawab Akbar Bugti, Sardar Athaullah Mengal, Nawab Khair Bakhsh Mari and the family of Mir Ghous Bakhsh Bizenjo in the political process of the state was also a gesture from the Baloch nationalists that they were united for a peaceful and honorable solution of the Baloch national question in Pakistan through political means.

However, the running of the government was not smooth and relations between the governments in Quetta with that of Islamabad were not cordial. On May 28, 1998, the Pakistani government exploded several nuclear devices in the Chagai District of Balochistan. The Balochistan government protested that they had not been informed regarding the tests. The BNP and other nationalist parties declared May 28 as the Black Day, initiating a series of rallies and demonstrations against nuclear tests on Baloch soil. This was more than the military establishment could tolerate. With the active manipulations of state secret agencies, BNP was divided. Sardar Akhthar Mengal stepped down from the position of Chief Minister in 1998, on the pretext that he had not been kept in the loop on the nuclear tests carried out in Balochistan.

With the end of the Baloch nationalist government, it appeared that the gesture on behalf of the Baloch leadership towards the state in their acceptance of participation in the political process of the state in order to seek a peaceful political solution to the Baloch national question, was altogether rejected by the state and a new showdown became inevitable between the Baloch and Pakistan.

Sardar Athaullah Mengal and Nawab Khair Bakhsh Mari after failing to secure any international support for the Baloch struggle were compelled to end their exile, returned and participated in the political process of Pakistan. Their return was due to unexpected political developments in regional and international polity. With the sudden collapse of the Soviet Union, the position of the Afghan revolutionary government became untenable. An imminent takeover of Afghanistan by Mujahideen forced Nawab Khair Bakhsh Mari and his followers to end their stay in Afghanistan. Sardar Athaullah Mengal became disappointed by any prospect of Western support for an independent Balochistan and had no option but to return. On the other hand, the Pakistani establishment was not ready to show any gesture of compromise in response to the conciliatory gestures and actions of the Baloch leaders. Instead, the establishment was busy in creating rifts and divisions in the Baloch polity.

After the unceremonious fate of the last Baloch nationalist government and the role of the secret agencies in the division of the main Baloch nationalist parties-BNP and BNM, the Baloch nationalists became engaged in a seemingly endless political, intellectual and academic debate. This concerned the merit and demerit of boycotting all state institutions and adopting armed resistance as the only viable method to achieve the desired objective of national salvation. Announcements regarding the exploration of natural resources without taking into consideration the reservations shown by the Baloch leadership, plans for colonizing the coastal regions of Balochistan with non-Baloch from Punjab and other areas of the country in order to bring about demographic changes and preparations for the establishment of military cantonments in Balochistan were factors which prompted the Baloch nationalists to take immediate measures. Ultimately a series of events created the situation in which a bloody showdown became inevitable between Pakistan and the Baloch. In the contemporary conflict which practically began in 2002, the Baloch are suffering immense losses in men and material while the state is continuing its policy of ruthlessly crushing the Baloch national aspirations using excessive force. To counter the designs of the establishment, the Baloch nationalist parties began a process of political mobilization. As a result, the Baloch and the state security forces became involved in a head-on collision. A bloody and protracted resistance movement began in Balochistan with tales of much horror and brutalities.

The state establishment adopted the strategy of not only weakening the hold of Nawab Mari, Sardar Mengal and Nawab Bugti on their respective tribes but in order to dilute and create confusion among the masses regarding the national struggle, a two-pronged strategy was adopted. First, they successfully created a Baloch nationalist party of their own. In this context, many among the Baloch nationalists believed that National Party (NP) was formed with the active support of the establishment by uniting a section of BNM with the Balochistan National Democratic Party (BNDP) as its political front. BNDP was earlier formed by some activists of the BNP, who left the party in 1998 and was headed by the sons of Mir Ghous Bakhsh

Bizenjo. Second, the establishment openly patronized the religious elements in Balochistan. This was felt necessary in order to achieve the objective of weakening the nationalist support among the Baloch masses; as the whole philosophy of Baloch resistance was based on a struggle against the illegal occupation of their land by a state that was created in the name of religion. Rivals of Nawab Mari, Sardar Mengal and Nawab Bugti, in their respective tribes, were encouraged and brought into the fold of the anti-nationalist camp. A section of the Mari tribe headed by Mir Hazaar Khan Rahmakani began an active collaboration with the military establishment. The Kalpar and Missouri clans of the Bugti tribe were given assistance to oppose Nawab Akbar Bugti and a family from the Mengal tribe was openly groomed to counter Sardar Athaullah Mengal.

On the political front, the rhetoric that the Baloch struggle is not for the well being of the people, but for taking of favors for tribal leaders and their families was propagated through state-controlled media. The newly formed pro-establishment party, the National Party (NP), was portrayed by the state media, as the true representative of the Baloch national aspirations. Jamiat Ulema Islam, Jamaat e Islami, and several other religious groups were given all-out support by the army. The military regime made it certain that these religious parties under the umbrella of a united front, Muthahida Majlis e Amal (MMA), secure a reasonable number of seats in Balochistan in the general elections held in 2002. Security agencies/ establishment created several religious organizations. These were used against the Baloch nationalists. With the establishment of madrasas (religious schools) in every town and village, political patronage and massive funding from multiple sources, the social standing of the Mullah (clergy) was upgraded and the role of the clergy was increased in such a way that was unprecedented in a Baloch society of the liberal and secular mind-set. This was to neutralize the 'infidel led' Baloch resistance with the 'force of Allah'.

Beginning from the dismissal of Sardar Akhthar Mengal's government in 1998, tensions between the Baloch and the state increased. Exploration of the natural resources of Balochistan, bringing about demographic changes in the guise of developing the coastal region together with the establishment of three more military cantonments in Balochistan, were the main elements of the new strategy of the state to deal with the Baloch national question. The gold and uranium deposits of a huge area in the Chagai District were already depleted by the Chinese. Negotiations were underway for the exploration of other natural resources with different Chinese companies and corporations. The Oil and Gas Development Corporation of Pakistan (OGDC) and Pakistan Petroleum Limited (PPL) were planning to begin a new phase of oil and gas exploration in the Mari, Bugti, and Jahlawaan regions. In the guise of developing the fishing port of Gwadar into a deep seaport, hundreds and thousands of acres of land were forcibly acquired from the local population. In 2002, Shoukat Aziz, the finance minister of the military regime announced a plan to relocate 2.5 million people from outside Balochistan into the Gwadar area by 2025. This was considered by the Baloch as a blatant move to bring about demographic changes in Balochistan. It was announced that three new army cantonments and a naval base would be established in Balochistan. This was considered an act of war against the Baloch.

The Baloch opinion regarding the state strategies was divided. Some of the Baloch nationalists were of the opinion that the objective conditions for a new armed confrontation with the state were not favorable as the Western world is behind the military establishment. According to them, the only feasible method of resistance at present should be political agitation. Another segment, however, was of the opinion that it was a "now or never" situation with the Baloch. This view was espoused by Nawab Mari and his supporters and a section of the BSO and BNM. Even Sardar Athaullah Mengal who was considered to be the most pragmatic of contemporary Baloch leaders expressed his dismay over the behavior of the state establishment. He observed that Baloch have tried their utmost to develop friendly relations with the Punjab-dominated establishment but in response, they had been pushed against the wall, and the idea of full autonomy for Balochistan would never be considered voluntarily by the state. Sardar Akhthar Mengal asserted that the Baloch now felt that all doors for a peaceful solution were closed and it was certain that they would need to resort to other methods to preserve the Baloch national identity and to save their natural resources. Nawab Akbar Bugti called for safeguarding the Baloch coast and resources in whatever way possible.

Although, the atmosphere in Balochistan was of generalized anger; nevertheless, the immediate response from the Baloch against state provocation was the beginning of political agitation. At the end of the Baloch nationalist government in 1998, the political forces had already initiated a process of political mobilization in Balochistan under the banner of PONM. Sardar Athaullah Mengal was instrumental in the formation of the Pakistan Oppressed Nations Movement (PONM), with a manifesto of demanding a confederation of all nationalities comprising Pakistan. The PONM became the umbrella group of parties from minority national entities and was to struggle for the reconstitution of Pakistan on the basis of March 23, 1940, Lahore resolution passed by Muslim League, the proponent party of Pakistan, as a blueprint of a constitutional arrangement for a future Pakistan. PONM became ineffective during the Martial Law regime of General Pervez Musharraf when Sardar Athaullah Mengal again went into exile and lived in the UK for many years.

In 2001, the security forces entered the house of Nawab Khair Bakhsh Mari in Quetta and arrested him on the murder charges of a high court judge. This was perceived by the Baloch as the state policy of humiliating revered Baloch leaders and sending signals to the Baloch that the state was not ready to treat them with honor and dignity. The arrest of Nawab Khair Bakhsh Mari in such a manner was the turning point of the Baloch resistance after a pause of two decades during which the Baloch kept a low profile regarding their grievances against the state and they tried to participate in the political process of the state.

The Baloch political mobilization was led by a four-party alliance. It was composed of Jamhoori Wathan Party (JWP) of Nawab Akbar Bugti, Balochistan National Party (BNP) of Sardar Athaullah Mengal, National Party (NP) of Dr. Abdul Hayee and Baloch Haq Tawar of Nawab Khair Bakhsh Mari. In 2004, the alliance tried to formulate recommendations as to the basis of a negotiated settlement on the issue, with the military regime. However, as the establishment had already opted for a violent confrontation, political moves were soon overtaken by aggressive behavior and saber-rattling by the establishment and security agencies.

The military-installed hapless civilian government headed by Shoukat Aziz, appointed a parliamentary committee on September 23, 2004 'to deal with the issue of Balochistan and inter-provincial harmony'. Its two subcommittees were to make appropriate recommendations on the situation in Balochistan and make recommendations 'to promote inter-provincial harmony and protect the rights of provinces, with a view to strengthening the federation'. The committee's recommendations were rejected by both parties in the conflict; the four-party Baloch Alliance, and the military establishment. In 2006, the former chief minister of Balochistan and a leader of the four-party alliance, Sardar Akhthar Mengal called for a joint meeting of the Pakistan Oppressed Nations Movement (PONM) and the Baloch Alliance to chalk out a joint strategy against what he called government's extra-constitutional measures. He accused the intelligence agencies of harassing and victimizing families of those Baloch leaders, who had raised voices against the government's excesses in Balochistan.

Attempts were also made for the creation of a single Baloch nationalist party. Although Nawab Bugti and Sardar Athaullah Mengal were hopeful of forming a single party of Baloch nationalists, for reasons still unknown, this move could not be finalized. Indeed, with the murder of Nawab Akbar Bugti and Mir Balaach Mari, the four-party alliance disintegrated as Nawab Mari was no longer interested in participating in the political process of the state and National Party headed by Dr. Abdul Hai Baloch came into open with its support to the establishment.

Nawab Akbar Bugti took the responsibility of leading the mass mobilization efforts on his shoulders. This made Nawab Akbar Bugti an irritant in the eyes of the military establishment. There was another reason for the establishment to be angry with Nawab Akbar Bugti. Nawab Akbar Bugti was not flexible in relaxing the Baloch demand for increased royalties from the gas fields, neither he was ready to grant any rights for new exploration in the Bugti area.

On the one hand, the civilian face of the military establishment, the ruling Pakistan Muslim League pretended to settle outstanding issues between the Baloch and the state through political means, whilst on the other hand, the army was mobilized in every district of Balochistan for a military showdown. The state media was given the task by the regime to portray the Baloch political mobilization against military cantonments, Gwadar project, and issues of Gas royalty and exploration rights as anti-development and anti-state activities by certain tribal chiefs. Quoting military and civilian intelligence agencies, the media and establishment affiliated political parties, were busy convincing the Pakistani public, on a ubiquitous "foreign hand" which was responsible for all troubles in Balochistan. There began vigorous propaganda that the international conspiracy was to dismantle the only 'Allah given country' on this planet Earth and that the Baloch nationalists were tools of foreign enemies of Pakistan.

Tension increased between the Bugti tribe and the military stationed in Dera Bugti and Sui and there was an overall intensification of political activities from the Baloch nationalist parties on Gwadar and other related issues. In the meantime, the case of Dr. Shazia Khalid occurred which further inflamed the situation. The person accused of the rape of Dr. Shazia Khalid was a major rank officer in the Pakistani army and the military ruler General Pervez Musharraf wasted no time, and publicly affirmed the officer's innocence.

Instead of addressing the Baloch grievances through negotiations, the military government resorted to greater use of force. General Musharraf added fuel to the fire when he publicly gave an ultimatum to the Baloch by saying that "Don't push us. This isn't the 1970s when you can hit and run and hide in the mountains. This time you won't even know what hit you." This statement further fuelled the already inflammable situation as the Baloch took it as an insult and a threat to their national honor by a ruler who originated from Indian immigrants (Muhajir) and was the son of a dancer girl, whom they did not consider as equal to a Baloch in social standings.

Negotiations ultimately failed between Nawab Akbar Bugti and the government regarding a new agreement for oil and gas exploration in the Bugti region. The army units were deployed and troops blockaded the town of Dera Bugti, alleging that the head of the Bugti tribe was protecting rebels who were sabotaging the infrastructure for the extraction of natural gas. Sporadic clashes were reported between the Baloch militants and army units.

On March 17, 2005, the paramilitary forces shelled the residence of Nawab Bugti and its surrounding areas for many hours. Nawab Akbar Bugti was not hurt but 67 people died and more than a hundred were injured. Several houses and a Hindu temple were reduced to rubbles.

In December 2005, the military regime accused the Baloch militants of an attack on General Pervez Musharraf's public meeting in Kohlu. Reacting to this, the Pakistani military ruler promised to "fix" Baloch leaders. The army launched retaliatory operations against the Mari tribe in which many hundreds were killed and injured. In July 2006, General Pervez Musharraf reiterated his government's stance that his regime was determined to re-establish its control on Balochistan and would protect national installations in Balochistan at all costs and ensure full security for the development activities and for Chinese investors there.

The 80 years old Nawab Akbar Bugti was forced to leave Dera Bugti. He camped himself in the Chalgri area of the Bhamboor hills of Dera Bugti. On August 24, 2006, the army launched a massive operation in the area. Nawab Bugti was killed, along with 37 of his companions on August 26, 2006. In the wake of increased armed activities and a massive crackdown on Baloch activists throughout Balochistan, he had earlier predicted his murder. In April 2006, Nawab Bugti observed that the army units have been given instructions that he and Mir Balaach Mari (Balaach was the son of Nawab Khair Bakhsh Mari, murdered a year after Nawab's martyrdom) — the two of us should be eliminated.

The way Nawab Bugti died elevated him to the pantheon of Baloch heroes and martyrs. His death inspired a broad section of the Baloch youth. The Baloch all over the world expressed their grief over his murder by taking out rallies and demonstrations. The four-party Baloch Alliance announced a 15-day mourning period and declared that protests would continue across the region. The alliance held a massive protest rally in Quetta, the capital city of Balochistan. On September 4, 2006, the Balochistan National Party announced the resignations of its members from the federal Parliament and the Balochistan Assembly in protest against the murder of Nawab Bugti. In October 2006, the Baloch nationalists in a grand Jirga of tribal elite and political parties in Kalat demanded that Pakistani army should vacate Balochistan and the status of Balochistan in Pakistan should be renegotiated between the representatives of the Baloch and the state. The Jirga tasked Mir Suleiman Daud, the grandson of the last Khan of the Baloch state, to plead the case for the independence of Balochistan in the International Court of Justice in The Hague.

For the last fifteen years, Balochistan is engulfed in a protracted and bloody conflict with no visible end to the miseries and sufferings of the people. Compared to all other periods of active hostility between the Baloch and Pakistan, the highest numbers of casualties, disappearances, and displacement of the population occurred in the present conflict. Thousands have been killed, disappeared, and displaced. Indiscriminate arrests, unlawful custody and the use of inhuman torture of the Baloch political activists and mutilation of their bodies were the hallmarks of the adopted strategies against the Baloch resistance. Thousands of political activists were rounded-up by security agencies under the anti-terrorism law. In a planned way, the security agencies tried to physically wipe out the intellectual, writers, poets, and opinion leaders who are the cream of society. Anti-social and extremist religious elements organized by security agencies in various parts of Balochistan were used in identifying, kidnapping and dumping bodies of the Baloch activists. They are popularly known as the 'death squads'. The Baloch nationalists are identifying several organizations run by security agencies to assist them in arresting their workers, torturing them, and dumping their bodies. The "Squads" were successful in some areas in creating confusion and even disrupting the activities of resistance groups. Four main organizations are said to be operating in Balochistan today; although, they change names frequently. The Baloch Musala Defaie Thanzeem operates in the Jahlawaan area while Sarawaan Aman Force has been active in the Sarawaan region. Sepah e Shuhda e Balochistan and Lashkar e Khurasan are other militia outfits operating against the Baloch in southern Balochistan. In recent years, the secret agencies are also using extremist religious outfits like Lashkar e Janghwi and Thehrik e Thaliban e Pakistan in various operations against the Baloch political activists.

On November 21, 2007, Mir Balaach Mari, who was believed to be the commander of the Balochistan Liberation Army (BLA), one of the armed resistance groups, died in mysterious circumstances. The majority of the Baloch believe that he was murdered by Pakistani secret agencies in Afghanistan where he had sought refuge following the crackdown in the Mari and Bugti areas in the wake of the murder of Nawab Akbar Bugti in 2006. His death was a serious blow to the resistance struggle. After his death, divisions appeared in ranks of the Baloch resistance and between his brothers which caused serious damage to the national struggle.

When BNM leaders merged BNM with BNDP to found National Party, Ghulam Muhammad Baloch parted ways with his colleagues and reorganized the BNM and was elected as the Chairman of the party. Ghulam Muhammad Baloch and the leader of a breakaway faction of BSO, Dr. Allah Nazar were of the opinion that establishment using National Party would try to replace genuine Baloch nationalist parties with so-called representatives of a Baloch nationalism that would become totally subservient to Islamabad. On 9 April 2009, Ghulam Muhammad Baloch, Lala Muneer Baloch, and BRP Joint Secretary Sher Muhammad Baloch were picked up by the security agencies when they were conferring with their solicitor, after attending a court proceeding. Their mutilated bodies were found in Murgaap 10 kilometers away from Turbat.

Nawab Khair Bakhsh Mari remained a symbol of Baloch national resistance from the 1960s until his death in 2014. His Mari tribe spearheaded the Baloch armed resistance during the 1970s in alliance with the Mengal tribe of Sardar Athaullah Mengal. Age, political and personal losses, exile, and arrests in no way mellowed him. He continued to cherish the dream of liberating the Baloch till his last breath. Nawab Mari was arguably a towering figure in Baloch national resistance. However, many Baloch analysts believe that the failure to organize his nationalist activities on a political platform was one of the weaknesses in Nawab Mari's long political career. After his death, there occurred damaging divisions among his sons and tribal followers. A gathering of Mari tribesmen held on June 20, 2014, in Quetta 'elected' his eldest son Mir Jangeez Mari as the new chief of the tribe. However, other brothers of Mir Jangeez Mari and elders of Mari tribe loyal to late Nawab Mari rejected his appointment as chief of their tribe. They alleged that Jangeez Mari had been appointed the chief at the behest of the state establishment. A meeting of Mari tribal elders in Kahaan in July 2014, decided to appoint Mir Mehraan Mari as the new chief of the tribe.

After the end of the military regime of General Pervez Musharraf, the powerless civilian governments were not in a position to initiate any reconciliatory process in the province. The so-called civilian government of President Asif Zardari attempted to resolve the crisis by announcing some half-hearted measures. In early November 2009, the so-called "Balochistan Package" was announced. Included in the plan were proposals such as the return of political exiles, freeing of jailed Baloch political activists, the withdrawal of the army from some key areas, a reform of the federal resources allocation mechanism, efforts to create jobs for the Baloch youth, and greater control of resources by the provincial assembly. However, the de facto ruler of the state, the military establishment was not ready to concede anything substantial to the Baloch. The Balochistan Package was never implemented. The establishment also rejected a six-point confidence-building agenda presented by BNP chief, Sardar Akhthar Mengal in 2013 in order to pave the way for a peaceful resolution of the issue. In a reconciliatory gesture, the BNP decided to take part in the parliamentary elections of 2018. But elections were rigged and despite winning the majority of seats in Baloch regions the party was allowed to retain an insignificant number of seats in the provincial and national assembly. It was a clear indication from the establishment that it is not ready to end the conflict through peaceful means.

The state establishment is continuing with the implementation of its own 'fight to finish' policy and on the face of it, there is no hope of a peaceful end to the bloody, protracted and devastating confrontation with no side appearing as the winner at present. The state establishment has apparently been successful in containing the Baloch national resistance by adopting various time-tested strategies. These include divide and rule, unleashing unprecedented terror, adopting assimilation strategies and introduction of religious fundamentalism into the Baloch society. However, despite the claim of the state establishment that it has crushed the fifth Baloch insurgency, there is no winner in the contemporary conflict. The reality is that neither the armed resistance has been crushed nor the Baloch armed resistance been able to inflict a major blow on the security forces. The present situation can be described as an impasse or a situation of stalemate. The regional and international political situation has also changed during the last two decades. There have been new alignments of regional and international forces in Asia. In this crossroad of history, the future strategies of the Baloch nationalists and the state establishment will decide not only the future of Balochistan and Pakistan but of the whole region.

The situation for the Baloch in western Balochistan has not been promising. Baloch nationalist leadership who settled in the West after initially migrating to Pakistan, Afghanistan and the Arab countries during the 1980s tried to retain their organizations; however, these organizations once again underwent serious transformations from the 1990s. They could not stop the phenomenon of division among their ranks. Baloch Raaj e Zrombesh (BRZ) was divided and the Balochistan Peoples Party of Iran was formed in 2003, while a small section retained the name of Baloch Raaj e Zrombesh. Balochistan United Front formed in 2003 was a serious attempt in the direction of uniting all the Baloch political organizations working in various Western countries. Prominent in the formation of Balochistan United Front were Dr. Habibullah Malik, Dr. Abdul Doshaki, Ghulam Raza Hosseinbhor, Jamshed Amiri, Aziz Daadyar, Anwar Dehwaari, Dr. Noor Muhammad Maliki, Hasan Kamali, and Naser Mubaraki. The Front disintegrated in 2005.

At present, the most active organization is the Balochistan Peoples Party led by Naser Buledai. Its main activities include highlighting the grave human rights situation in Balochistan and advocacy for the Baloch cause among the political and humanitarian institutions of the West. In 2005, with the initiative of the Balochistan Peoples Party of Iran, Balochistan has been successful in gaining the membership of the prestigious Unrepresented Nations and Peoples Organization (UNPO). There are many other organizations of the Baloch in Diaspora that has not been particularly active in recent years.

The Baloch nationalists, belonging to several different organizations of Western Balochistan and based in European capitals are hopeful that their struggle will get the required support from the international community, as Iran is increasingly being seen as a threat to world peace and internally it is racing towards economic, social and political chaos.

There are ongoing debates and discussions among the Baloch nationalist circles on how to proceed in order to achieve the objective of national salvation, bearing in mind the prevailing situation in Western Balochistan. Some of the groups insist on an autonomous Balochistan in a federated Iran. They argue that keeping in mind the objective reality of the progress of the Baloch national resistance in Iran and the conditions and circumstances relating to it, federalism for Iran and the demand for autonomous status are the only feasible options. While for a significant section of the Baloch, an independent and united Balochistan is the sole objective of the Baloch national resistance.

Another phenomenon is taking root in Western Balochistan and that is the emergence of the clergy in Baloch politics. In recent years, the Baloch Mullahs have replaced the traditional Baloch nationalist political activists and tribal leadership. In the initial period of the regime of Ayathullahs, the Baloch religious groups, under the leadership of Moulvi Abdul Aziz and the banner of Hezb e Ithihad al-Muslemin, tried to mobilize the masses exploiting the imbalance regarding various Islamic sects in the Iranian constitution. This was also joined by the nationalist and left-wing forces, mainly by supporters and cadres of Sazman e Democratic Murdom e Balochistan. This mobilization, apart from demands for cultural, religious and political rights, was based on awakening the masses for an ultimate struggle for Baloch sovereignty. Demonstrations throughout Balochistan were held. However, soon the agitation became violent and dozens of people were killed in skirmishes between Baloch demonstrators and the state security forces. The Ayathullahs adopted a policy of zero tolerance towards the Baloch, regardless of them being religious, secular, left or right-wing. Some of the religious leaders were persecuted by the regime and many went into exile but a significant section of the religious leaders remained in Balochistan and practically replaced the nationalist and tribal leadership of the Baloch national resistance.

From 2003, a religious group, Jundullah, began militant activities in many regions of Western Balochistan targeting the state security apparatus. The organization claimed to continue fighting for national and religious rights of the Baloch and to resist Shia encroachments on the Sunni beliefs. Its leader, Abdul Malik Reki was arrested in February 2010 and executed in June 2010 on charges of waging war against the Islamic Republic of Iran. The organization still carry out small-scale ambushes on convoys of Iranian security forces, assassinations, and abductions of government officials or people affiliated to the government under the new leadership of Muhammad Zahir Baloch. Jundullah included Baloch nationalism in its narratives and tried to rename itself as the Peoples Resistance Movement of Iran. Jundullah declared that in such conditions, faced by the Baloch in Iran, it was not easy for the Baloch to live peacefully; asserting that they had a moral right to defend their community, nation, and country. Iran has accused Pakistan of supporting Jundullah activities, which are emanating from bases in Eastern Balochistan. The Iranians are also accusing the US intelligence agencies, Saudi Arabia, Qatar, Israel, and the United Kingdom as countries supporting the Baloch religious groups fighting against them. However, on the ground, there has been no substantial evidence to prove any Western involvement.

Several other Baloch religious groups have emerged since 2012 are claiming responsibility for activities against security forces in the

Sistaan wa Balochistan province of Iran. One among them is Jaish ul-Adl (Army of Justice) founded by former members of Jundullah, vowed to retaliate against oppression and crimes being committed against the Sunni community in Iran including the Baloch, Kurds, and Ahwazi. Iran has accused Saudi Arabia of funding Jaish ul-Adl and Pakistan of turning a blind eye to its base in Pakistani Balochistan. During 2015 and 2016, Jaish ul-Adl carried out many serious hits and run attacks on security forces in Western Balochistan and appeared to be the only potent armed group against the regime of Ayathllahs. Harkat-e-Ansar e Iran was another splinter group of Jundullah. The group merged with Hizbul-Furqan and formed Ansar Al-Furqan in late 2013. The Iranians blame Qatar, Saudi Arabia, and Pakistan for giving financial and logistic support to the group. It is generally believed that all religious groups are in one way or another, had connections with radical groups such as Sepah-e Sahabah and Lashkar-e Jangawi and Thaliban in Afghanistan and Pakistan, indicating a strong connection between Pakistani security agencies and the religious organizations in Western Balochistan.

In the 21st century, the Baloch in Western Balochistan, under perpetual Persian occupation, have found themselves suppressed and oppressed to varying degrees. They are deprived of their cultural, social and economic rights. Treated as third-class citizens, the Baloch in Iran are struggling to preserve the basic elements of their national identity. They are forced to adopt Persian names and are deprived of using their mother tongue as the medium for instruction at schools. The use of the Balochi language in public places is being discouraged. Policies of the Ayathullahs regarding the Baloch and other national minorities are clear manifestations of chauvinistic Persian nationalism. The regime is carrying out policies of previous regimes including demographic manipulations in order to make the Baloch a minority in their own homeland. With the influx of Persians, cities such as Zahaadan (Duzzap) and Chahbaar are increasingly losing their characteristics as Baloch cities.

A disconnect has been created between the Baloch activists in exile and those acting inside Western Balochistan as a result of the long absence of leadership. A difference of opinion on strategy can be observed between Baloch organizations operating in exile and those participating in the political process of the Persian state inside Balochistan. Some of those involved in the political activities in Iran calling themselves national democrats. They believe in participating in the political process of the state in order to gain opportunities for the greater political mobilization of the Baloch masses. Those who call themselves federalists believe that the Baloch should accept being a federating unit of Iran as the first step in their struggle for national self-determination, however, some of the Baloch activists who call themselves pro-independent, believe that there is no point in joining any state political process, as it is counterproductive for the Baloch national struggle and brings opportunistic tendencies among the Baloch.

Circumstances have never been favorable for the Baloch to achieve their desired goal of overthrowing the yoke of subjugation, nor has their resistance been able to secure any constitutionally sanctioned degree of autonomy as a result of their political or armed resistance. However, despite being divided, weak and seeing no help from international community for their national cause, the Baloch parties, groups, and personalities hope to achieve their objective. They believe that it is only a matter of channeling the Baloch nationalist sentiments in a united organization to launch an effective resistance. They believe that soon the Baloch nationalist parties will engage the oppressors in a meaningful political and armed resistance.

CHRONOLOGY OF EVENTS

1666	The Baloch Confederacy in Kalat established by Mir Ahmad.
1839	(13 November) Mir Mehraab Khan, the Khan of Kalat killed in battle with British troops in Kalat.
1854	(14 May) The British Government enters into an agreement with Mir Naseer Khan II of Kalat, recognizing the independent status of Kalat.
1871	Border settlements between Baloch
1886	Confederacy and Persia under British
1905	auspices.
1867	(26 January) Mir Ghulam Husain Bugti Killed along with 257 men in the battle fought against British forces in Chachar gorges near Dera Ghazi khan.
1876	British Government enters into an agreement with Khan of Kalat, Mir Khudadaad Khan reaffirming the earlier treaty of friendship, recognizing the sovereign status of Baluchistan.
1893	Mir Khudadaad Khan, Khan of Kalat, detained by the British government in Quetta. He was replaced by Mir Mahmud Khan, his son.
1894	Rebel leader, Mir Gohar Khan killed by British forces in the battle of Garmaap.
1898	(27 January) Mir Baloch Khan was killed along with 250 fighters by British troops in the battle of Gokprosh.
1901	Mir Sheraan Daad Kareem, a Baloch rebel was hanged by the British government.

1917	The Baloch rebel Noora Mengal arrested by Nawab Habibullah Khan Nosharwani in Kharan and handed over to the British.
1921	Noora Mengal dies in a British jail in Hyderabad.
1928	Amir Dost Muhammad Barakzai arrested by Iran and subsequently hanged in 1931.
1932	(December) The Karachi weekly AL Baloch carries a map defining the Boundaries of greater Balochistan.
1932	(27 December) The Baloch Conference held in Jacobabad, attended by delegates from Balochistan and other parts of British India.
1933	Anjuman-e-Ithihad-e-Balochaan launched by Mir Yosuf Ali Magsi and Mir Abdul Aziz Kurd.
1933	The second all Baloch Conference held in Hyderabad.
1937	(5 February) The Kalat State National Party formed at Sibi.
1939	(20 July) The Kalat State National Party declared illegal by the Kalat Government.
1947	(29 June) Controversial vote of Shahi Jirga ceding British Balochistan to Pakistan.
1947	(4 August) The Tripartite Agreement (the Standstill Agreement) between Britain, Pakistan, and Balochistan. The agreement recognizes the sovereign and the independent status of Balochistan.
1947	(11 August) The Khan of Kalat, Ahmad Yar khan declares independence for Balochistan.
1947	(30 September) Afghanistan votes against Pakistan's admission to the United Nations.
1947	(August) The Khan holds elections to the Bi-Cameral legislature of Balochistan. National Party members contesting the polls in their individual capacity and returned to the Lower House with majority securing 39 seats in the 52-member house.
1947	(14 December) Discussions on the question of the merger with Pakistan in the Balochistan Assembly. Mir Ghous Bakhsh Bizenjo, the leader of the majority party spoke against the accession proposal, favoring an independent and sovereign Balochistan.

1947	(December) The Balochistan Lower House recommends that Balochi should be declared the official and the national language of Balochistan.
1948	(4 January) The Upper House of Balochistan Parliament unanimously rejects the proposal of the accession of Balochistan to Pakistan. Mir Ghous Bakhsh Bizenjo tables a resolution signed by all the members of the Assembly, opposing Balochistan joining Pakistan.
1948	(26 March) Pakistan's Prime Minister, in a meeting with his army commanders, decides to send troops to the Balochistan to take the counrty forcefully.
1948	(March) The Government of Pakistan orders its troops stationed in Quetta to march on Kalat on April Ist 1948 if the Khan of Kalat does not sign the instrument of accession.
1948	(27 March) Khan of Kalat declares the accession of Balochistan into Pakistan.
1948	(April) Leaders of National Party arrested, including Mir Ghous Bakhsh Bizenjo and Mir Gul Khan Naseer.
1948	(8 May) Abdul Ghaffar Khan forms Pakistan Peoples Party.
1948	(26 May) Prince Abdul Kareem revolts and crosses the border into Afghanistan.
1948	(June) The Kalat State National Party declared illegal by the Government of Pakistan.
1948	(8 July) Prince Abdul Kareem returns to Balochistan from Afghanistan along with his followers and taken into custody.
1948	(July) Pakistan Government declares the Khudai Khidmathgaar of Abdul Ghaffar Khan, illegal.
1948	(4 December) Abdul Kareem and Muhammad Husain Unqa sentenced to ten years of rigorous imprisonment on charges of treason.
1949	(26 July) The Afghan National Parliament, Loya Jirga, votes national support for Pakhtunistan and officially rejects the 1893 Durand agreement and all subsequent agreements with the British on Pakhtun status.

1950	Balochistan Peace Committee formed by Abdul Kareem Showrish.
1950, 1951	Afghanistan organizes tribal raids into Pakistan.
1954	Wrore Pakhtuns, The Pakhtun Brotherhood, formed by Abdul Samad Achakzai, a leader of former British Balochistan.
1954	The Baloch opposed the proposed merger of the Pakhtun speaking districts, of former British Balochistan with the Balochistan States Union.
1955	(1st January) The ex-Khan of Kalat, Ahmad Yar Khan signs an agreement with the Government accepting the merger of Balochistan and the leased areas into the One-Unit system.
1955	(30 March) Pakistan Embassy in Kabul attacked and the flag of Pakhtunistan hoisted on the Embassy flag –pole.
1955	(14 July) Usthuman Gal formed by Prince Abdul Kareem.
1955	A joint Pak-Iran Border Commission demarcated Perso-Baloch borders on 6 January 1958.
1955	(14 October) provinces in the western part of Pakistan integrated into One-Unit, to be known as West Pakistan.
1956	Pakistan National Party formed by the merger of six political groups of west Pakistan.
1957	(24 March) Daadshah Kamaal ambushes and kills an American near Chahbaar.
1957	(July) National Party renamed a National Awami Party of Pakistan in the convention of political workers in Dacca.
1958	(6 October) The ex Khan of Kalat, Ahmad Yar Khan arrested after an army attack on Kalat.
1958	(7 October) President Skandar Mirza of Pakistan abrogates the constitution and imposes Martial Law.
1959	Pakistan Government hands over a Baloch rebel, Ahmad Shah to the Iranian Government.
1960	(15 July) Seven Baloch rebels executed in Hyderabad and Sukkar jails.
1961	Warna Waaninda Gal, formed in Quetta.

1961	(August) Military ruler, General Muhammad Ayub Khan threatens the Baloch with total extinction if they continue their resistance.
1962	(6 November) The ex-Khan of Kalat, Ahmad Yar Khan released from Prison.
1963	(July) The Baloch leader, Mir Abdul Baqi Baloch moves a writ in High court challenging the Government the decision to transfer a large area of Baloch territory to Persia.
1964	Mir Norouz Khan dies in Prison.
1964	RCD, Regional Co-Operation for Development, formed between Pakistan, Iran, and Turkey.
1966	(23rd March) the Awami League leader, Sheikh Mujeebur Rehman announced his six-point program demanding more powers to the federal units.
1967	(26 November) The Baloch Students Organization formed after a three-day convention in Karachi.
1967	The BSO splits into two factions; an "Anti-Sardar" group formed.
1968	(29 May) Police raided the students' hostels in Quetta killing one student, Zarif, and injuring two others.
1970	(3 January) Military ruler, General Yahya Khan meets former heads of constituent states of Kalat to discuss the breakup of the One-Unit.
1970	(July) One-Unit system in West Pakistan dissolved.
1971	(26 November) General Yahya imposes a ban on the NAP.
1971	(20 December) Ban on NAP removed by President Zulfiqar Ali Bhutto.
1972	(April) National Awami party Government headed by Sardar Athaullah Mengal installed in Balochistan. Mir Ghous Bakhsh Bizenjo takes over as Governor.
1972	(September) Pakistani press report an alleged conspiracy by the Baloch and Pakhtun leaders to disintegrate Pakistan; naming it "the London Plan".
1973	(10 February) Arms recovered in Iraqi Embassy in Islamabad. The Pakistan Government alleges that these were meant for anti-state activities in Balochistan and NWFP.

1973	(14 February) Governor Bizenjo dismissed and Mengal ministry dissolved. Akbar Bugti takes over as Governor of Balochistan.
1973	(15 February) NAP-JUI coalition government in NWFP resigns in protest against the dismissal of Mengal ministry.
1973	(18 May) The first major encounter of the Baloch guerillas with Pakistani troops, killing eight soldiers.
1973	(7 August) Mir Lawang Khan killed in a midnight attack on his house in Dasht- e-Goran by Pakistani troops.
1973	(August) Baloch leaders, Mir Ghous Bakhsh Bizenjo, Sardar Khair Bakhsh Mari and Sardar Athaullah Mengal arrested.
1973	(19 August) Ali Muhammad Mengal along with many others killed in an army raid on his village.
1973	(31 December) Governor Bugti resigned and the ex-ruler of Kalat, Ahmad Yar Khan takes over as Governor of Balochistan.
1974	PFAR, Popular Front for Armed Resistance, formed by Baloch exiles.
1974	(14 April) The Government announces a general amnesty in Balochistan.
1974	(August) Majeed Lango, a BSO activist, killed in Quetta when a hand grenade intended for Premier Bhutto explodes in his hand.
1974	(19 October) The Government of Pakistan publishes a White Paper on Balochistan.
1975	(10 February) Government declares National Awami Party illegal.
1975	(30 October) The Supreme Court upholds the Government's decision to ban the NAP. NAP leaders boycotted the entire court proceedings.
1975	(6 November) NAP workers formed the National Democratic Party.
1975	(20 December) Hyderabad Special Tribunal constituted to try the Baloch and Pakhtun leaders on charges of Treason.
1976	(6 February) Asadullah Mengal and Ahmad Shah kidnapped and killed by army commandos from Karachi.

1976	(8 April) The Prime Minister announced his government's decision to abolish the Sardari System in Balochistan.
1976	(15 April) Special Tribunal in Hyderabad starts proceeding against Baloch and Pakhtun leaders.
1977	(August) Safar Khan, a guerilla commander killed in an encounter with the army.
1977	(9 December) Abdul Wali Khan and other Pakhtun leaders involved in Hyderabad Conspiracy Case were released on bail while the Baloch leaders refused to be bailed out. They demanded the withdrawal of the cases, unconditional release of all political prisoners.
1978	(1 January) Hyderabad Special Tribunal dissolved and conspiracy case was withdrawn by the military regime of General Zia ul Haq. Baloch leaders released from prison.
1978	(27 April) President Daud of Afghanistan killed in coup d'état. Noor Muhammad Taraki of the Khalq faction of the Afghan Communist Party took over as President of the country.
1978	(20 June) Balochistan Exile Liberation Front formed in London.
1979	(19 April) Baloch leaders quit the NDP ending the Baloch-Pakhtun political alliance.
1979	(1 June) Baloch leaders form Pakistan National Party (PNP).
1979	(July) BSO manifesto amended by its National Council to include the provision for the right of national self-determination for the Baloch.
1979	(October) 7 student leaders tried by a military tribunal and collectively sentenced to one-year rigorous imprisonment.
1981	(11 June) Hameed Baloch, a BSO activist, hanged in Mach jail.
1983	(March-April) The Peoples' Front, London, the mouthpiece of the Baloch nationalists in exile declares its aim of creating an independent Balochistan. The declaration also defines the territorial limits of a unified Balochistan.
1983	(25 September)"Awami" faction of the BSO merge with the Baloch Students Organization.

SELECT BIBLIOGRAPHY

Abdullah, Ahmad: The Clash Over the Identity of Pakistani Culture. Dawn, Karachi, 3rd March 1975.

Afzal, M. Rafique: Political Parties in Pakistan. Islamabad 1976.

Ahmad, N.D: The Survival of Afghanistan. Lahore, 1973.

Ali, Tariq: Can Pakistan Survive? Death of a State. london,1983.

Arberry, A.J. (ed): The Legacy of Persia. London, 1953.

Arfa, Hasan: The Kurds-A Historical ad Political Study. London, 1968.

Baloch, Inayatullah: The Balochi Question in Pakistan and the Right of Self-determination: Pakistan in its Fourth Decade. Wolfgang peter Zingel (ed) Hamburg, 1983.

Baloch, Muhammad Sardar Khan: History of the

Baloch Race and Balochistan. Karachi, 1958.

The Great Baloch. Quetta,1965.

A literary History of the Balochi. (Vol I) Quetta,1977.

Baloch, Siddique: Heat Waves: A Script for the Balochi Language. Dawn Karachi, 27th June 1982.

Balochistan Through Ages, A selection from the Government Record. (Vol I & II) Quetta, 1979.

Barker Ernest: National Character and Factors of Formation. London,1948.

Barker, Muhammad Abdur Rehman, and Aqil Khan Mengal: A Course in Balochi (Vol I), Montreal,1969.

Bedaar, Bashir: Gwarbaam. Turbat,1982.

Bellow, H.W: An Inquiry into the Ethnography of Afghanistan. London,1891.

Afghanistan- Country and People. London, 1920.

Binder, Leonard: Religion and politics in Pakistan. California,1963.

Brailvi, Mujahid: Balochistan – what is the Issue? Quetta 1984.

Bray, Denys: The Brahui Language. (Vol I & II) re- printed, Brahui Academy, Quetta, 1978.

Bugti, Aziz: Tharikh e Balochistan: Shakhsiat Ke Aeene Mien. Quetta.1984.

Burki, H.K: Punjabi Chauvinism. Pakistan Times, Lahore, 29 June 1975.

Burnes, Alexander: Travels into Bukhara and a Voyage on the Indus (Vol I). London,1934.

Burton, Richard F: Sindh and the Races that Inhabit the Valley of the Indus. London,1951.

Caroe, Olaf: The Pathans. London,1958.

Choudhary, G.W: The Last Days of United Pakistan. London, 1974.

Cragg, Kenneth: Counsels in Contemporary Islam. Islamic Survey No,3 Edinburgh, 1965.

Dashti, Naseer: The Baloch and Balochistan: A Historical Account from the Beginning to the Fall of the Baloch State. Trafford, Publishing, North America,2012

Dashti, Naseer: Baloch Conflict With Iran and Pakistan. Trafford, Publishing, North America,2017

Dashti, Naseer: Tears of Sindhu: Sindhi National Struggle in the Historical Context. Trafford, Publishing, North America, 2018

Dastural Amal Baloch Students Organization. Karachi, 1968.

Dost, Dost Muhammad: The Language and Races of Afghanistan. Kabul, 1975.

Dodge, Bayard: The Significance of Religion in Arab Nationalism. In J. Harris Proctor (ed) Islam and International Relations. New York, 1965

Dullin, David J: Soviet Foreign Policy After Stalin. New York, 1961.

Elfenbein, J. H: The Balochi Language; A Dialectology with Text. Royal Society Monographs (Vol XXVII) London 1966.

Elphinstone, Mountstuart: The Kingdom of Kabul (Vol I). London 1815.

Emerson, Rupert: From Empire to Nation. Massachusetts,1960.

Fareedi, Noor Ahmad: Baloch Koum Aor Uski Tharikh. Multan.1968.

Ferrier, J.P: A Caravan Journey and Wanderings in Persia, Afghanistan and Balochistan. London,1857.

Gankovsky, Yu V: The People of Pakistan. Moscow 1971.

Gankovsky, Yu V and Moskelenko, VN.: The Three Constitutions of Pakistan. Lahore,1979.

Gibb H.A.R: "Religion and politics in Christianity and Islam". In J. Harris Proctor (ed.) Islam and International Relations. New York 1965.

Grierson, George Abraham: Linguistic Survey of India-Specimens of languages of the Iranian Family (Vol X). Calcutta, 1921

Griffiths, John C: Afghanistan: Key to a Continent. London,1981.

Grunebaum, Gustave E. Von: Medieval Islam. Chicago,1961.

Halliday Fred: A threat from the East? Soviet Policy from Afghanistan and Iran to the Horn of Africa. London, 1982.

Hasan Muhammad: Attarawien Sadi Mien Dehli Ke Afrad aur Muashira Ka Thaaruf. Qalam Qabeela (compilation of Articles) Quetta,1983.

Hasan, Sabthe: Naveed e Fikr. Karachi,1982.

Harris, Errol E: Annihilation and Utopia-The principles of International Politics. London.1966.

Harrison Selig S: Nightmare in Balochistan. Foreign Policy, fall, 1978.

In Afghanistan's Shadow-Baloch Nationalism and Soviet Temptation. New York, 1981.

Heikal, Muhammad: The Return of the Ayatollah. London, 1984

Hithoram, Lala: Tharikh e Balochistan. Quetta,

Holdich, Thomas: The Gates of India – Being a historical Narrative. London, 1877.

Hobson J.A: Imperialism- A Study. London,1968.

Hughes, A. W: The Country of Balochistan. London, 1965.

Huq, M.U: Muslim Politics in Modern India. Lahore

Imperial Gazetteer of India, provincial series, Balochistan. Calcutta,1908.

Isayev. M. L: National Languages in USSR: Problems and Solution. Moscow,1977.

Kaushik, Devendra: Central Asia in Modern Times: A history from the 19th century. Moscow, 1970.

Kedourie, Elies (ed): Nationalism in Asia and Africa. New York, 1970.

Khadhuri, Majid: "Islamic theory of international relation" in J. Harris Proctor (ed.) Islam and International Relations. New York, 1965.

Khan, Ahmad Yar: Mukhthasar Tharikh Koume Baloch o Khawanien e Baloch. Quetta, 1972.

Khan, Muhammad Asghar: Generals in Polities- Pakistan: 1958-1982 Delhi, 1982: What is the Ideology of Pakistan? Peshawar Time, 4 April 1970:

The Voice of the Pakhtuns. Lahore 1972:

The Pakhtunistan Bogey. Khyber Mail, 16 January 1969.

Kinnane, Derk: The Kurds and Kurdistan. London,1970.

Kissinger, Henry: The White House Years. London,1979.

Kochanek, Stanley A: Interest Groups and Development of Business and Politics in Pakistan. Karachi,1983.

Kohn, Hans: Nationalism: It's Meaning and History. Princeton,1965. The Idea of Imperialism. New York, 1944.

Kousar, Inam ul Haq: Pakistan Movement in Balochistan. Islamabad.

Levy, Reuben: The Social Structure of Islam. London,1965.

Lenesleosky, George: The Middle East in World Affairs. London,1982.

Le Page R. B. The National Language Question. London. 1964.

MacIver, R.M: The Modern State. London, 1955.

Mari, Khuda Bakhsh: The Baloches through the Centuries- History Vs legend. Quetta.

Mari, Khuda Bakhsh: Searchlight on the Balochees and Balochistan. Karachi, 1974.

Masson, Charles: Narrative of a Journey to Kalat.London, 1843.

Morgenestierne, George: Report on a Linguistic Mission to North-Western India. Kulturforskning, 1932.

Mullah G.R: Bazhn. Karachi,1981.

Munn Mac: Afghanistan-From Darius to Amanullah. London, 1919.

Myrdal, Gunnar K: The Asian Drama (Vol I). Massachusetts, 1968.

Myres. J. L: The Dawn of History. London,1918.

Naseer, Gul Khan: Balochi Razmia Shairi. Quetta,1979

Naseer, Gul Khan: Balochistan Ki Kahani Shaeroun Ki Zubani. Quetta

Naseer, Gul Khan: Balochistan: Qadeem Aur Jadeed Tharikh Ki Roshni Mien. Quetta,1982.

Naseer, Gul Khan: Tharikh-e-Balochistan (Vol II). Quetta,1956.

Oliver, Edward E: Across the Border-Pathan and Baloch. London, 1890.

Philips C.H. (ed.) The evolution of India and Pakistan, 1958 to 1947. Select Documents. London, 1962.

Popowski, Joseph: Rival Powers in Central Asia. Quetta 1977.

Prasad, Bisheshwar: The Foundations of India's Foreign Policy 1860 – 1962 Delhi,1978.

Raverty. Henry George: Notes on Afghanistan and Balochistan. London 1921.

Rawlinson, George: The Five Great Monarchies of theAncient Eastern World. London,1892.

Razvi, Mujtaba: The Frontiers of Pakistan. Karachi, 1971.

Randal, Johathan C: Iran seeks to curb separatist feeling Among Balochi. Washington Post, 12 March 1979.

Rihkye Ravi: The Fourth Round: Indo-Pak War 1984, Future history. Singapore, 1982.

Roman, Anwar: Aina e Baloch. Qasar-e-Adab, Multan,

Ross, Arthur: In Afghanistan's Shadow. Washington Quarterly, Autumn, 1982.

Runciman, S: Byzantine Civilazation. London,1933.

Saabir, Qazi, Abdur Rahim: Balochistan Ke Janbaaz. Karachi, 1979.

Saabir, Sultan: Pashthu Culture. Saqafat of Adab Wadi e Bolaan Mien. Quetta,1966.

Salam, Elie: Nationalism and Islam. Muslim World, October 1962.

Sayad, Zahoor Shah: Sisthagien Dasthunk. Karachi, 1962.

Angar or Throngal. Karachi, 1962.

Thrampkunien Thramp. Karachi, 1962.

Saahir, Muraad: Pahaar, Karachi

Sayeed, Khalid B: Politics in Pakistan. Nature and the direction of Change, New York, 1980.

Siddiqui, Abdur Rahman: Afghanistan Crisis and Subcontinental Security. Defense Journal (No.8) Karachi, 1983.

Afghan Refugees in Pakistan: Problems and Prospects. Defense Journal (No.10-11), Karachi,1983.

The Military Option. Defense Journal, Karachi, November,1978 Siddiqui, Kalim: Conflict, Crisis, and War in Pakistan. London,1972.

Sampson, Anthony: A new Escalation of Craziness. Newsweek, 28 May 1984.

Smith, Anthony D: Theories of Nationalism. London1971.

Sulzberger, C. Belief in Crude Reality. New York Times, 22 April 1973.

Sutherland Denial: Key Men Caught in Balochistan Storm. Christian Science Monitor,14 December 1973.

Tate G.P: The Frontiers of Balochistan: Travels on the borders of Persia and Afghanistan. London 1909.

The Amnesty International Reports on the Islamic Republic of Pakistan. 1976.

Toynbee, Arnold j: A Study of History. Moscow,1971.

Tytler, W.K. Fraser: Afghanistan- A study of political development in Central Asia. London,1968.

Vatikiotis, P. J: 'Islam and the Foreign Policy of Egypt', in J. Harris Proctor (ed.) Islam and International Relations. New York,1965.

Waheed Sheikh A: The Kurds and Their Country. Lahore, 1955.

Walker, Walter: The Next Domino? London,1982.

Waldport, Stanley: Roots of Conflict in South Asia Afghanistan, Pakistan, India, and the Super Powers. New York,1982.

White Paper on Balochistan. Islamabad, 19 October 1974.

Wirsing, Robert G: The Balochis and the Pathan. London,1981.

Zamaan, Waheeduz(ed) The Quest for Identity. Islamabad, 1981.

Ziring, Lawrence: Pakistan-Enigma of Political Development. Kent,1980.

NEWSPAPERS AND PERIODICALS

Azaad Balochistan (Monthly), London.
Azan (Monthly) Multan, September 1979.
Balochi (Monthly) Karachi and Quetta.
Baam (Irregular), Organ of Baloch Students Organization.
Baluchi Dunya (Monthly), Multan.
Bramsh (Irregular Magazine), Karachi
Dawn, Karachi.
Girouk (Irregular), Organ of the Baloch Students Organization.
Jang, Karachi, Quetta.
Labzaank (Irregular), literary magazine brought out by BSO.
Mashriq, (Quetta.)

Makkuraan (Irregular), Tehran.

Nokien Dour, Quetta.

Nida-e-Balochistan (Monthly), London.

Ouman (Monthly), Karachi

Peoples Front (Monthly) London.

Pajjaar (Irregular), Organ of the Baloch Students Organization.

Saugaath (Irregular), Organ of Baloch Students organization.

Shubenag (Irregular).

Sanj, Sayad Hashmi Academy, Karachi

Sougaath (Monthly), Karachi.

Ulus Balochi (Monthly) Quetta.

Youth literary Circle, Turbat (Irregular), Organ of Baloch Students Organization.

Zamana (Monthly), Quetta.

GOVERNMENT PUBLICATIONS

Development statistics of Balochistan 1980-1983 Bureau of Statistics, Planning and Development Department, Government of Balochistan.

The official reports of Discussions in the Balochistan Assembly on a resolution to end the Sardari, Tribal and Jirga system, June 1972.

OTHER SOURCES

A large number of pamphlets, leaflets and unprinted material on Kalat State National Party, Baloch Students Organization and insurgency in Balochistan were consulted.

INDEX

285

Printed in the United States
By Bookmasters